# Philadelphia County, Pennsylvania Land Records 1706-1713

*Mary M. Brewer*

HERITAGE BOOKS
2008

# HERITAGE BOOKS
*AN IMPRINT OF HERITAGE BOOKS, INC.*

**Books, CDs, and more—Worldwide**

For our listing of thousands of titles see our website
at
www.HeritageBooks.com

Published 2008 by
HERITAGE BOOKS, INC.
Publishing Division
100 Railroad Ave. #104
Westminster, Maryland 21157

Copyright © 2000 Mary M. Brewer

Other books by the author:

*Land Records of Sussex County, Delaware, 1681-1725*
*Land Records of Sussex County, Delaware: Various Dates: 1693-1698, 1715-1717, 1782-1792, 1802-1805*
*Kent County, Delaware, Land Records, Volume 1, 1680-1701*
*Kent County, Delaware Land Records. Volume 2: 1702-1722*
*Kent County, Delaware Land Records. Volume 3: 1723-1734*
*Kent County, Delaware Land Records. Volume 4: 1735-1743*
*Kent County, Delaware Land Records. Volume 5: 1742-1749*
*Kent County, Delaware Land Records. Volume 6: 1749-1756*
*Kent County, Delaware, Land Records. Volume 7: 1756-1764*
*Kent County, Delaware, Land Records. Volume 8: 1764-1768*
*Land Records of Sussex County, Delaware, 1681-1725*
*Land Records of Sussex County, Delaware: Various Dates: 1693-1698, 1715-1717, 1782-1792, 1802-1805*
*Land Records of Sussex County, Delaware, 1763-1769*
*Land Records of Sussex County, Delaware, 1753-1763*

All rights reserved. No part of this book may be reproduced or transmitted in any form or by any means, electronic or mechanical, including photocopying, recording or by any information storage and retrieval system without written permission from the author, except for the inclusion of brief quotations in a review.

International Standard Book Numbers
Paperbound: 978-1-58549-594-8
Clothbound: 978-0-7884-7074-5

## Preface

The information abstracted by this book is found in LDS microfilm #21875, Philadelphia, Pennsylvania City Hall Deed Book E3. Researchers are advised to consult the originals whenever possible.

29 Jun 1706. Deed. Whereas WILLIAM PENN proprietary and governour by a patent dated 2 Oct 1704 gave to his son WILLIAM PENN the younger a 7480 a. tr of land situate on the River Schuylkill in Phila . . . WILLIAM PENN the younger on 7 Oct 1704 conveyed the 7480 a. to WILLIAM TRENT and ISAAC NORRIS ackn in Phila 7 --- 1704 . . . WILLIAM TRENT and ISAAC NORRIS of Phila merchants for 213 pounds sold to JOSEPH HARVEY of Darby in Chester Co wheelwright pt/o the afsd tr of land . . . bounded by land sold to JOHN CICLE . . . 710 a. Wit: DAVID LOYD, DAVID POWELL, RICHARD HATH. Ackn 2 Jul 1706 before NATHAN STANBURY justice of the peace. MAURICE LIELE dep recorder of deeds. (E3:pg 1)

6 Jun 1706. Deed. THOMAS FAIRMAN of Phila Co gent and JOHN HART of Bucks Co yeoman executors named in the will of ANNIE SALTER, late of Phila Co Taconis Twp decd, dated 17 Nov 1688 ackn that ANNA by an exchange made with OLIE NELLSON alias USTENBURG for the use of his son ERICK NELSON alias USTENBURG did sell a 70 a. tr of land of the sd USTENBURG's (USTENBURGH) ne side of Quessensomings Cr which she afterwards sold unto THOMAS LOYD . . . also a tr of land sw side of Pemepedia Cr which she purch of CASPER FISH (FISHER) then of Lacony pt/o which land for want of skill of the conveyance escaped the grant of the sd ANNA SALTER whereby the sd ERICK USTENBURG hath not the consideration contracted for, therefore we the sd THOMAS FAIRMAN and JOHN HART for 5 shillings confirm unto ERICK USTENBURG 100 a. pt/o 500 a. afsd surveyed by WALTER WARTON in 1675 a share of the sd CASPER FISH's . . . adj PETER RAMBOE, [?] KEEN, JOSEPH ASHTON, LASSE BOORE and THOMAS THOMPSON's widow . . . and a small strip of land apppproiated to the use of STACK BOTTIMS . . . . Wit: THOMAS TRESSE, WILLIAM FISHER, THOMAS TRESSE Junr. Ackn 4 Jun 1706 before NATHAN STANBURY justice of the peace of Phila Co. MAURICE LIELE dep recorder. (E3:pg 3)

1 Mar 1705/6. Deed. ANTHONY MORRIS of Phila Co merchant for 2 pounds 6 shillings paid on two days, 1 Sep and 1 Mar next ensuing, sold to RICHARD ARMITT of the city taylor a piece of ground s side of Morris' alley in Phila . . . adj JOHN REDMAN . . . pt/o a front lott which THOMAS LOYD by his deed poll dated 4 Oct 1687 conveyed unto ANTHONY MORRIS (Book E rol 5 pg 523) . . . adj Front St and Second St . . . . Wit: SAMUELL POWELL, RICHARD HEATH. Ackn 6 Jul 1706 before NATHAN STANBURY justice of the peace. MAURICE LISLE dep recorder of deeds. (E3:pg 5)

25 Apr 1706. Deed. THOMAS ENGLAND of Phila shopkeeper for 120 pounds sold to GRIFFITH OWEN of Phila practiconer in physick a lott of land w side of Second St in Phila bounded by the lott late of CHARLES [illegible] and WILLIAM CARTER granted by patent 27 May 1693 (41 ft breadth 200 ft length) unto JOHN SOUTHWORTH who on 6 Jun 1693 conveyed it unto WILLIAM BEVAN of Phila shoemaker and MARY his wife, and he on 10 Oct 1694 conveyed it unto WILLIAM CARTER of Phila blockmaker, and he on 11 Jan 1698/9 conveyed it unto MARTIN JERVIS of Phila, and he on 7 Mar 1699/1700 conveyed it unto JACOB USHER of Phila carpenter, and he on 1 Mar 1702/3 conveyed pt/o the ground, 20 ft breadth and 97 ft length, unto THOMAS ENGLAND, with pt/o the lott now in the tenure of JOHN LONGHURST . . . . Wit: JOSEPH PEMBERTON, WILLIAM CARTER, JOHN LONGHURST, BENJAMIN MARTIN. Ackn 6 Jul 1706 before DAVID LLOYD justice of the peace. MAURICE LISLE dep recorder of deeds. (E3:pg 7)

4 Apr 1706. Deed. ABELL COTLEY of Phila watchmaker for 10 pounds sold to HENRY CARTER of same city brickmaker a piece of ground 5 foot in breadth and 62 foot in length adj Second St, house & ground now of the sd ABELL COTLEY & ground late of ALEXANDER BADCOKE but now of the sd HENRY CARTER, which is pt/o a lott of land which RICHARD HILL of Phila merchant by his indenture of 4 Mar 1702/3 sold to ABELL COTLEY . . . . Wit: EDWARD EVANS, RICHARD HEATH. Ackn 15 Jul 1706 before DAVID LLOYD justice of the peace of Phila. MAURICE LISLE dep recorder of deeds. (E3:pg 9)

29 Jul 1706. Deed of Gift. EDWARD SHIPPEN the elder of Phila merchant for natural love and affecon gave to his dau ANN w/o THOMAS STORY of same city gent (she being his only dau) pt/o a lott of land . . . whereas WILLIAM PENN proprietary and governour of PA by a patent dated 10 Jul 1684 (recorded Patent Book A vol i pg 37 10 Dec 1684) did grant unto JOHN MOOR then of Phila gent a lott of land on Walnutt St and Chestnutt St 51 ft breadth and from Second St to the swamp 243 ft length bounded with a lott of ANDREW GRISCOMB (GRISCOM) & a lott then in the tenure of JOHN GOODSONN (now of the sd EDWARD SHIPPEN) . . . JOHN MOOR built a messuage upon the lott and soon after died, after whose decease the messuage lott of land descended to ELIZABETH MOOR his sole dau and heir, and the sd ELIZABETH having intermarryd with one HENRY HAWKINS of the city of Bristoll in England merchant, they after she arrived to full age of 21 for 160 pounds on 3 Feb 1698 did release unto JOHN MOOR of Phila Co brewer the house and lott (ackn 8 Mar 1699 & recorded Book E3 vol 5 pg 368 25 Jun 1700), and the afsd JOHN MOOR on 9 Mar 1699 for 200 pounds sold unto EDWARD SHIPPEN the afsd messuage lott of land with brewhouse

building improvements (ackn 4 Sep 1701) . . . . Wit: JOSEPH SHIPPPEN, NEHEMIAH ALLEN, THOMAS MOURRY, JOHN BLANEY. Ackn 29 Jul 1706 before NATHAN STANBURY justice of the peace. MAURICE LISLE dep recorder of deeds. (E3:pg 11)

23 Nov 1706. Deed. PHILLIP ROMAN of Chichester, Chester Co, PA cordwayner for 18 pounds sold to THOMAS CHALKLEY of Phila sawyer a lot of land 150 ft breadth and 306 ft length bounded by High St & GEORGE HARMON . . . whereas by indenture of lease & release dated 23&24 Sep 1681 WILLIAM PENN proprietary and governor of PA did sell unto JOHN HARRIS of Goatacre, Co of Wilts, in England clothier 1500 a., and whereas JOHN HARRIS of Goatacre clothier son & heir of the sd JOHN HARRIS (then deceased) and EDWARD HARRIS of Foxhall, Co of Wilts, by their life indentures bearing date 31&30 Oct 1701 did convey unto the sd PHILIP ROMAN 1000 a. pt/o the 1500 a. . . . whereas by virtue of certain constitutions bearing date 11 Jul 1681 between the sd WILLIAM PENN and the sd JOHN HARRIS the father & others the originall grantees of the lands, there belonged unto the sd JOHN HARRIS severall lots of land in that tr surveyed for the site of the city of Phila as appurtenant to the sd 1500 a., the other 500 a. pt/o the 1500 a. being sold by the sd JOHN HARRIS the father in his life time . . . at the request of the sd PHILIP ROMAN & by virtue of a warrant dated 8 Nov 1703 there was surveyd unto the sd JOHN HARRIS on 16 Nov 1703 a lot of land s side of Mulbery St in Phila 150 ft breadth and 306 ft length bounded by High St & GEORGE HARMON . . . . Wit: WILLIAM TILL, GRIFFITH[?] LEWELYN. Ackn 3 Dec 1706 before THOMAS MASTERS justice of the peace. THOMAS STORY recorder of deeds. (E3:pg 14)

20 Aug 1706. Deed. JACOB GODSHALK of Germantown Phila Co turner for 25 shillings sold to ISSAC SHOEMAKER of same place turner, CASPAR HOODT of Phila taylor, GEORGE GRAY of same place merchant, SOLOMON CRESSON of same place turner, DAVID BREINTNALL of same place shopkeeper & THOMAS STORY of same place . . . a parcell of land, to build a building for the making of oyle of linseed, in Germantown adj 3 a. late of the sd ISSAC SHOEMAKER sold to the sd grantees and other land of the sd GODSHALK . . . 14 perches pt/o 50 a. granted by the sd ISSAC SHOEMAKER to the sd JACOB GODSHALK 21 Oct 1702 . . . JACOB GODSHALK hath made JOHN NOOKS his atty to ackn these presents. Wit: GEORGE KEEN, MATHEW PETERS. Ackn 6 Dec 1706 before NATHAN STANBURY justice of the peace. THOMAS STORY recorder of deeds. (E3:pg 16)

1 Oct 1706. Deed. WILLIAM CARTER of Phila blockmaker sold to DANIEL GAUNT of same city cordwiner a piece of ground in Phila 13 ft 6 inches breadth 51 ft length bounded by Chesnutt St, CALEB CASH, lott late of

HENRY TREGRANEY & house now of WILLIAM RUDD, which CALEB CASH executed by his deed poll the day next before the day of the date hereof with yearly rent of 7 pounds payable to JOSHUA CARPENTER & WILLIAM TRENT by an indenture dated 31 Aug 1702 made between JACOB COFFING of Phila clothier and the sd JOSHUA CARPENTER and WILLIAM TRENT ackn 9 Dec 1703 . . . yearly rent of 2 pounds 4 shillings 9 pence 1/2 penny on 25 Mar & 29 Sep by equal portions . . . and also DANIEL GAUNT shall erect 1 brick messuage within 12 months . . . . Wit: GRIFFITH OWEN, CALEB CASH, RICHD HEATH. Ackn 9 Dec 1706 before NATHAN STANBURY justice of the peace. THOMAS STORY recorder of deeds. (E3:pg 19)

5 Dec 1706. Deed. SAMUEL HARRIOT of Phila marriner for 155 pounds sold to GEORGE FITZWATER of same city collarmaker 1/4 pt/o a messuage and land called "The Globe" in Phila between Fronts St and King St now in the possession of GRIMSTON BOWDE containing 17 ft 5 inches in length 30 ft breadth bounded by JEFFRY POLLARDS & the sd SAMUEL HARRIOTT . . . which was formerly conveyed to the sd SAMUEL HARRIOTT by SAMUEL CARPENTER of Phila & afterwards confirmed to the sd SAMUEL HARRIOTT by patent dated 28 Oct 1701 (Patent Book A vol 3 pg 197) . . . 1/2 pt/o the sd messuage next adjoining to the lott formerly of JOHN DELAVALL then in the possession of RICHARD HILL, the sd SAMUEL HARRIOTT did 18 Jul 1706 convey unto JEFFRY POLLARD of Bucks Co merchant . . . . Wit: JAMES SPENCER, ANN STURBARY, THO CLARKE. Ackn 11 Dec 1706 before NATHAN STANBURY justice of the peace. THOMAS STORY recorder of deeds. (E3:pg 22)

9 Dec 1706. Deed. Whereas DIRICK SIPMAN, by virtue of indentures of lease & release dated 9&10 Mar 1682 made between WILLIAM PENN proprietary & governour of PA & the sd DIRICK SIPMAN, became seized in 5000 a. and sold the same to MATHIAS VAN BEBBER, and by virtue of certain other indentures dated 10&11 Jun 1683 made between the sd WILLIAM PENN and GOVERT RAINKES, the sd GOVERT RAINKES became seized of 1000 a. and sold the same to the sd DIRICK SIPMAN who sold the same to MATHIAS VAN BEBBER, and whereas WILLIAM PENN under patent dated 22 Feb 1702 confirmed unto the sd MATHIAS VAN BEBBER the sd 6000 a. together with 160 a. of over measure found upon resurvey (Patent Book A vol 2 pg 463) . . . MATHIAS VAN BEBBER late of Phila & now of Cecill Co MD merchant for 38 pounds sold to THOMAS WISEMAN of Germantown Phila Co husbandman a tr of land pt/o the afsd 6000 a. adj CLAUS JOHNSTON, MATHIAS VAN BEBBER & EDWARD BEERS . . . 190 a. Wit: JOHN KREY, DAVID LLOYD, RICHD HEAT. Ackn 13 Dec 1706 before THOMAS MASTERS justice of the peace of Phila. THOMAS STORY recorder of deeds. (E3:pg 24)

10 Dec 1706. Deed. THOMAS WISEMAN of Germantown Phila Co husbandman for 38 pounds sold to MATHIAS VAN BEBBER of Cecill Co MD merchant a tr of land in Phila Co bounded by CLAUS JOHNSON, the sd MATHIAS VAN BEBBER & EDWARD BEERS . . . 190 a. . . . . Wit: JOHN KREY, DAVID LLOYD, RICHD HEATH. Ackn 14 Dec 1706 before THOMAS MASTERS justice of the peace. THOMAS STORY recorder of deeds. (E3:pg 26)

19 Nov 1706. Deed. THOMAS MORRIS of Phila Co yeoman for 140 pounds sold to THOMAS DAVIDS batchlour a piece of land adj NICHOLAS MOORE by Southampton Twp . . . 245 a. the sd THOMAS MORRIS purch the sd tr 2 Jun 1702 of REES PREES of Phila decd and by virtue of another deed from JOHN PREES son of REES PREES dated 30 Apr 1706 ackn 23 May 1706 (Book B vol 2 pg 417) and THOMAS MORRIS purch the same for the only proper use of the sd THOMAS DAVIDS . . . . Wit: NATHLL TOMS, JAMES D[?], GRIFFITH JOHN. Ackn 16 Dec 1706 before WILLIAM CARTER justice of the peace. THOMAS STORY recorder of deeds. (E3:pg 28)

25 Feb 1702. Deed. MATHIAS VAN BEBBER (VANBEBBER) of Phila merchant for 48 pounds sold to CLAUSE (CLAUS) JOHNSON of Crevelt Phila Co yeoman a parcell of land adj JOHN KREY & other land of MATHIAS VAN BEBBER . . . 306 a. which is pt/o 6166 a. granted unto the sd MATHIAS VAN BEBBER by WILLIAM PENN proprietary & govenour of PA 22 this instant Feb (Patent Book A vol 2 pg 463-465) . . . MATHIAS VAN BEBBER hath made HENRY SELLEN of Creishym in German Twp his atty to ackn these presents in court . . . . Wit: NATHAN ALLEN, MAURICE LISLE. Ackn 17 Dec 1706 before WILLIAM CARTER justice of the peace. THOMAS STORY recorder of deeds. (E3:pg 30)

25 Feb 1702. Deed. MATHIAS VANBEBBER of Phila merchant for 39 pounds 7 shillings 6 pence sold to JOHN KREY (KEY) of Kreysham German Twp Phila Co yeoman a parcell of land adj HENRY PANNEBECKER, other land of MATHIAS VANBEBBER & CLAUS JOHNSON . . . 306 a. . . . which is pt/o a 6166 a. tr of land granted unto the sd MATHIAS VANBEBBER by WILLIAM PENN proprietary & governour of PA by patent dated 22 Feb now currant (Patent Book A vol 2 pg 463-465) . . . MATHIAS VANBEBBER hath made HENRY SELLEN his atty to ackn these presents in court . . . . Wit: NATHAN ALLEN, MAURICE LISLE. Ackn 18 Dec 1706 before THOMAS MASTERS justice of the peace. THOMAS STORY recorder of deeds. (E3:pg 32)

9 Dec 1706. Deed. MATHIAS VANBEBBER (VAN BEBBER) late of Phila but now of Cecill Co MD merchant for 38 pounds sold to EDWARD BEER of Phila Co husbandman a tr of land pt/o 6000 a. adj THOMAS WISEMAN, other land of MATHIAS VANBEBBER & JOHN NEWBERRY . . . 190 a.. . . whereas DIRICK SIPMAN, by vertue of indentures of lease & release dated 9&10 Mar 1682 made between WILLIAM PENN proprietary & governour of PA and sd DIRICK SIPMAN, became seized in 5000 a. and sold same to the sd MATHIAS VANBEBBER, and by other indentures dated 10&11 Jun 1683 made between the sd WILLIAM PENN and GOVERT RAMKES, GOVERT RAMKES became seized in 1000 a. and sold same to the sd MATHIAS VANBEBBER, and a patent dated 22 Feb 1702 was granted to the sd MATHIAS VANBEBBER for 6000 a. together with 166 a. of overmeasure (Patent Book A vol 2 pg 465). Wit: JOHN KREY, DAVID LLOYD, RICHD HEATH. Ackn 19 Dec 1706 before WILLIAM CARTER justice of the peace of Phila. (E3:pg 33)

10 Dec 1706. Deed. EDWARD BEER of Phila Co husbandman for 38 pounds sold to MATHIAS VANBEBBER of Cecill Co MD merchant a tr of land in Phila Co adj THOMAS WISEMAN . . . 190 a. . . . . Wit: JOHN KREY, DAVID LLOYD, RICHD HEATH. Ackn 20 Dec 1706 before THOMAS MASTERS justice of the peace. THOMAS STORY recorder of deeds. (E3:pg 35)

9 Dec 1706. Deed. MATHIAS VANBEBBER of Bohemia River MD merchant for 54 pounds sold to DIRK & WILLIAM RENBERG (RENNBERGE) (RENBERGE) both of Millhenn upon the Scullkill Phila Co yeoman a tr of land in Bebbers Twp Phila Co adj JOHN NEWBERRY & other land of MATHIAS VANBEBBER . . . 300 a. pt/o a 6000 a. tr of land . . . . Wit: HENRIETTA LOWTHER, JOHN NEWBERRY, GEORGE LOWTHER. Ackn 23 Dec 1706 before WILLIAM CARTER justice of the peace. THOMAS STORY recorder. (E3:pg 36)

21 Dec 1706. Deed. GEORGE HARMER of Phila horner for 21 pounds sold to THOMAS CHALKLEY of sd city sawyer a lott 49 1/2 ft breadth 306 ft length . . . by virtue of a warrant dated 26 Oct 1702 there was surveyed unto WILLIAM GARRETT (by DAVID POWEL on 12 Apr 1703) a lott of ground in sd city bounded by Fifth St, DE, Mullberry St & High St and whereas the sd WILLIAM GARRETT on 17 May 1703 did convey the same unto the sd GEORGE HARMER (ackn 8 Jun 1704 in court) . . . . Wit: WILLIAM TILL, THOMAS WILSON. Ackn 23 Dec 1706 before THOMAS MASTERS justice of the peace. THOMAS STORY recorder of deeds. (E3:pg 38)

8 -- 1706. Deed. MATHIAS VANBEBBER of Sicil Co MD merchant sold to GARRETT INDENHOOF a tr of land in Phila Co adj DIRICK RAMSBRYE & other land of MATHIAS VANBEBBER . . . 420 a. pt/o 6166 a. . . . . Wit: GEORGE LOWTHER, DA POWELL, HENRY PANNEBECKERS. Ackn 24 Dec 1706 before WILLIAM CARTER justice of the peace. THOMAS STORY recorder of deeds. (E3:pg 40)

19 Dec 1706. Deed. JOHN AUSTIN of Phila shipwright & JANE his wife & ELIZABETH BENNETT of same city widow for 36 pounds sold to JAMES DAVID of Great Valley Chester Co yeoman . . . [illegible] . . . 100 a. whereas THOMAS LLOYD & JAMES CLAYPOOLE two of the commissioners of WILLIAM PENN proprietary & governour of PA by their warrant dated 12 -- 1684 granted unto the sd ELIZABETH by the name of ELIZABETH POTTS 100 a. [illegible] & 25 May 1703 the 100 a. was resurveyed and returned to be situated in the Welch Tr in Chester Co adj GRIFFITH JOHN, LOETITIA [?]'s Manner of [blank] & JOHN ROBERTS . . . the grantors have made JOHN DOE their atty to deliver these presents in court. Wit: JEREMIAH JANNAN, GRIFFITH LEWELLYN. Ackn 25 Dec 1706 before THOMAS MASTERS justice of the peace. THOMAS STORY recorder of deeds. (E3:pg 42)

18 Nov 1706. Deed. WILLIAM SOUTHEBE of Phila yeoman for 11 pounds 10 shillings sold to SOLOMON CRESSON of sd city hairmaker . . . [illegible] . . . purch by LAWRENCE COCK [illegible] . . . . Wit: EDWARD TEW, ELIZABETH TEW. Ackn 26 Dec 1706 before THOMAS MASTERS justice of the peace. THOMAS STORY recorder of deeds. (E3:pg 44)

8 Dec 1706. Deed. MATHIAS VANBEBBER of Sicel Co MD for 82 pounds sold to JOHN NEWBRY of Phila husbandman a tr of land adj EDWARD BEER, other land of MATHIAS VANBEBBER & [?] RANBERY . . . 450 a. pt/o 6166 a. . . . [illegible] . . . whereas WILLIAM PENN by his present commissioners EDWARD SHIPPEN, GRIFFITH OWEN, THOMAS STORY & JAMES LOGAN by a patent dated 22 Feb 1702 did grant unto the sd MATHIAS VANBEBBER 6000 a. as by resurvey found containing 6166 a. (Book A vol 2 pg 463-465) . . . [illegible] . . . . Wit: GEO LOWTHER, DAVID POWELL. Ackn 26 Dec 1706 before WILLIAM CARTER justice of the peace. THOMAS STORY recorder of deeds. (E3:pg 45)

30 Sep 1706. Deed. Whereas JAMES FOX became seized in 2 lotts and by his will dated 8 Sep 1699 appointed his wife ELIZABETH FOX and his son JAMES FOX executors and SAMUEL CARPENTER, DAVID LLOYD & ISAAC NORRIS trustees, & JAMES FOX the son also dyed, and ELIZABETH FOX on 1 Mar 1701 conveyed the land unto EDWARD

SHIPPEN (Book B vol 3 pg 156) . . . EDWARD SHIPPEN of Phila merchant for 800 pounds sold to JOHN CRAPP of same city merchant two lotts of land in Phila the one 30 ft breadth 250 ft length bounded by lott late of CHARLES PICKERING, Front St, ALICE GUEST & River DE, the other 30 ft breath 250 ft length bounded with lott late of DANIEL SMITH, lott late of CHARLES PICKERING & River DE . . . . Wit: DAVID LLOYD, NATHAN STANBURY, MAURICE LISLE, JOHN JONES, RICHD HEATH. Ackn 26 Dec 1706 before NATHAN STANBURY justice of the peace. THOMAS STORY recorder of deeds. (E3:pg 47)

13 Sep 1706. NATHAN STANBURY of Phila merchant executor of the will of ELIZABETH FOX who was surviving executrix of the will of JAMES FOX her late husband decd paid 800 pounds to EDWARD SHIPPEN of Phila merchant & hereby ackns that 575 pounds pt/o the 800 pounds is in satisfaction of the debt of 425 pounds & interest and 228 pounds being the residue was paid unto NATHAN STANBURY towards payment of the rest of the sd JAMES FOX's debts . . . whereas the sd ELIZABETH with the consent of sd JAMES FOX by her deed poll dated 3 Mar 1702 did convey to sd EDWARD SHIPPEN two lotts upon the payment of 420 pounds due him from the sd JAMES FOX's estate, and EDWARD SHIPPEN by his indenture [see above] for 800 pounds to be paid by JOHN CRAPP of Phila merchant did convey unto sd JOHN CRAPP the sd lotts and it was agreed between the sd EDWARD SHIPPEN, NATHAN STANBURY and the trustees that all the money they should receive be imployed for the payment of the sd JAMES FOX's debts . . . . Wit: SAMUELL BORDEN, RICHD HEATH. Ackn 26 Dec 1706 before THOMAS MASTERS justice of the peace. THOMAS STORY recorder of deeds. (E3:pg 49)

14 Aug 1706. Deed of Mortgage. EDWARD JAMES of Phila bricklayer & ANN his wife sole executrix of the will of WILLIAM HUDSON late of Phila bricklayer her former husband decd under the direction of ANN PARSONS of same city widow sole executrix of the will of JOHN PARSONS her late husband decd sold to DAVID LLOYD of Phila gentlemen a messuage & lott of ground bounded on Chestnutt St in Phila 49 ft 6 inches breadth 245 ft length adj lott late of THOMAS JONES & lott now in possession of JOSHUA CARPENTER . . . whereas WILLIAM HUDSON by his will dated 29 Aug 1694 did give unto his son JOHN HUDSON 20 pounds to be paid him when he shall arrive at the age of 21 and next he gave his dau ELIZABETH 20 pounds to be paid her when she arrive at the age of 21 and if either of his children dies before the age it will return to the survivor and if both happen to die then unto their mother, and after WILLIAM's decease, ANN his relict did deposit 40 pounds in the hands of sd JOHN PARSONS for securing the payment of the legacies, and whereas the sd EDWARD JAMES & ANN his

wife have received from the sd JOHN PARSON's the most pt/o the 40 pounds & interest in his life time and the residue from the sd ANN PARSONS since his decease . . . this indenture EDWARD JAMES for securing the payment of 40 pounds to the children and for securing the payment of a debt of fifty pounds due the sd DAVID LLOYD of Phila gent by the sd EDWARD JAMES . . . if EDWARD JAMES shall pay unto DAVID LLOYD 50 pounds with interest upon 15 Nov 1707 and if EDWARD JAMES shall pay unto JOHN HUDSON & ELIZABETH HUDSON the legicies given them by their father's will then this indenture shall cease . . . . Wit: SAMUELL POWELL, RICHD HEATH. Ackn 28 Dec 1706 before THOMAS MASTERS justice of the peace. THOMAS STORY recorder of deeds. 7 Dec 1715 before CHARLES BROCKDON dep recorder of deeds, DAVID LLOYD released ye mortgage. (E3:pg 50)

11 Aug 1701. Deed. THOMAS WHARTON of Phila taylor for 100 pounds sold to THOMAS EVERNDEN of Annamessin Somersett Co MD yeoman 46 ft breadth 20 ft length . . . whereas WILLIAM PENN propriatary & governour of PA by indenture of lease & release granted 5000 a. unto CHRISTOPHER TAYLOR & by virtue of a patent he became seized in lotts in Phila and sold same to THOMAS LLOYD, and he sold pt/o the lotts (55 ft breadth 396 ft length) to ANTHONY MORRIS of Phila merchant, and ANTHONY MORRIS on 20 Dec 1692 granted unto the sd THOMAS WHARTON a piece of the lott (46 ft length 20 ft breadth) bounded by Second St, EDMUND DUCASTELE & the great lott in the hand of sd ANTHONY MORRIS. Wit: GEORGE GRAY, WM FISKBOURN. Ackn 30 Dec 1706 before WILLIAM CARTER justice of the peace. THOMAS STORY recorder of deeds. (E3:pg 52)

23 Jul 1706. Deed. JOHN POWELL of Phila Co yeoman & ROBERT BONELL of Phila yeoman for 120 pounds sold to SAMUEL PRESTON of same city merchant a messuage & lott of land . . . whereas JOHN FINNEY high sheriff of Phila Co by his deed poll dated 11 Nov 1704 sold to JOHN POWELL & ROBERT BONELL a messuage with a lott in the sd city 51 ft 6 inches breadth & 178 ft length bounded by MARY MALTBY, Chestnut St, ENOCH STORY & High St . . . . Wit: RO HEATH, DAVID EVANS, DAVID LLOYD, RICHD HEATH. Ackn 5 Jan 1706 before GRIFFITH JONES justice of the peace. THOMAS STORY recorder of deeds. (E3:pg 54)

2 Jan 1706. Deed. THOMAS POTTS of Bristoll Twp Phila Co yeoman for 250 pounds sold to EVERARD BOLTON of Chiltenham same co yeoman 1/4 pt/o 3 parcells of land in Bristol Twp Phila Co adj CHRISTOPHER SIPTHORP . . . 13 1/2 a. and 15 a. 36 perches being pt/o 2 trs one 100 a. conveyed unto the sd THOMAS POTTS by JACOB SHOEMAKER 22 Jun 1699, the other 19 1/2 a. conveyed by the sd JACOB SHOEMAKER unto sd THOMAS POTTS

1 Sep 1705, and the 15 a. 36 perches stand erected 2 grist mills under one roof called "Potts Mills" which the sd THOMAS POTTS was lately seised as by indenture dated 2 Jul last past which granted 1/2 of the land & mills unto GEORGE GRAY of Phila merchant and by one other indenture dated same day for 250 pounds granted 1/4 pt/o the sd lands, mills & premisses unto the sd EVERARD BOLTON (Book B vol 3 pg 23 4 Aug last) . . . . Wit: THOMAS SHUTE, SAML BORDEN. Ackn 10 Jan 1706 before JOHN JONES justice of the peace. THOMAS STORY recorder of deeds. (E3:pg 56)

16 May 1706. Deed. JACOB COFFING late of Phila weaver but now of Glocester Co w NJ for 450 pounds sold to RICE PETERS of same place cordwainer 200 a. . . . whereas WILLIAM JAMES of Cheltnam Twp Phila Co yeoman by his deed poll dated 21 Apr 1704 did give unto sd JACOB COFFING his plantation & tr of land bounded by EVERARD BOLTON, JOHN SONGHURST, JOHN DAY & WILLIAM BROWN . . . 200 a. pt/o 500 a. granted to one WILLIAM BROWN by sd WILLIAM BROWN & one JOHN BERTLES, & by them unto PATRICK ROBINSON, who sold the same unto the sd WILLIAM JAMES, and he unto the sd JACOB COFFING . . . . Wit: WILLIAM HEAVERD, FRANCIS COOK. Ackn 27 Jan 1706 before THOMAS MASTERS justice of the peace. THOMAS STORY recorder of deeds. (E3:pg 60)

28 Jan 1706. Deed of Gift. Whereas Capt LASSEY COCK of Phila Co on 14 Jul 1704 sold unto WILLIAM SNOWDEN son of WILLIAM SNOWDEN decd a parcell of land in Passyunck with one home lott between ANDREW BANKSON & MATHIAS HOWLSTED 100 a. (ackn in court 6 May 1685), and WILLIAM SNOWDEN on 20 Oct 1694 sold 61 a. pt/o the afsd land and 2 a. more at Malsurars Point & a piece of meadow between PETER COCK & the sd MATHIAS HOLSTED at Sephickan Cr in Parsyunck Twp unto MATHIAS HOWLSTED . . . this indenture MATHIAS HOWLSTED of Passyunck Phila Co farmer & WILLIAM SNOWDEN of Phila husbandman for natural affection gave to LAWRENCE HOWLSTED of Passyunck eldest sonn of the sd MATHIAS HOWLSTED a parcel of land adj other land of sd MATHIAS HOWLSTED, bank of Sculkill & the reputed BANKSON's lott . . . 48 1/2 a. and a piece of meadow 1 1/2 a. . . . . Wit: RICHARD RODES, FREDERICK HOLSTEN. Ackn 1 Jan 1706 before WILLIAM CARTER justice of the peace. THOMAS STORY recorder. (E3:pg 62)

25 Jan 1706/7. Deed of Gift. CASPAR FISH & WILLIAMKA his wife of Burlington Co w NJ & MATHIAS KEEN, JONAS KEEN & GEORGE KEEN of PA yeomen for love, good will & affection give to our son & brother ERICK KEEN of Oxford Twp Phila Co yeoman a tr of land in Oxford Twp at the mouth of Sissowakissink Cr adj widow HARMON, which was first purch

from Sir EDMUND ANDREAS under the seal of NY 25 Mar 1676 (Patent Book A pg ---) unto MICHAEL FREDRICKS, & he conveyed 1/2 of the tr unto ERICK MULLEKER 10 Apr 1688, and he conveyed the tr unto the sd MATHIAS KEEN 5 Jun 1696 . . . . Wit: JOHN MERRICK, HENRY STRIKE. Ackn 8 Feb 1706 before THOMAS MASTERS justice of the peace. THOMAS STORY recorder of deeds. (E3:pg 64)

25 Jan 1706/7. Deed. GARTHO ENOCH widow & relict of HERMON ENOCH late of Taconey Oxford Twp Phila Co decd & ENOCH ENOCH son of the sd HERMON ENOCH for 3 pounds sold to MATHIAS KEEN of same place yeoman 1 lott in Longfloughton Meadow adj sd MATHIAS KEEN 1 a. pt/o a tr purch by MICHAEL FREDRICKS by patent from Sir EDMUND ANDROS esqr of NY 25 Mar 1676 (Patent Book A pg ---), and MICHAEL FREDRICKS conveyed the tr unto the sd HERMON ENOCH 1 Sep 1705 and by power of administration the sd GARTHO & ENOCH sell to the sd MATHIAS KEEN . . . . Wit: ERICK KEEN, HENRY STRIKE. Ackn 9 Feb 1706 before THOMAS MASTERS justice of the peace. THOMAS STORY recorder of deeds. (E3:pg 66)

-- 1706/7. Deed. Whereas JACOB HALL decd of Oxford Twp Phila Co did in his lifetime sell unto MATHIAS KEEN of same place yeoman, but did not make any title, certain lotts . . . JACOB HALL son of the afsd JACOB HALL for 9 pounds paid unto JACOB HALL Senr decd 3 Aug 1696 sold unto MATHIAS KEEN the afsd lotts adj widdow NEEL . . . [illegible] . . . 3 1/4 a. Wit: ERICK KEEN, HENRY STRIKE. Ackn 11 Feb 1706 before THOMAS MASTERS justice of the peace. THOMAS STORY recorder of deeds. (E3:pg 67)

9 Sep 1706. Deed. ANTHONY MORRIS of Phila merchant sold to NATHAN STANBURY & PENTECOST LEAGUE of same city merchants for the use of ANTHONY MORRIS his son . . . 1/2 of a messuage, brewhouse, lott, wharfs, buildings, improvements, stock, negroes, debts, goods & chattels in the sd city adj River DE, Front St, King St, JOSEPH KIRK & JACOB REIGNIER . . . [illegible] . . . . Wit: HUGH CORDRY, PHILIP HILLIARD, MAURICE LISLE. Ackn 12 Dec 1706 before JOHN JONES justice of the peace. THOMAS STORY recorder of deeds. (E3:pg 69)

23 Jan 1706/7. Deed. RICHARD HILL of Phila merchant & HANNAH his wife sold to JAMES BARRETT of same city cordwiner pt/o a piece of ground adj Wallnutt St, GRIFFITH JONES, lott late of JOHN FELLOWS, lott late of JOHN OTTER now of sd RICHARD HILL, & THOMAS GRIFFITH . . . whereas on 13 Jan 1693 sd GRIFFITH JONES of Phila merchant conveyed unto HANNAH HARRIS by the name of HANNAH DELAVAL widow &

relict of JOHN DELAVALL late of Phila merchant decd a piece of ground [illegible] . . . . Wit: JAMES LOGAN, CHARLES PLUMLY, RICHD HEATH. Ackn 13 Feb 1706 before WILLIAM CARTER justice of the peace. THOMAS STORY recorder of deeds. (E3:pg 72)

30 Jan 1706/7. Deed. RICHARD HILL of Phila merchant & HANNAH his wife executrix of the will of JOHN DELLAVALL late of same city merchant her former husband decd sold to CHARLES PLUMLY of same city joiner pt/o a tr of land . . . whereas by an indenture dated 12 Sep 1689 JOHN OTTER sold to JOHN DELAVALL of NY merchant (Book E vol 5 pg 144) a lott in Phila 21 ft breadth 396 ft length adj JOSHUA CART, [blank] JONES, Front St & Second St, and JOHN DELAVALL being seized of the lott made his will & did bequeath all his land to his wife HANNAH to hold until his son JOHN came to the age of 21, he getting 1/2 of the estate, if the son should die then 1/4 of the estate to be divided equally between his two sisters REBECCA & MARGARETT and 3/4 to remain to his wife . . . the son JOHN dyed before he attained the age of 21, and REBECCA also dyed after whose decease the sd MARGARET together with her husband THOMAS CODRINGTON did release unto HANNAH all their right to the estate . . . [illegible] . . . for the rent of 3 pounds 13 shillings 6 pence all arrears shall be fully satisfyed . . . . Wit: JAMES LOGAN, JAMES BARRETT, RICHD HEATH. Ackn 15 Feb 1706 before WILLIAM CARTER justice of the peace. THOMAS STORY recorder of deeds. (E3:pg 75)

27 Dec 1701. Deed. THOMAS FAIRMAN of Phila Co gent for 25 pounds sold to SILAS PRYER of Chester Co husbandman 200 a. pt/o 5000 a. which he purch from THOMAS HARTLEY esqr who originally purch same from WILLIAM PENN proprietary & governour of PA. Wit: JOHN REDMAN, HENRY FLOWERS. Ackn 1 Mar 1706 before NATHAN STANBURY justice of the peace. THOMAS STORY recorder of deeds. (E3:pg 77)

15 Aug 1706. Deed. JOSEPH HARVEY of Darby Chester Co wheelwright for 106 pounds 10 shillings secured to be paid to WILLIAM TRENT & ISAAC NORRIS both of Phila merchants by JOHN CARTRIDGE of Plymouth Phila Co yeoman, sold to JOHN CARTRIDGE a tr of land excepting 10 a. reserved to sd JOSEPH HARVEY, bounded by Scullkill River, land of WILLIAM TRENT & ISAAC NORRIS & land sold to JOHN COCK . . . 1/2 of 710 a. pt/o 7480 a. granted by WILLIAM PENN prprietary & governour of PA to his son WILLIAM PENN Junr by warrant 13 Sep 1683, also by warrant to resurvey 2 May 1704 confirmed by patent to sd WILLIAM PENN Junr 2 Oct 1704 (Book A vol 2 pg 703-4) and the sd WILLIAM PENN sold the tr to WILLIAM TRENT & ISAAC NORRIS 7 Oct 1704, they sold 710 a. to sd JOSEPH HARVEY 29 Jun 1706 . . . . Wit: EDMUND CARTLIDGE, JOHN

HOOD. Ackn 1 Mar 1706 before THOMAS MASTERS justice of the peace. THOMAS STORY recorder of deeds. (E3:pg 78)

5 Oct 1706. Deed. JOHN CARTLIDGE of Plymouth Phila Co yeoman & JOSEPH HARVEY of Darby Chester Co wheelwright for 60 pounds sold to DAVID THOMAS of Darby Chester Co blacksmith a tr of land e side of River Scoolkill adj WILLIAM TRENT & ISAAC NORRIS . . . 200 a. pt/o 710 a. sold to the afsd JOSEPH HARVEY from WILLIAM TRENT & ISAAC NORRIS both of Phila merchants 29 Jun 1706 (Book E3 vol 6 pg 1&2) and the sd JOSEPH HARVEY sold 1/2 pt/o the 710 a. excepting 10 a. to JOHN CARTLIDGE 15 Aug 1706 . . . . Wit: JOHAN REDWITSIOR, HUGH JONES. Ackn 3 Mar 1706 before THOMAS MASTERS justice of the peace. THOMAS STORY recorder of deeds. (E3:pg 79)

20 Mar 1705/6. Deed. JOHN HUMPHREY of Gwynedd Twp Phila Co yeoman for 30 pounds sold to HUGH GRIFFITH the younger of same place yeoman . . . a parcell of land in Gwynedd adj JOSEPH FISHER, EDWARD ROBERTS, sd JOHN HUMPHREY & OWEN EVANS . . . 129 a. pt/o 574 a. granted unto the sd JOHN HUMPHREY by patent 8 Feb 1702 (Patent Book A vol 2 pg 453) . . . . Wit: MATHEW ROBINSON, DAVID POWEL. Ackn 8 Jul 1706 before THOMAS MASTERS justice of the peace. THOMAS STORY recorder of deeds. (E3:pg 81)

6 Dec 1706. Deed. ABRAHAM CARLILE (CARLIELL) (CARLIEL) of Phila cooper sold to THOMAS GRIFFITH of same city cordwainer a piece of ground s side of Walnutt St in Phila 47 ft length 20 ft breadth bounded by JOSEPH CLAYPOOLE, RUTH DUCKETT & sd ABRAHAM CARLILE pt/o land which HENRY BADCOCK (BADCOKE) of Phila brewer on 25 Mar 1704 sold to ABRAHAM CARLILE . . . . Wit: SAML POWEL, RICHARD HEATH. Ackn 17 Mar 1706 before NATHAN STANBURY justice of the peace. THOMAS STORY recorder of deeds. (E3:pg 82)

24 Dec 1706. Deed. JACOB USHER of Phila carpenter for 29 pounds and the arrearage rent sold to HENRY FLOWER of same city barber a lott . . . whereas on 1 Jun 1703 JACOB USHER conveyed to DANIEL FLOWER of same place carpenter a lott in Phila 40 ft breadth 178 ft length bounded by High St, lott late of JOSEPH AMBLERS, Chestnut St with the rent of 1 pound 15 shillings on 24 Dec & 24 Jun yearly forever with a clause of distress for nonpaymt . . . . Wit: WILLIAM COLEMAN, RICHARD HEATH. Ackn 19 Feb 1706 before THOMAS MASTERS justice of the peace. THOMAS STORY recorder of deeds. (E3:pg 85)

25 Sep 1706. Deed. SAMUEL CARPENTER of Phila merchant, DAVID LLOYD of Phila gent, ISAAC NORRIS of Phila merchant, NATHAN

STANBURY of Phila merchant executor of the will of ELIZABETH FOX late of Phila widow decd and JOHN CRAPP (CRAP) of Phila merchant for a valuable consideration sold to HENRY FLOWER of Phila barber a lott . . . whereas JAMES FOX late of Phila merchant by deed poll executed under the hand of CASPAR HOODT of Phila taylor 6 Feb 1693/4 became in his life time seised in a piece of ground in Phila 152 ft length 25 ft 6 inches breadth bounded by Second St, lott late of CRISTOPHER SIBTHORP, sd CASPAR HOODT & lott late of ABRAHAM HARDIMAN, and the sd JAMES FOX made his will dated 8 Sep 1699 making his wife ELIZABETH & son JAMES executors to sell the land to pay his debts . . . and whereas the sd ELIZABETH and son JAMES are since decd so the whole power of the sale rests with the sd SAMUEL CARPENTER, DAVID LLOYD & ISAAC NORRIS . . . at the request of NATHAN STANBURY for the payment of sd JAMES FOX's debts did sell but not convey the sd lott unto the sd JOHN CRAPP . . . . Wit: EDWARD EVANS, RICHARD HEATH. Ackn 20 Feb 1706 before THOMAS MASTERS justice of the peace. THOMAS STORY recorder of deeds. (E3:pg 86)

4 Nov 1706. Deed. BENJAMIN CHAMBERS of Phila Co yeoman for 32 pounds 15 shillings sold to THOMAS PASCOLL of same co yeoman a tr of land w side of Scullkill in Kinses Twp Phila Co being the lower end of a neck of land fomerly belonging to PETER YOCOM the elder since decd, who sold the same to the sd BENJAMIN CHAMBERS by two deeds, one 7 Jun 1699 the other 8 Jan next following, bounded by the Great Damm, the Little Dam & the house where widow JENNER formerly dwelt . . . 14 a. . . . . Wit: RICHARD MORRIS, ELIZABETH JENKINS. Ackn 22 Feb 1706 before NATHAN STANBURY justice of the peace. THOMAS STORY recorder of deeds. (E3:pg 88)

22 Nov 1706. Deed. BENJAMIN CHAMBERS of Phila Co yeoman for 20 silver money sold to STEPHEN JACKSON of Phila merchant two lotts on Front St 140 ft breadth 250 ft length bounded by DE River & JAMES MOOR, granted by two patents to BENJAMIN CHAMBERS one 5 May 1694 & the other 9 Jun 1694 (Patent Book A pg 367-369) . . . . Wit: SAMUEL PRESTON, ELIAS HUGG. Ackn 23 Mar 1706 before NATHAN STANBURY justice of the peace. THOMAS STORY recorder of deeds. (E3:pg 89)

25 Sep 1705. Deed. SAMUEL MILES (MEALS) of Phila cooper for 22 shillings sold to BENJAMIN CHAMBERS of Phila Co yeoman in his procuring for the sd SAMUEL MILES a warrant survey & return of 50 a. as well as for 12 shillings discharged by the sd BENJAMIN CHAMBERS . . . which land was granted to SAMUEL MILES by warrant 3 Sep 1705 directed to ISAAC TAYLOR surveyor of Chester Co & resurveyed in Bensalem Twp

Chester Co & certifyed by JACOB TAYLOR . . . bounded by ABRAHAM MARSHALL (which he lately purch of sd BENJAMIN CHAMBERS) & RICHARD PEIRS . . . 50 a. . . . . Wit: HENRY BADCOCK, BENJAMIN MORGAN. Ackn 25 Mar 1706 before NATHAN STANBURY justice of the peace. THOMAS STORY recorder of deeds. (E3:pg 90)

28 Sep 1706. Deed. HENRY FLOWER of Phila barber sold to CALEB RANSTED of same city chairmaker a piece of ground . . . whereas on 25 Sep instant SAMUEL CARPENTER of Phila merchant, DAVID LOYD of Phila gent, ISAAC NORRIS of Phila merchant, NATHAN STANBURY of Phila merchant executor of the will of ELIZABETH FOX late of Phila widow decd and JOHN CRAPP of Phila merchant conveyed to sd HENRY FLOWER a piece of ground in Phila 25 ft 6 inches breadth 152 ft length bounded by Second St, lott late of CHRISTOPHER SIBTHORP, CASPER HOODT & lott late of ABRAHAM HARDIMAN . . . . Wit: NATHAN STANBURY, DAVID LLOYD, RICHD HEATH. Ackn 28 Mar 1707 before DAVID LLOYD justice of the peace of Phila. THOMAS STORY recorder of deeds. (E3:pg 91)

29 Mar 1707. Deed. JOHN CADWALLAD (CADWALAD) of Phila Co yeoman for 45 pounds sold to JOHN MORGAN of Abbington Phila Co taylor a parcell of land adj sd JOHN CADWALLAD & the Mannor of More Land . . . 70 a. pt/o 192 a. which WILLIAM SALSBERRY late of Phila carpenter 27 Dec 1700 conveyed unto the sd JOHN CADWALLAD . . . . Wit: DAVID LLOYD, EDWARD BUZBY, HENRY WILLIS. Ackn 21 Mar 1706 before DAVID LLOYD justice of the peace. THOMAS STORY recorder of deeds. (E3:pg 93)

7 Jul 1704. Deed. RUDOLPH (RANDOLPH) BONDELIN of Germantown Phila Co yeoman for 2 score 5 pounds sold to CLAUSS BRUNS of Chesnut Hill in Germantwp Phila Co yeoman a tr of land at Somerhousen Germantwp between JUSTUS FALCKNER & GEORGE MILLER called "Chestnut Hill" 100 a. . . . which are now in the tenure of the sd RUDOLPH BONDELIN by virtue of an indenture of sale from DANIEL FALCKNER of Germantown yeoman 29 Feb 1703/4 formerly granted unto him by JOHANN JAWERT, partner & atty of Francfort Company 4 Mar 1702/3 . . . . Wit: WILLIAM STORNYGARD, GEORGE MILLER. Ackn 2 Apr 1706 before NATHAN STANBURY justice of the peace. THOMAS STORY recorder of deeds. (E3:pg 94)

9 Dec 1703. Deed. Whereas JOHN LEAPLIDGE citizen & skinner of London in the Court of Common Pleas held 5 Mar 1701 did recover against SARAH SANDERS of Phila widow executrix of the will of CHARLES SANDERS late of Phila merchant decd a debt of 154 pounds 1 shilling 3 pence & damages of

42 shillings 6 pence . . . JOHN LEAPLIDGE by his atty THOMAS MURRAY and the late sherriff THOMAS FARMER then returned that he had seized in execution a messuage & tr of land 500 a. at Pemapecka which was of the sd CHARLES SANDERS decd (valued at 590 pounds) but remained in his hands unsold for want of buyers . . . JOHN FINNEY esqr now high sherriff of Phila Co conveyed to sd JOHN LEAPLIDGE 1/4 pt/o the 500 a. . . . . Wit: THOMAS CLARK, CHR PHILIPSON, DAVID LLOYD. Ackn 11 Jan 1703 ROBERT ASHETON prothonotary. Recorded 3 Apr 1707. (E3:pg 95)

9 Dec 1703. Deed. Whereas WILLIAM SANDERS citizen & cooper of London at the Court of Common Pleas held 5 Mar 1701 did recover against SARAH SANDERS of Phila Co widow executrix of the will of CHARLES SANDERS late of Phila merchant decd a debt of 109 pounds 9 shillings 3 pence & damages of 40 shillings 6 pence & a debt of 105 pounds 9 shillings 5 pence & damages of 42 shillings 6 pence . . . WILLIAM SANDERS by his atty THOMAS MURRAY & the late sherriff THOMAS FARMER then returned that he had seized in execution a messuage tr of land 500 a. at Pemapecka which was of the sd CHARLES SANDERS decd (valued at 590 pounds) but remained in his hands unsold for want of buyers . . . JOHN FINNEY esqr now high sheriff of Phila Co conveyed to sd WILLIAM SANDERS 1/5 pt/o the 500 a. . . . . Wit: THO CLARK, CHR PHILIPSON, DAVID LOYDD. Ackn 11 Jan 1703 ROBERT ASHETON prothonotary. Recorded 4 Apr 1707. (E3:pg 96)

9 Dec 1703. Deed. Whereas WILLIAM SHARDLOW of London merchant at the Court of Common Pleas held 5 Mar 1701 did recover against SARAH SANDERS of Phila widow executrix of the will of CHARLES SANDERS late of Phila merchant decd a debt of 119 pounds 18 shillings & damages of 42 shillings 6 pence . . . WILLIAM SHARDLOW by his atty THOMAS MURRAY & the late sherriff THOMAS FARMER then returned that he had seized in execution a messuage & tr of land 500 a. which was of the CHARLES SANDERS decd (valued at 590 pounds) . . . JOHN FINNEY esqr now high sheriff of Phila Co conveyed to WILLIAM SHARDLOW 1/5 pt/o the 500 a. . . . . Wit: THO CLARK, CHR PHILIPSON, DAVID LOYD. Ackn 11 Jan 1703 ROBERT ASHETON prothonotary. Recorded 5 Apr 1707. (E3:pg 98)

12 Apr 1707. Deed. JOHN HAVARD of Phila Co yeoman for 200 pounds sold to DAVID POWEL of Phila yeoman a tr of land in Cheltenham Twp bounded by RICE PETERS, RICHARD HALL & EVERARD BOLTON . . . 229 a. 40 perches which land was granted unto the sd JOHN HAVARD by patent 23 Feb 1701 (Patent Book A vol 2 pg 303) . . . . Wit: ROBERT WILLIAMS,

WILLIAM HAVARD, RICHARD HEATH. Ackn 14 Apr 1707 before THOMAS MASTERS justice of the peace. THOMAS STORY recorder of deeds. (E3:pg 99)

3 Apr 1707. Quit Claim. Whereas THOMAS POTTS Junr late of Germantown & now of Phila yeoman was seized of a tr of land bounded by JOHN ROBERTS, SILAS CRISPIN, land late of PHILIP THLEMAN & land late of JOHN SIBLEY . . . 135 a. and by indenture 1 Jan 1700/1 for 60 pounds conveyed same to JAMES SAMSON of Phila merchant, the sd THOMAS POTTS being under the age of 21 at the time of the conveyance, all which land the sd JAMES SAMSON by deed poll 8 May 1703 conveyed unto JOHN GARRATT (GERRATT) of Phila Co yeoman . . . the sd THOMAS POTTS now of the full age of 21 & upward for the confirmation of the land unto sd JOHN GARRATT for 5 shillings hath quit claimed unto JOHN GARRATT the afsd land . . . . Wit: JOHN MORGAN, JOHN PENNEL. Ackn 14 Apr 1707 before THOMAS MASTERS justice of the peace. THOMAS STORY recorder of deeds. (E3:pg 101)

26 Mar 1707. Deed. RICHARD THOMAS of Phila Co carpenter son & heir of RICHARD ap THOMAS decd for 94 pounds 10 shillings sold to JOHN WATSON of Phila lawyer a lott of land . . . w side of Front St in Phila 51 ft breadth 501 ft length bounded by Second St & GRIFFITH JONES which GRIFFITH OWEN, THO STORY & JAMES LOGAN by patent under their hands 8 Nov 1703 did grant to the sd RICHARD THOMAS in right of & as appurtenant to his sd late father RICHARD ap THOMAS's purch of 5000 a. . . . . Wit: JOHN MIFFLIN, THOMAS SHUTE, DAVID LLOYD, RICHARD HEATH. Ackn 21 Apr 1707 before THOMAS MASTERS justice of the peace. THOMAS STORY recorder of deeds. (E3:pg 102)

10 Feb 1706/7. Quit Claim. CASPAR HOODT of Phila taylor for 5 shillings quit claim unto CALEB RANSTEDD (RANSTED) of Phila turner a piece of ground in Phila 25 1/2 ft breadth 150 ft length bounded by Second St, lott late of CHRISTOPHER SIBTHORP, sd CASPAR HOODT & lott late of ABRAHAM HARDIMAN . . . . Wit: DANIEL RADLEY, DAVID LOYD, RICHARD HEATH. Ackn 15 May 1707 before NATHAN STANBURY justice of the peace. THOMAS STORY recorder of deeds. (E3:pg 104)

25 Mar 1707. Deed. JOHN HART of Phila Co yeoman for 42 pounds sold to JOHN TURNER of Biberry Twp Phila Co yeoman two parcells of land, the first bounded by NATHANIEL WALTON & ANDREW BANKSON . . . 29 a. the other parcell bounded by sd ANDREW BANKSON, sd JOHN TURNER & the first tr . . . 19 a. both being pt/o 484 a. granted to the sd JOHN HART in right of his purch of 1000 a. by virtue of a patent dated 31 May 1703 (Patent

Book A vol 2 pg 329-330) .... Wit: WILLIAM LEE, HANS LICON. Ackn 16 May 1707 before THOMAS MASTERS justice of the peace. THOMAS STORY recorder. (E3:pg 105)

Deed. RICHD MORRIS for 40 pounds sold to EDWARD ENDEHAVE ... [illegible] ... conveyed unto GEORGE PALMER, and GEORGE PALMER being seized of 5000 a. by his will dated 4 Jun 1682 did devise unto his son WILLIAM PALMER a share of the 5000 a., and WILLIAM PENN in his patent dated 7-- 1702 confirmed unto the sd WILLIAM PALMER the tr of land ... [illegible] ... 832 a. and WILLIAM PALMER on 7 Jul 1703 conveyed the afsd tr unto PHILIP PRIE of Upper Mizion Twp, and PHILIP PRIE on 5 Aug 1703 conveyed 417 a. pt/o the tr unto RICHARD MORRIS . .. bounded by WILLIAM THOMAS, sd EDWARD ENDEHAVE, CHARLES MOLEN & other land of sd RICHARD MORRIS ... 100 a. .... Wit: JOHN HUMPHREY, GARRETT ENDEHAVE, DAVID POWEL. Ackn 17 May 1707 before THOMAS MASTERS justice of the peace. THOMAS STORY recorder of deeds. (E3:pg 107)

8 Feb 1706/7. Deed. THOMAS BURGLEY of Phila Co husbandman for 65 pounds sold to ABRAHAM GRIFFITH of Phila Co cordwinder a tr of land . .. whereas JOHN WEBSTER of Bucks Co husbandman by his deed poll 16 Nov 1703 sold unto THOMAS BURGLEY a messuage & plantation 50 a. in Biberry Twp bounded by WILLIAM HIBBS, JOSIAS ELLIS & GILES KNIGHT ... pt/o 250 a. granted by patent 15 Jul 1684 unto THOMAS CROSS, and he conveyed the same unto MICHAEL BUTCHER, and he conveyed the same unto WILLIAM WALTON, and he unto NICHOLS WILLIAMS, and he unto the sd JOHN WEBSTER, and from him to the sd BURGLEY .... Wit: HENRY MALLOWS, JOHN HOOL, JOHN BROWN. Ackn 19 May 1707 before NATHAN STANBURY justice of the peace. THOMAS STORY recorder deeds. (E3:pg 109)

17 Dec 1706. Deed. SAMUEL CARPENTER of Phila merchant, DAVID LLOYD of Phila gent, ISAAC NORRIS of Phila merchant and NATHAN STANBURY of Phila merchant executor of the will of ELIZABETH FOX late of Phila widow decd sold to JOHN CRAPP (CRAP) of Phila merchant a tr of land ... whereas JAMES FOX late of Phila merchant by a deed poll executed under the hand & seal of WILLIAM HONNEY late of Phila taylor dated 13 Nov 1694 became in his lifetime seised of a lott of land under the bank of the River DE in Phila & also in a messuage & wharf thereon, 20 ft breadth 250 foot length, bounded with the house, lott & granary late of sd JAMES FOX but now of sd JOHN CRAPP & Front St ... JAMES FOX made his will dated 8 Sep 1699 ... ELIZABETH his wife & JAMES his son are since decd so the power of the sale rests with sd SAMUEL CARPENTER, DAVID LLOYD &

ISAAC NORRIS .... Wit: HENRY FLOWER, OWEN THOMAS, RICHD HEATH. Ackn 3 Apr 1707 before WILLIAM CARTER justice of the peace. THOMAS STORY recorder of deeds. (E3:pg 111)

6 Feb 1706/7. Deed. JOHN CRAPP of Phila merchant for 175 pounds sold to EDWARD CHURCH of same city cordwiner a messuage in Phila with a piece of ground 20 ft breadth 30 ft length bounded by Front St, King St & ground late of JAMES FOX now of sd JOHN CRAPP . . . pt/o land which SAMUEL CARPENTER, DAVID LLOYD & ISAAC NORRIS trustees of JAMES FOX late of Phila merchant decd & NATHAN STANBURY executor of the will of ELIZABETH FOX who was executor of the sd JAMES FOX on 17 Nov last past did convey to JOHN CRAPP .... Wit: DAVID LLOYD, THOMAS GRIFFITH, RICHARD HEATH. Ackn 23 Apr 1701 before DAVID LLOYD justice of the peace. THOMAS STORY recorder of deeds. (E3:pg 113)

21 May 1707. Deed. THOMAS CHALKLEY of Phila sawyer for 43 pounds 16 shillings 6 pence sold to WILLIAM HUDSON of same city tanner a lott . . . [illegible] . . . whereas PHILIP ROMAN of Chihester Chester Co cordweyner on 23 Nov last for 18 pounds conveyed unto the sd THOMAS CHALKLEY a lott s side of Mulbery St in Phila 150 ft breadth 306 ft length bounded by High St & GEORGE HARMER . . . [illegible] .... Wit: THOMAS HARP, SAMUEL BORDEN. Ackn 23 May 1706 before THOMAS MASTERS justice of the peace. THOMAS STORY recorder of deeds. (E3:pg 116)

1 Mar --. Deed. SAMUEL CARPENTER of Phila merchant & JAMES LOGAN of same city gent attys to DANIEL WHARLEY of Chalfont, St Giles Bucks Co England gent & SAMUEL WALDINGFEILD & HENRY GOLDNEY of London linin drapers sold to GUNNER RAMBOE of Phila Co yeoman a tr of land . . . whereas WILLIAM PENN esqr proprietary & governour of PA by deeds of lease & release dated 22 Oct 1687 did grant unto his dau LOETITIA PENN 5000 a. & by virtue of a warrant were surveyed & laid out in 1693 w side of River Skuylkill & resurveyed in 170- & found to contain 7800 a. ... by mistake of the surveyor divers parcells of land of other purchasers & renters many years before were included ... one tr of 500 a. was confirmed by patent 25 Oct 1701 to the sd LATITIA PENN & having intermarried with WILLIAM AUBREY of London merchant & by their deed of lease & release dated 3&4 May 1703 (Book A vol 1 pg 265&266) did convey to the sd DANIEL WHARLEY, SAMUEL WALDENGFEILD & HENRY GOLDNEY the 5000 a., and the sd DANIEL WHARLEY, SAMUEL WALDINGFEILD & HENRY GOLDNEY on 24 Sep 1703 (Book A vol 1 pg 268) appointed sd SAMUEL CARPENTER & JAMES LOGAN their attys to convey the 5000 a. ... whereas by virtue of a warrant in 1684 laying out unto

LASSE COCK & Company a tr upon the River Scuylkill there was surveyed a tr 1000 a. to the sd GUNNER RAMBOE 26 May 1701 bounded by PETER COCK & JOHN HUGHS . . . 500 a. pt/o the 5800 a. . . . as of the reputed Manner of Springtown in Chester Co . . . . Wit: THOMAS FAIRMAN, JOHN BRUCE, JOHN JOHNSTON. Ackn 26 May 1707 before WILLIAM TRENT justice of the peace. THOMAS STORY recorder of deeds. (E3:pg 118)

20 Dec 1706. Deed. ROBERT ap EVAN of Gwynedd Twp yeoman for 90 pounds sold to JOHN DAVIES of same twp carpenter a tr of land adj ROBERT ap EVAN, CADWALLADER ROBERTS & OWEN EVANS . . . 200 a. pt/o 1034 a. . . . whereas by patent dated 15 Mar 1702/3 a 1034 a. tr of land was granted unto sd ROBERT ap EVAN in Gwynedd Twp (Patent Book A vol 2 pg 477) . . . . Wit: CADWALLADER EVAN, DAVID LLOYD, RICHARD HEATH. Ackn 29 May 1707 before THOMAS MASTERS justice of the peace. THOMAS STORY recorder of deeds. (E3:pg 121)

8 Mar 1706/7. Deed of Mortgage. JOHN DAVIES of Gwynedd Twp carpenter for 89 pounds sold to ROBERT ap EVAN of same place yeoman the [above] tr of land . . . if the sd JOHN DAVIES shall pay unto the sd ROBERT ap EVAN 103 pounds 4 shillings 8 pence (7 pounds 2 shillings 4 pence on 25 Mar 1708 & 96 pounds 2 shllings 4 pence residue on 25 Mar 1709) then this indenture shall cease . . . . Wit: CADWALLADER EVAN, DAVID LLOYD, RICHARD HEATH. Ackn 30 May 1707 before THOMAS MASTERS justice of the peace. THOMAS STORY recorder of deeds. (E3:pg 124)

7 May 1707. Deed. GEORGE SMEDLEY of Westown Chester Co yeoman for 90 pounds sold to RICHARD MARTIN of Abbington Phila Co yeoman 200 a. . . . whereas THOMAS FAIRMAN of Phila Co gent on 12 Jan 1705 conveyed unto the sd GEORGE SMEDLEY 200 a. bounded by THOMAS MATLOCK, WILLIAM HENDRICKS, JOSEPH FISHER & ROBERT HEATON (Book B vol 2 pg 308) . . . . Wit: JOHN LEA, THOMAS SMEDLEY. Ackn 1 Jun 1707 before THOMAS MASTERS justice of the peace. THOMAS STORY recorder of deeds. (E3:pg 126)

31 May 1707. Deed. JACOB USHER of Phila carpenter for 10 shillings & extinquishing the yearly rent of 2 pounds 4 shillings sold to RALPH JACKSON of same city blacksmith & for the revesting of the sd land & premises in the sd RALPH JACKSON in the same condition the same were in . . . whereas sd RALPH JACKSON on 5 Sep last past for 2 pounds 4 shillings conveyed unto the sd JACOB USHER a parcell of land 11 ft breadth 102 ft length bounded by THOMAS BROWN, other pt/o the whole lott of sd RALPH JACKSON, High St & JOHN LEWDEN (Book B vol 3 pg 159) . . . .

Wit: PENTECOST LEAGUE, SAMUEL BORDEN. Ackn 2 Jun 1707 before THOMAS MASTERS justice of the peace. THOMAS STORY recorder of deeds. (E3:pg 129)

10 Mar 1706/7. Deed of Release. SAMUEL CARPENTER of Phila merchant & JAMES LOGAN of same city gent attys to DANIEL WHARLEY of Chalfont, St Giles Bucks Co gent, SAMUEL WALDENFEILD & HENRY GOLDNEY of London linnen drapers in consideration of 150 a. laid off to RICHARD ORME in Goshen Twp & 13 pounds 10 shillings release unto sd RICHARD ORME 200 a. ... whereas WILLIAM PENN esqr proprietary & governour of PA by deeds of lease & release the release dated 22 Oct 1681 granted unto his dau LOETITIA PENN 5000 a. which by virtue of a warrant was surveyed & laid out in one tr in 1683 w side of River Skuylkill which by another warrant resurveyed in 1701 & found to contain 7800 a. including by mistake of the surveyor divers parcells which had been surveyed to other purchasers & renters many years before, the said tr was confirmed by patent 24 Oct 1701 to the said LOETITIA PENN, and sd WILLIAM PENN by deeds of lease & release dated 14&15 Sep 1681 granted to JOHN ap JOHN & THOMAS WYNE 5000 a. which THOMAS WYNE sold pts/o his 1/2 to divers persons, [i.e.] to RICHARD ORME of Chester Co 150 a. which not being confirmed were conveyed to sd RICHARD by JONATHAN WYN son & heir of sd THOMAS on 2 Jun 1704 besides which he had given him 50 a. more ... whereas there was surveyed the 200 a. tr of land called "Welch Tr" in Chester Co which has since been found to be within the lands granted to said LOETITIA PENN adj JAMES DAVID ... and LOETITIA having since intermarried with WILLIAM AUBREY of London merchant they by their deeds of lease & release dated 3&4 May 1703 (Book A vol 1 pg 265&266) conveyed to the sd DANIEL WHARLEY, SAMUEL WALDENFEILD & HENRY GOLDNEY the 5000 a., and whereas the sd DANIEL WHARLEY, SAMUEL WALDENFEILD & HENRY GOLDNEY on 24 Sep 1703 (Book A vol 1 pg 268) appointed sd SAMUEL CARPENTER & JAMES LOGAN their attys to convey the 5000 a. ... the sd RICHARD ORME being disappointed of the land first surveyed to him did by warrant dated 26 Jun 1704 for laying off to him in the sd "Welch Tr" 150 a. from THOMAS WYNNE in Goshen Twp Chester Co adj GRIFFITH OWEN & executors of THOMAS LLOYD ... RICHARD ORME desired to release in consideration of like quantity pt/o the afsd 200 a. purch of us the remaining 50 a. ..... Wit: SAMUEL PRESTON, JOHN HOUGH, HUGH MIDDLETON. Ackn 4 Jun 1707 before WILLIAM TRENT justice of the peace. THOMAS STORY recorder of deeds. (E3:pg 130)

27 -- 1706/7. Deed of Release. RICHARD ORME of Ridnor Twp Chester Co cordwayner release unto SAMUEL CARPENTER & JAMES LOGAN 157 a.

. . . [see above] . . . . Wit: THOMAS FAIRMAN, PETER CHAMBERLIN, JOHN JOHNSTON. Ackn 4 Jun 1707 before WILLIAM TRENT justice of the peace. THOMAS STORY recorder of deeds. (E3:pg 133)

1 Feb 1706/7. Deed of Mortgage. JOHN THOMAS of Parsyanik Twp Phila Co for securing the payment of 175 pounds unto JOHN VAUGHAN sold to sd JOHN VAUGHAN a messuage & tr of land where the sd JOHN THOMAS now dwells bounded by HENRY BADCOKE & Sickhansing Cr . . . 171 a. . . . whereas the sd JOHN THOMAS has become bound unto WILLIAM CARTER of Phila blockmaker in 290 pounds by obligation dated 18 Aug 1703 and conditioned for payment of 145 pounds with interest on or before 1 Nov 1704, whereas the sd JOHN VAUGHAN at the like request for the debt of sd JOHN THOMAS is bound together with the sd JOHN THOMAS unto the sd WILLIAM CARTER in 290 pounds by obligation dated 18 Aug 1703 condition for payment of 145 pounds on 1 Jul next ensuring, and whereas the sd JOHN VAUGHAN at the like request for the proper debt of the sd JOHN THOMAS is become bound together with the sd JOHN THOMAS unto THOMAS MASTERS of Phila merchant in 44 pounds in obligation bearing date 29 Dec 1704 conditioned for the payment of 22 pounds on -- Jun next ensuing, and whereas the sd JOHN VAUGHAN at the like request for the debt of sd JOHN THOMAS is bound together with sd JOHN THOMAS unto EDWARD SHIPPEN of Phila by obligation dated 11 Feb 1705 & conditioned for payment of 10 pounds with interest on 11 Aug next ensuing, and whereas the sd JOHN THOMAS is justly indebted to the sd JOHN VAUGHAN for 175 pounds afsd . . . if JOHN THOMAS shall pay unto sd JOHN VAUGHAN the 175 pounds with interest (87 pounds 10 shillings 1 Feb next ensuing and 87 pounds 10 shillings residue with interest in 1708) then this indenture to cease . . . . Wit: FRANCIS COOKE, THOMAS GRIFFITH, DAVID LLOYD, RICHARD HEATH. Ackn 5 Jun 1707 before NATHAN STANBURY justice of the peace. THOMAS STORY recorder of deeds. 11 Jul 1713 before CHARLES BROCKDEN dep recorder of deeds came SAMUEL PRESTON of sd city merchant & HENRY LAWRENCE of Haverford Chester Co yeoman executor of will of JOHN VAUGHAN decd late mortgagee & ackn they had received of JOHN THOMAS 175 pounds with interest & discharge the mortgage. (E3:pg 135)

31 Jan 1706/7. Deed. JOHN VAUGHAN of Phila carpenter for 145 pounds sold to JOHN THOMAS of Parsyunck Phila Co yeoman 171 a. bounded by HENRY BADCOKE & Sickhansing Cr . . . whereas WILLIAM CARTER of Phila blockmaker & WILLIAM GREGORY late of Parsyunck carpenter by their deed poll dated 18 Aug 1703 conveyed unto the sd JOHN VAUGHAN & JOHN THOMAS severall parcels of land within Parsyunck Twp . . . . Wit: FRANCIS COOK, THOMAS GRIFFITH, DAVID LOYD,

RICHARD HEATH. Ackn 6 Jun 1707 before THOMAS MASTERS justice of the peace. THOMAS STORY recorder of deeds. (E3:pg 138)

1 Mar 1706/7. Deed. ARNOLD CASSELL of Phila Co yeoman for 60 pounds 10 shillings sold to ISAAC DEAVES of Phila Co husbandman a tr of land in Kresheim Phila Co adj CORNELIUS SIVERT, line dividing Sommerhausen & Kresheim, Germantown line, JOHN KREY & CORNELIUS SWERT . . . 75 a. conveyed with other land unto the sd ARNOLD CASSELL by JOHN KAIGHIN of Glouester w NJ & SARAH his wife 4 Jun 1702 . . . . Wit: EDWARD EVANS, DAVID LLOYD, RICHARD HEATH. Ackn 7 May 1707 before NATHAN STANBURY justice of the peace. THOMAS STORY recorder of deeds. (E3:pg 140)

13 Jan 1706/7. Deed. CASPAR HOODT of Phila taylor for 84 pounds sold to GEORGE GRAY of same city merchant, DAVID BREINTNALL of same city shopkeeper, SOLOMON CRESSON of same city turner & THOMAS STORY of same city gent an undivided 1/6 pt/o a parcell of ground in Germantown between the land late of ISSAC SHOEMAKER & JACOB GODSHALK . . . 3 a. and 1/6 pt/o another piece through which the Ayl Mill Race now runneth adj afsd tr & Mill St, and also 1/6 pt/o another piece adj afsd trs . . . 14 perches, and also 1/6 pt/o a tr adj afsd tr & land late of WALTER SIMONS (SYMONS) . . . 44 sq perches, and also 1/6 pt/o the two mills on the 3 a., [i.e.] one oylmill & one water corner mill or grist mill, both under one roof called the "Oyl Mill" in the tenure of sd CASPAR HOODT in partnership with the grantees and also 1/6 pt/o the proffitts of the sd mills . . . . Wit: ABELL PRESTON, JAMES PEMBERTON. Ackn 9 Jun 1707 before NATHAN STANBURY justice of the peace. THOMAS STORY recorder of deeds. (E3:pg 141)

13 Jan 1706/7. Deed. ISAAC SHOEMAKER of Germantown Phila Co turner for 71 pounds 11 shillings sold to GEORGE GRAY of Phila merchant, DAVID BREINTNALL of same city shopkeeper, SOLOMON CRESSON of same city turner & THOMAS STORY of same city gent [same as above] . . . . Wit: ABELL PRESTON, JA PEMBERTON. Ackn 11 Jun 1707 before NATHAN STANBURY justice of the peace. THOMAS STORY recorder of deeds. (E3:pg 144)

21 Dec 1706. Deed. GEORGE GUEST of Phila cooper sole executor of the will of ALICE GUEST late of Phila widow his late mother decd to secure a legacie farm letts unto JOHN WEBB of same city taylor a messuage e side of Front St & w side of King St in Phila called the "Sign of the Crooked Billett" bounded by JOHN CRAPP & lott late of PHILIP JAMES . . . [illegible] . . . whereas sd ALICE GUEST by her will dated 30 Aug 1705 did bequeath unto

severall persons sundry sums of money . . . and whereas the legacie given unto PHOEBE the now w/o ANTHONY MORRIS Junr is paid . . . [illegible] . . . after the decease of the survivor of sd GEORGE & ELIZABETH his wife the rent does not exceed 20 pounds . . . . Wit: JOHN REDMAN, JOSEPH REDMAN, JOHN GUEST, RICHD HEATH. Ackn 12 Jun 1707 before NATHAN STANBURY justice of the peace. THOMAS STORY recorder of deeds. (E3:pg 146)

24 Apr 1707. Deed. ABRAHAM OPDEN GRAEF of Germantown Phila Co weaver for 105 pounds sold to JOSEPH SHIPPEN of Phila merchant a tr of land in Germantown adj JOHN NEUS & sd JOSEPH SHIPPEN formerly of HERMAN OPDEN GRAEF 50 a. pt/o 828 a. granted unto the sd ABRAHAM OPTEN GRAEF & his two brothers HERMAN & DIRK OPDEN GRAEF by JACOB FELNOR by deed dated 4 Apr 1689 (Book C2 vol 3 fol 124-125) . . . . Wit: JOSEPH COULSON, FRANCIS DANIEL PASTORIUS. Ackn 14 Jun 1707 before THOMAS MASTERS justice of the peace. THOMAS STORY recorder of deeds. 4 Apr 1707 ABRAHAM OP DEN GRAEF received of JOSEPH SHIPPEN 105 pounds. Wit: RICHARD HEATH, JOSHUA LAWRENCE. (E3:pg 149)

6 Jun 1707. Deed. SAMUEL ROWLAND of Phila mariner for 121 pounds sold to JOHN SNOWDEN of Bucks Co tanner a tr of land . . . whereas JAMES CLAYPOOL, ROBERT TURNER commissioners of WILLIAM PENN proprietary & governour of PA on 12 May 1686 granted unto GEORGE BARTHOLOMEW in right of JAMES BOYDEN purchaser a tr of land in sd city on Second St (Patent Book A vol 1 pg 148), and sd GEORGE BARTHOLOMEW on 3 Jun 1686 conveyed with other land unto GRIFFITH JONES of Phila merchant with redemption of the premises at a day then to come upon paying a certain sum of money, but the sd GEORGE BARTHOLOMEW soon after departing this life and the sd sum not paid, the estate of the sd GEORGE BARTHOLOMEW became vested in sd GRIFFITH JONES & peaceably yielded up into the actual possession of the sd GRIFFITH JONES by JANE the relict of sd BARTHOLOMEW 20 Dec 1689, the sd GRIFFITH JONES on 19 Aug 1690 conveyed sd land unto THOMAS BUDD of Phila (Book E3 vol 5 pg 27), and sd THOMAS BUDD on 2 Jan 1690 conveyed the land unto the sd SAMUEL ROWLAND, whereas SAMUEL CARPENTER, WILLIAM MARKHAM, ROBERT TURNER & JOHN GOODSON commissioners of property on 13 Dec 1690 conveyed unto sd SAMUEL ROWLAND the sd tr of land bounded by JAMES BOYDEN (Patent Book A vol 4 pg 13-14) . . . . Wit: EDWARD CHURCH, NICHOLAS MORE, JAMES BINGHAM. Ackn 15 Jun 1706 before THOMAS MASTERS justice of the peace. THOMAS STORY recorder of deeds. (E3:pg 150)

9 Apr 1707. Deed. JOHN HART of Phila bricklayer for 85 pounds sold to JOHN MILLS of Phila bricklayer a messuage a lott of land . . . whereas THOMAS WHARTON of Phila taylor on 5 Jan 1703/4 conveyed unto the sd JOHN HART a messuage & lott of land between Fourth & Fifth Sts 30 ft breadth 178 ft length adj High St, lott late of WILLIAM NICOLLS & Chestnutt St . . . . Wit: SAMUEL POWELL, DAVID LLOYD, RICHARD HEATH. Ackn 19 Jun 1707 before NATHAN STANBURY justice of the peace. THOMAS STORY recorder of deeds. (E3:pg 154)

18 Jun 1707. Deed. JOHN SWIFT of Southampton Bucks Co yeoman for 60 pounds sold to LIONELL BRITTON of Phila shopkeeper a tr of land . . . whereas WILLIAM PENN propietary & governour of PA by his commissioners of property EDWARD SHIPPEN, GRIFFITH OWEN, THOMAS STORY & JAMES LOGAN granted a patent dated 8 Jun 1702 unto the sd JOHN SWIFT for a lott of land w side of Second St in Phila 34 ft breadth 303 ft length bounded by PHILIP HOWELL & THOMAS JONES (now called the parsonage land) (Patent Book A vol 2 pg 328) . . . . Wit: GRIFFITH JONES, JOSEPH WILLCOX, DAVID LLOYD. Ackn 3 Jul 1707 before THOMAS MASTERS justice of the peace. THOMAS STORY recorder of deeds. (E3:pg 156)

20 Jun 1707. Deed. THOMAS BIRD of Phila carpenter for 45 pounds sold to JONATHAN COCK of same city carpenter a lott in Phila 20 ft breadth 66 ft length bounded by Third St & lott formerly belonging to JOHN AUSTIN . . . purch 25 Mar last of JOSEPH YARD of Phila bricklayer . . . . Wit: HENRY PAULL, DAVID LOYD, RICHARD HEATH. Ackn 12 Jul 1707 before NATHAN STANBURY justice of the peace. THOMAS STORY recorder of deeds. (E3:pg 158)

16 May 1707. Deed of Gift. ALEXANDER EDWARDS of Gwynedd Twp Phila Co yeoman for love & affection gave to his son ALEXANDER EDWARDS the younger a tr of land near Gwynedd bounded by land he sold to RICHARD ap HUGH, ROBERT FAIRMAN, JOB BATES & THOMAS EDWARDS . . . 200 a. pt/o 990 a. patented 12 Oct 1702 to sd ALEXANDER EDWARDS the father (Book A vol 2 pg 379) . . . . Wit: DAVID POWELL, NATHAN ROBINSON. Ackn 14 Jul 1707 before THOMAS MASTERS justice of the peace. THOMAS STORY recorder of deeds. (E3:pg 160)

7 Jul 1707. Deed. JOSEPH REDMAN of Phila bricklayer sold to JOHN WEBB of same city taylor a lott . . . whereas WILLIAM TRENT of sd city merchant on 15 May 1705 sold to sd JOSEPH REDMAN a lott bounded by JOHN REDMAN & THOMAS ENGLAND . . . [illegible] . . . . Wit: JOSHUA

JOHNSON, SAMUEL BORDEN. Ackn 15 Jul 1707 before NATHAN STANBURY justice of the peace. THOMAS STORY recorder of deeds. (E3:pg 162)

1 Feb 1702. Deed. DANIEL FLOWER sold to CORNELIUS STURGS [illegible] ... with the lott late of JOHN DAY ... [illegible]. Wit: SAMUEL MEALS, BENJAMIN MORGAN. Ackn -- -- -- before NATHAN STANBURY justice of the peace. THOMAS STORY recorder of deeds. (E3:pg 165)

-- -- --. Deed. CORNELIUS STURGES sold to DANIEL HODGSON & SARAH HODGSON a lott ... [illegible] ... bounded by Third St, EMANUAL WALKER. GEORGE HARMER, SAMUEL CHANDLER, ANTHONY STURGES & lott late of JOHN DAY ... [illegible] .... Wit: ANTHONY TAYLOR, RICHARD SUTTON, FRANCIS COOK. Ackn 9 Sep 1703, ROBT ASHTON protonotary. Ackn 18 Jul 1707 before NATHAN STANBURY justice of the peace. THOMAS STORY recorder of deeds. (E3:pg 166)

23 Jun 1707. Deed. GABRIEL COCK of Phila Co yeoman ... by virtue of a patent under the hand of FRANCIS LOVELACE late governor of NY dated 1 Oct 1669 confirmed unto PETER COCK father of sd GABRIEL COCK an island at the mouth of Skoolkill adj DE River 50 a. bounded by ANDREW BONN's kill ... and by the will of sd PETER COCK devised pt/o the same called "Skoolkill Island" to his sd son GABRIEL COCK devided from the other part by Eagles Cr ... 400 perches, and sd GABRIEL COCK on 1 Sep 1705 for 120 pounds sold to JOHN FISHER of Phila blacksmith "Skoolkill Island" ... [illegible] .... Wit: MORICE SMITH, FRANCIS COOK. Ackn 19 Jul 1707 before THOMAS MASTERS justice of the peace. THOMAS STORY recorder of deeds. (E3:pg 168)

10 Feb 1706/7. Deed. WILLIAM TRENT of Phila merchant sold to NICHOLAS WANSFORD of same city blacksmith ... on 13 Jul last JOHN MARTIN of Phila merchant sold to the sd WILLIAM TRENT ... [illegible] ... late in possession of JOHN COLLEE ... [illegible] ... the sd PHILIP JAMES by the commissioners of WILLIAM PENN proprietary & governour ... [illegible] .... Wit: LOWRY HAYS[?], DAVID LLOYD, RICHD HEATH. Ackn 22 Jul 1707 before THOMAS MASTERS justice of the peace. THOMAS STORY recorder of deeds. (E3:pg 170)

20 Jul 1707. Deed. SAMUEL FINNEY of Taconey Phila Co esqr for 25 pounds sold to GABRIEL WILKINSON of Phila yeoman a lott ... whereas WILLIAM PENN proprietary & governour of PA by his commissioners of

property EDWARD SHIPPEN, GRIFFITH OWENS & JAMES LOGAN by patent dated 8 Feb 1705 confirmed unto sd SAMUEL FINNEY a lott of ground e side of Third St from the bank of DE in Phila 60 ft breadth 196 ft length bounded by lott late of sd GABRIEL WILKINSON & Second St (Patent Book A vol 3 pg 244) . . . . Wit: JOSEPH WILLCOX, DAVID LLOYD, RICHD HEATH. Ackn -- -- -- before THOMAS MASTERS justice of the peace. THOMAS STORY recorder of deeds. (E3:pg 173)

9 May 1707. Deed. JOHN CRAPP of Phila merchant for 715 pounds sold to WILLIAM TRENT of same city merchant the first & third lotts & residue of the second lott e side of King St . . . whereas SAMUEL CARPENTER, WILLIAM MARKHAM, ROBERT TURNER & JOHN GOODSON the late commissioners of property of WILLIAM PENN proprietary & governour of PA by a patent dated 5 Mar 1690/1 granted unto WILLIAM LEE of Phila a lott of land on the bank of DE in Phila 30 ft breadth 250 ft length bounded by CHARLES PICKERING & Front St (Patent Book A pg 350) . . . WILLIAM LEE on 25 Feb 1697/8 conveyed unto JAMES FOX of Phila merchant the sd lott (Book E3 vol 5 pg 124) and the sd commissioners by another patent dated 27 Aug 1689 granted unto CHARLES PICKERING late of Phila another lott on the bank of DE in Phila 20 ft breadth 250 ft length bounded by the afsd lott . . . [illegible] . . . CHARLES PICKERING conveyed unto sd JAMES FOX the afsd lott . . . on 27 Feb 1690 the commissioners granted unto JOHN ROBERTS a lott of land on the bank of DE in Phila 30 ft breadth 250 ft length bounded by the afsd lott . . . on 2 Mar 1690/1 sd JOHN ROBERTS sold to sd JAMES FOX the afsd lott, by virtue of several conveyances sd JAMES FOX became seised in the severall lotts . . . sd JAMES FOX made his will dated 8 Sep 1699 the lotts to be sold to pay his just debts, his wife ELIZABETH FOX & his son JAMES FOX executors, the son JAMES after dyed, and the sd ELIZABETH, SAMUEL CARPENTER, DAVID LLOYD & ISAAC NORRIS on 3 Mar 1701/2 conveyed the first & third lotts unto EDWARD SHIPP of Phila merchant (Book B vol 3 pg 156) . . . on 13 Sep last past sd EDWARD SHIPPEN conveyed to sd JOHN CRAPP two lotts of land (Book E3 vol 6 pg 47) and after the decease of sd ELIZABETH FOX the sd SAMUEL CARPENTER, DAVID LLOYD & ISAAC NORRIS together with NATHAN STANBURY executor of the will of sd ELIZABETH on 17 Dec last past conveyed to sd JOHN CRAPP the second lott (Book E3 vol 6 pg --) and sd JOHN CRAPP hath sold the last mentioned lott unto EDWARD CHURCH of Phila cordwiner 6 Feb last past and sd JOHN CARPENTER hath erected a slaughter house upon the wharf on the first lott . . . . Wit: WILLIAM CARTER, DAVID LLOYD, LAWRY HAIG, RICHARD HEATH. Ackn 24 Jul 1707 before THOMAS MASTERS justice of the peace. THOMAS STORY recorder of deeds. (E3:pg 175)

10 May 1707. Deed of Mortgage. WILLIAM TRENT of Phila merchant sold to JOHN CRAPP of same city merchant several lotts of land ... whereas the sd JOHN CRAPP sold to sd WILLIAM TRENT severall lotts of land [see above] ... if sd JOHN CRAPP shall pay unto sd WILLIAM TRENT the sum of 715 pounds 3 shillings 6 pence with interest on 10 May 1708 then WILLIAM TRENT will transfer the recited premisses unto the sd JOHN CRAPP .... Wit: WILLIAM CARTER, DAVID LLOYD, LAWRY HAIG, RICHARD HEATH. Ackn 29 Jul 1707 before THOMAS MASTERS justice of the peace. THOMAS STORY recorder of deeds. [10 May 1707 Endorsement on Back]: If WILLIAM TRENT pays 57 pounds 4 shillings 3 pence on 10 Nov & 10 May yearly for 3 years then sd WILLIAM TRENT shall not during the sd term take advantage of the nonpayment of 715 pounds 3 shillings 6 pence. (E3:pg 181)

7 Feb 1706/7. Deed. EDWARD CHURCH of Phila cordwiner for 175 pounds sold to WILLIAM TRENT of sd city merchant two messuages & two pieces of ground ... whereas on 30 Mar 1702 JOHN GUEST of Phila esqr conveyed unto sd EDWARD CHURCH a parcell of ground in Phila 16 ft 4 inches breadth 100 ft length abutting GEORGE EAGLESFIELD, Front St & JOHN SMART and sd EDWARD CHURCH erected a brick messuage on sd ground ... before date hereof JOHN CRAPP of Phila conveyed to sd EDWARD CHURCH a messuage with lott on King St 20 ft breadth bounded by lott of JAMES FOX but now of sd JOHN CRAPP & Front St .... Wit: DAVID LLOYD, LAWRY HAIG, RICHARD HEATH. Ackn 13 Jul 1707 before THOMAS MASTERS justice of the peace. THOMAS STORY recorder of deeds. (E3:pg 184)

5 Jan 1706/7. Deed. JOHN ARTHUR late of Phila Co but now of Salem Co w NJ yeoman for 100 pounds sold to DAVID POWELL (POWEL) of Phila Co surveyor a tr of land adj GARRETT PETERSON, JOHN BARNES, JONAS POTTS & ROBERT TURNER 300 a. which THOMAS FAIRMAN of Shakamaxun on 4 Nov 1703 conveyed unto the sd JOHN ARTHUR .... Wit: WILLIAM HALL, NATHANIEL BRADING, WILLIAM GRIFFIN. Ackn 30 Jul 1707 before NATHAN STANBURY justice of the peace. THOMAS STORY recorder of deeds. (E3:pg 186)

16 Jan 1702/3. Deed of Mortgage. GRIFFITH JONES of Phila Co merchant sold to THOMAS SHUTE (SUIT) of same co yeoman a lott of ground pt/o his Front St lott 40 ft fronting Second St & 100 ft backwards bounded by JONES's alley, DAVID LLOYD's lot now in possession of KATHERINE BLANEY & JOHN COLLEY's pt/o same lott now in possession of sd GRIFFITH JONES ... the sd GRIFFITH JONES to pay rent of 6 pounds 10 shillings every year to be paid in one intire payment on 1 May 1704 ....

Wit: JOHN MOORE, JOHN BURTHRN. Ackn 1 Aug 1707 before NATHAN STANBURY justice of the peace. THOMAS STORY recorder of deeds. (E3:pg 188)

29 Nov 1705. Deed. BARTHOLOMEW PENROSE of Phila shipwright for 37 pounds 10 shillings 2 pence sold to GILES (GYLES) GREEN of sd city joyner a bank lott of land on Front St in Phila 29 ft length 22 1/2 ft breadth bounded by GABRIEL WILKINSON & sd BARTHOLOMEW PENROSE . . . . Wit: CLEMENT PLUMSTED, ROBERT ASHTON, TOBY LEESH. Ackn 1 Aug 1707 before THOMAS MASTERS justice of the peace. THOMAS STORY recorder of deeds. (E3:pg 189)

9 May 1707. Receipt. Received of WILLIALL TRENT 715 pounds by JOHN CRAPP. Wit: DAVID LLOYD, WILLIAM CARTER, LOWRY HAIG, RICHARD HEATH. Recorded 1 Aug 1707. [deed JOHN CRAPP to WM TRENT E3:pg 175] (E3:pg 190)

26 Jun 1705. Deed. THOMAS PASCHALL of Phila pewterer & HENRY FLOWERS of sd city barber for 16 pounds sold to JAMES POULTER of sd city wheelwright a lott of land . . . whereas WILLIAM SMITH late of Bristol City England merchant was seised of a lott of land in Phila 49 ft 6 inches breadth 306 ft length bounded by Mulberry St & lott late of NICHOLAS RANDALL & by his lease & release dated 17&18 Feb -- conveyed unto THOMAS PASCHALL & HENRY FLOWERS 250 a. of woodland in Chester Co in special trust that they should make sale of the lands (Book E B vol 5 pg 461) . . . we have made DAVID LLOYD our atty to ackn this deed in court. Wit: FRANCIS COOK, SAMUEL PROELL. Ackn 6 Aug 1707 before THOMAS MASTERS justice of the peace. THOMAS STORY recorder. (E3:pg 190)

29 Jul 1707. Deed. JOHN TURNER Bibary Twp Phila Co yeoman for 54 pounds sold to JOSEPH HALL of same place yeoman a tr of land . . . whereas by an indenture dated 17 Feb 1704/5 THOMAS WALTON of Bibary Twp yeoman conveyed unto sd JOHN TURNER a tr of land within the Mannor of Moreland adj HENRY COMELY's 300 a. tr, HUGH MORGAN, THOMAS WHITTON & THOMAS SCOTT . . . 65 a. . . . . Wit: WILLIAM BILES, DAVID LLOYD, RICHARD HEATH. Ackn 7 Aug 1707 before THOMAS MASTERS justice of the peace. THOMAS STORY recorder of deeds. (E3:pg 191)

15 May 1707. Deed. HUMPHREY MORREY of Phila Co merchant for 30 pounds sold to MATHIAS TISRON (TISRAN) of Abington Twp Phila Co yeoman a tr of land adj JOHN NASH . . . 50 a. pt/o 109 a. which JOHN

COLLEY of Phila hatter & SUSANNA his wife on 17 Oct 1692 conveyed to sd HUMPHREY MORREY (Book A No 1 pg 88) . . . . Wit: SAMUEL CART, WILLIAM HORMER, ANN MORREY. Ackn 11 Aug 1707 before THOMAS MASTERS justice of the peace. THOMAS STORY recorder of deeds. (E3:pg 193)

26 Mar 1707. Deed. NATHANIEL THORNTON of Phila yeoman for 40 pounds sold to JOHN HARRISON of same city carpenter a messuage and two lotts of land . . . whereas by patent dated 16 Jul 1684 granted to MILLISENT HODGKINS a lott of land in Phila 100 ft breadth 116 1/2 ft length bounded by Mulberry St, Fourth St & [illegible] . . . and sd MILLISENT HODGKINS on 30 Nov 1691 conveyed unto EVAN MORRIS of Phila the sd lott, and sd EVAN MORRIS sold but not conveyed the sd messuage & lott of land unto WILLIAM DAVIS who sold the same unto MICHAEL WALTON (WALLTON), and by another patent dated 4 Aug 1684 granted unto WILLIAM HARWOOD a lott of land in Phila 49 1/2 ft breadth 106 ft length bounded by JAMES CLAYTON Junr & Mulberry St . . . and sd WILLIAM HARWOOD on 26 Dec 1690 did convey the last mentioned lott unto the sd WILLIAM DAVIS, which sd WILLIAM DAVIS sold but not conveyed unto the sd MICHAEL WALTON, and whereas the sd EVAN MORRIS, WILLIAM DAVIS & MICHAEL WALTON on 25 Feb 1698/9 conveyed the messuage & two lotts of land unto the sd NATHANIEL THORNTON . . . . Wit: WILLIAM HALL, JOHN WILLIAMS, PHILLIP HOWELL. Ackn 10 Jul 1707 before THOMAS MASTERS justice of the peace. THOMAS STORY recorder of deeds. (E3:pg 195)

11 Aug 1707. Deed. JOHN MIFFLIN of Phila Co yeoman for 300 pounds sold to LIONEL BRITTON of Phila shopkeeper a brick messuage pt/o a lott of land . . . 16 ft breadth 49 1/2 ft length bounded by High St., Second St & sd JOHN MIFFLIN . . . whereas WILLIAM PENN proprietary & governour of PA granted a patent dated 29 Mar 1701 unto his dau LATITIA PENN for a lott of land 172 ft breadth 402 ft length bounded by High St, lott then in possession of widdow TENNET & Second St (Patent Book A vol 2 pg 12) and the sd LATITIA PENN by her atty JAMES LOGAN on 2 Nov 1702 conveyed unto JOHN MIFFLIN pt/o the sd lott 59 1/2 ft breadth 100 ft length (Book B vol 2 pg --) . . . . Wit: SAMUEL POWEL, DAVID LLOYD, RICHD HEATH. Ackn 18 Aug 1707 before NATHAN STANBURY justice of the peace. THOMAS STORY recorder of deeds. (E3:pg 197)

17 May 1707. Deed. ALEXANDER EDWARDS the younger of Gwynedd Phila Co yeoman for 42 pounds sold to DAVID HUGH GRIFFITH of same place yeoman a tr of land near Gwynedd adj RICHARD ap HUGHS & ROBERT FAIRMAN . . . 100 a. pt/o 200 a. which ALEXANDER EDWARDS

the father of sd ALEXANDER conveyed to sd ALEXANDER EDWARDS the younger day before these presents, the 200 a. is pt/o 990 a. which WILLIAM PENN proprietary & governour of PA by patent 12 Oct 1702 granted unto the sd ALEXANDER EDWARDS the elder (Patent Book A vol 2 pg 379) .... Wit: DAVID POWELL, OWEN EVAN, RICHARD HEATH. Ackn 19 Aug 1707 before THOMAS MASTERS justice of the peace. THOMAS STORY recorder of deeds. (E3:pg 199)

1 May 1707. Deed. JOSEPH JONES of Phila Co merchant sold to GERVAS BYWATER of Phila labourer & JOAN his wife a messuage & ground on Jones Alley in Phila 20 ft breadth 30 ft length bounded by JAMES PORTNES, WILLIAM BYWATER & THOMAS MILLAR which ground is pt/o a lott which GRIFFITH JONES (father of sd JOSEPH JONES) on 5 Aug 1704 conveyed to sd JOSEPH JONES his son ... [illegible] .... Wit: GRIFFITH JONES, HENRY PAULL, RICHARD HEATH. Ackn 21 Aug 1707 before DAVID LLOYD justice of the peace. THOMAS STORY recorder of deeds. (E3:pg 200)

1 Mar 1706. Deed. EDWARD SMOUT of Phila merchant for 230 pounds sold to BARTHOLOMEW PENROSE of same city shipwright a piece of ground in Phila on King St & bank of DE River 108 ft breadth 250 ft length bounded by JOSEPH BROWN, GABRIEL WILKINSON & Front St ... which parcell was granted to one BENJAMIN CHAMBERS who conveyed the same to sd EDWARD SMOUT by two indentures on 12 Feb 1696 and the other 6 Jun 1699 .... Wit: JOSEPH YARD, NATH SIKES, FO D[?], THOMAS CLARK. Ackn 23 Aug 1707 before DAVID LLOYD justice of the peace. THOMAS STORY recorder of deeds. Memo: Full & peaceable possession of the premises was given by sd EDWARD SMOUT unto sd BARTHOLOMEW PENROSE 24 Jul 1707. Wit: DAVID GRIFFIN, TOBY LEECH, THOMAS CLARK. (E3:pg 202)

20 Aug 1707. Deed. JONATHAN CORK of Phila carpenter for 45 pounds sold to EBENEZER LARGE of sd city currier a messuage & piece of ground in Phila 20 ft breadth 66 ft length bounded by Third St., lott formerly belonging to JOHN AUSTIN & other pt/o lott now in the tenure of JOSEPH YARD ... under the yearly rent of 1 pound 10 shillings payable to JOSEPH YARD of Phila bricklayer .... Wit: SAMUEL POWELL, HENRY PAULL, RICHD NEWCOMBER. Ackn 29 Aug 1707 before WILLIAM CARTER justice of the peace. THOMAS STORY recorder of deeds. (E3:pg 204)

16 -- 1707. Deed. PHILIP HOWELL of Phila taylor for 90 pounds sold to LIONELL BRITTON of same city shopkeeper a lott in Phila ... whereas WILLIAM PENN proprietary & governour of PA by his lease & release dated

7&8 Sep 1681 conveyed to FRANCIS SMITH of Newcastle Co gent 400 a. and sd FRANCIS SMITH on 13 May 1698 conveyed the lott to sd PHILIP HOWELL, and by virtue of a warrant dated 16 Feb 1701/2 the lott was surveyed & laid out unto sd PHILIP HOWELL s side of Second St 51 ft breadth 303 ft length bounded by DAVID POWELL, lott late of JOHN SWIFT but now of the sd LIONELL BRITTON & Third St, and WILLIAM PENN by his commissioners EDWARD SHIPPEN, GRIFFITH OWEN, THOMAS STORY & JAMES LOGAN by patent dated 8 Jun 1702 did grant the lott of land unto the sd PHILIP HOWELL (Patent Book A Vol 2 pg 327).... Wit: NICHOLAS HITCHCOCK, DAVID LLOYD, RICHARD HEATH. Ackn 1 Sep 1707 before DAVID LLOYD justice of the peace. THOMAS STORY recorder of deeds. (E3:pg 206)

6 Sep 1707. Deed. THOMAS SHUTE of Phila Co yeoman sold to JOHN PIGGOTT (PIGGOT) of Phila cordwiner a brick messuage & lott of ground in Phila 20 ft breadth 50 ft length bounded by Second St, bank of DE, ANDREW ROBESON, sd THOMAS SHUTE, JOHN COLLEE & Jones Alley . . . pt/o a lott which GRIFFITH JONES of Phila Co merchant on 16 Jan 1702/3 conveyed to sd THOMAS SHUTE (Book E3 vol 6 pg 700).... Wit: LAURY HAIG, RICHARD HEATH. Ackn 8 Apr 1707 before DAVID LLOYD justice of the peace. THOMAS STORY recorder of deeds. (E3:pg 208)

3 Sep 1707. Deed. For 121 pounds 13 shillings 5 pence paid to SAMUEL CARPENTER of Phila merchant by DANIEL JONES of sd city taylor at the special request of JOHN DENSEY (DENSIE) (DENZIE) of sd city carpenter & for 18 pounds 6 shillings 7 pence paid to the sd JOHN DENSEY by sd DANIEL JONES, the sd SAMUEL CARPENTER & JOHN DENSEY sold to sd DANIEL JONES a lott of land in Phila now in the tenure of sd JOHN DENSEY 20 1/2 ft breadth 80 ft length bounded with High St, SILAS CRISPIN, JOHN JAMES & GEORGE HARNER.... Wit: RICHD HEATH, WILLIAM HENLINGS. Ackn 10 Sep 1707 before DAVID LLOYD justice of the peace. THOMAS STORY recorder of deeds. (E3:pg 210)

10 Sep 1707. Deed. JOHN PIGGOTT of Phila cordwiner for 130 pounds sold to WILLIAM HUDSON of same city tanner a brick messuage & lott of ground 20 ft breadth 50 ft length . . . whereas GRIFFITH JONES late of Phila Co merchant on 16 Jan 1702/3 conveyed to THOMAS SHUTE (SUIT) of sd co yeoman a lott of ground pt/o his Front St lott 40 ft fronting Second St 100 ft backwards bounded by Jones Alley, DAVID LLOYD's ground in possession of KATHARINE BLANEY & JOHN COLLEY (Book E3 vol 6 pg 188), and THOMAS SHUTE on 6 Sep instant conveyed to JOHN PIGGOTT a messuage with lott (pt/o the afsd ground) 20 ft breadth 50 ft length bounded by the bank

of DE & ANDREW ROBISON (Book E3 vol 6 pg 208) . . . . Wit: DAVID LLOYD, RICHARD HEATH, EDWARD EVANS. Ackn 10 Sep 1707 before DAVID LLOYD justice of the peace. THOMAS STORY recorder of deeds. 10 Sep 1707 Received of sd WILLIAM HUDSON 130 pounds by JOHN PIGGOTT. Wit: DAVID LLOYD, DANIEL RADLEY. (E3:pg 212)

26 Mar 1707. Deed. THOMAS PRICE of Phila taylor & ELIZABETH his wife sole executrix of the will of CORNELIUS STURGES late of Phila felt maker her former husband decd and HENRY FLOWER of Phila butcher for 100 pounds sold to EDWARD FARMER of White Marsh Phila Co gent a messuage & tr of land . . . whereas CORNELIUS STURGES in his lifetime was seized in a messuage & plantation with a tr of land in Farmers Town near White Marsh adj THOMAS MILLAR, CASPER STALLS & JOHN ROADS and by his indenture dated 25 Nov 1703 conveyed the same unto the sd HENRY FLOWER under the condition to be void upon payment of 80 pounds & interest, which sd money & interest hath been paid and whereas CORNELIUS STURGES made his will dated 13 Apr 1706 and did "give his loving wife ELIZABETH all his land & plantation with all his personal estate in order to pay both mine & my fathers debts" . . . 150 a. . . . . Wit: DANIEL RADLEY, DAVID LLOYD, RICHARD HEATH. Ackn 24 Aug 1707 before DAVID LLOYD justice of the peace. THOMAS STORY recorder of deeds. (E3:pg 214)

27 Mar 1707. Deed of Mortgage. EDWARD FARMER of White Marsh Phila Co gent for 100 pounds sold to HENRY FLOWER of Phila barber a messuage & tr of land in Farmers Town near White Marsh adj THOMAS MILLAR, CASPAR STALLS & JOHN ROADES . . . 150 a. . . . if the sd EDWARD FARMER shall pay unto sd HENRY FLOWER 116 pounds on or before 25 Mar 1709 then this indenture shall cease . . . . Wit: DANIEL RADLEY, RICHARD HEATH. Ackn 12 Sep 1707 before DAVID LLOYD justice of the peace. THOMAS STORY recorder of deeds. 16 Dec 1743 before CHARLES BROCKMAN recorder of deeds came ENOCH FLOWER the surviving executor of the will of HENRY FLOWER mortgagee & ackn that EDWARD FARMER mortgagor pd 116 pounds with interest in full & discharges the mortgaged premises. (E3:pg 216)

1 May 1693. Deed. JOHN DUPLOVY (DUPLOUVY) of Phila baker for the yearly rent sold to THOMAS MASTERS of same place carpenter a DE Front St lott 40 ft breadth 396 ft length between WILLIAM SHANKLE & NATHANIEL SIKES bounded by Second St . . . [illegible] . . . against JACOB FELNER . . . . Wit: JOSEPH WILLCOX, PATRICK ROBINSON clerk-com. Ackn 22 Sep 1693. Recorded 25 Sep 1707. (E3:pg 218)

15 Sep 1707. Deed. FRANCIS RICHARDSON of Phila silversmith for 70 pounds sold to HENRY STEVENS of sd city master mariner & MARTHA his wife a lott of land . . . whereas WILLIAM MARKHAM & JOHN GOODSON commissioners of property of WILLIAM PENN proprietary & governour by patent dated 12 Jun -- granted unto NATHANIEL ALLEN a lott of land in said city 40 ft 9 inches breadth 396 ft length adj WILLIAM SHARDLOR & JOHN LOVE (Book A vol 1 pg 375) and sd NATHANIEL ALLEN on 18 Jun 1689 sold same unto ALBERTUS BRANDT (Book E vol 5 fol 146), and sd ALBERTUS BRANDT on 1 Mar 1692 did grant the lott unto JACOB TELNOR, and sd JACOB TELNOR on 10 Mar 1693 conveyed the sd lott & premises (with other lotts) unto JOHN DUPLOVY of Phila baker, and sd JOHN DUPLOVY on 1 May 1693 conveyed to THOMAS MASTERS of sd city carpenter 20 ft on s side of the lott . . . came into the possession of CLEMENT PLUMSTAD of sd city merchant . . . and sd JOHN DUPLOVY on 4 Apr 1695 sold same unto JACOB CULLOCH of Lewis Sussex Co cooper (Book E2 vol 5 pg 31), and sd JACOB CULLOCH on 16 Jun 1703 conveyed it unto the sd FRANCIS RICHARDSON . . . . Wit: CESAR CHISELUS, JOHN VANLEER. Ackn 5 Sep 1707 before NATHAN STANBURY justice of the peace. THOMAS STORY recorder. (E3:pg 220)

30 Sep --. Appointment. THOMAS STORY recorder of deeds to JOSEPH SHIPPEN of Phila gent . . . I have appointed you my dep . . . . (E3:pg 223)

12 Mar 1678/9. Deed. HANS OLESON (OLSON) of DE River in Andrica husbandman for certain sums of money sold to WILLIAM CLAYTON of same river carpenter 1/6 pt/o a tr of land w side of DE river called "Morretties Hook" the whole tr of 1000 a. granted by patent from the Hon Govr Sr EDMUND ANDROS 28 Mar 1676 to CHARLES IVENSEN, OLLE ROESSEN, OLLE NELLSEN, IAN HENDRICKSON & sd HANS OLESON . . . . Wit: EDMUND DRAUGHTON, EPH HERMAN clerk, JOHN TEST. Ackn 12 Mar 1678/9. (E3:pg 224)

10 Sep 1707. Deed. HERRIOTT ROCHFORD of Phila carpenter son & heir of MARY ROCHFORD decd . . . [illegible] . . . heirs of THOMAS HERRIOTT late of Hurst Sussex Co England yeoman decd for 20 pounds sold to THOMAS SHUTE of Phila yeoman 1/5 pt/o a tr of land . . . whereas by lease & release dated 10&11 Sep 1681 WILLIAM PENN proprietary & governour by the name of WILLIAM PENN of Worminghurst Sussex Co esqr conveyed to sd THOMAS HERRIOTT 2500 a., and by lease & release dated 13&14 Oct 1681 sd WILLIAM PENN conveyed unto sd THOMAS HERRIOTT 2500 a. . . . the sd THOMAS HERRIOTT died seized of 5000 a. which 1/2 descended to sd MARY his sister and 1/2 to the other sister and sd MARY having entermarryed with JERIOTT ROCHFORD of Phila merchant,

the late father of sd HERRIOTT ROCHFORD, & who died intestate having four sons to wit HERRIOTT, AMBROSE, DRUINS[?] & SOLOMON ROCHFORD now alive .... Wit: NICHOLAS WALN, FRANCIS COOK, RICHARD HEATH. Ackn 3 Oct 1707 before DAVID LLOYD justice of the peace. THOMAS STORY recorder of deeds. (E3:pg 225)

25 Sep 1707. Deed. SAMUEL CARPENTER of Phila merchant & JAMES LOGAN of sd city gent (attys of DANIEL WHARLEY of Chalfont St. Giles Bucks Co England gent, SAMUEL WALDENFIELD & HENRY GOLDNEY both of London linen drapers) for 120 pounds sold to THOMAS CHALKLEY of Phila lawyer pt/o a parcel of land bounded by WILLIAM TILL, NATHAN STANBURY, JOHN SMART & Second St . . . whereas WILLIAM PENN proprietary & governour of PA (of Worminghurst Sussex Co) esqr by indenture of lease & release dated 22 Oct 1681 released unto LATITIA PENN, his dau by GULIELINA MARIA then his wife, 5000 a. called "Mannor of Mount Joy" & by resurvey found to contain 7800 a. & confirmed to sd LATITIA PENN by patent dated 24 Oct -- (Patent Book A pg 405) . . . and WILLIAM PENN by his patent dated 29 Mar 1701 confirmed unto the sd LATITIA PENN a Front St lott 172 ft breadth 402 ft length bounded by High St, [blank] JENNETT widow & Second St (Patent Book A vol 2 pg 1-2) . . . whereas the sd LATITIA PENN is since intermarryed with WILLIAM AUBREY of London merchant who by their indenture of lease & release dated 4 May 1703 sold same to sd DANIEL WHARLEY, SAMUEL WALDENFIELD & HENRY GOLDNEY (Book A vol 1 pg 265-266) . . . . Wit: ALEXR PAXTON, BENJ GODFREY. Ackn 4 Oct 1707 before WILLIAM TRENT justice of the peace. THOMAS STORY recorder of deeds. (E3:pg 226)

27 Sep 1707. Deed. SAMUEL CARPENTER of Phila merchant & JAMES LOGAN of sd city gent (attys of DANIEL WHARLEY of Chalfont St. Giles Bucks Co England gent, SAMUEL WALDENFIELD & HENRY GOLDNEY both of London linen drapers) for 80 pounds sold to JOHN MIFFLIN of Phila yeoman pt/o a parcell of land . . . whereas [same as above] . . . bounded by Second St, WILLIAM TILL & sd JOHN MIFFLIN . . . [illegible] . . . . Wit: ALEXR PAXTON, BENJ GODFREY. Ackn 8 Oct 1707 before WILLIAM TRENT justice of the peace. THOMAS STORY recorder of deeds. (E3:pg 230)

25 Sep --. Deed. SAMUEL CARPENTER of Phila merchant & JAMES LOGAN of sd city gent (attys of DANIEL WHARLEY of Chalfont St Gyles Bucks Co England gent, SAMUEL WALDENFIELD & HENRY GOLDNEY both of London linnen drapers) for 80 pounds sold to WILLIAM TILL of Phila joyner pt/o a parcell of land bounded by JOHN MIFFLIN . . . whereas

[same as above] .... Wit: ALEXR PAXTON, BENJAMIN GODFREY. Ackn 9 Oct 1707 before WILLIAM TRENT justice of the peace. THOMAS STORY recorder of deeds. (E3:pg 234)

10 Sep 1707. Deed. JEREMIAH COLLETT of Chichesten[?] Chester Co gent son & heir & adminr of the estate of JEREMIAH COLLETT the elder late of Chichester gent decd for 287 pounds sold to WEYNTY (WEYNTIA) COLLETT of Phila widow relict of the sd JEREMIAH the father ... whereas WILLIAM PENN by patent dated 21 Aug 1690 granted unto THOMAS HOLM surveyor general a lott of land on the bank of DE, and whereas SILAS CRISP, PATRICK ROBINSON, ROBERT LONGALIN & JAMES ATKINSON attys of sd THOMAS HOLM on 1 Sep 1691 conveyed unto JEREMIAH COLLETT decd a piece of sd bank lott in Phila bounded by King St, Front St, JOHN GOODSON & Chestnut St .... Wit: JOHN VANLEAR, ANTHONY MORRIS Junr. Ackn 10 Oct 1707 before THOMAS MASTERS justice of the peace. THOMAS STORY recorder of deeds. (E3:pg 237)

29 Aug --. Deed. JOHN WEBB of Phila taylor for 30 pounds sold to THOMAS REDMAN of sd city bricklayer pt/o a lott of land fronting Mulberry St 24 ft length 102 ft breadth bounded by pt/o the great lott now in possession of ANDREW ROBISON, THOMAS PEARL & JOHN FARMAR ... whereas WILLIAM PENN proprietary & governour of PA by patent dated 27 Jun 1684 confirmed unto THOMAS HOLMS (HOLMES) (one of the first purchasers) a lott of land in Phila 102 ft breadth 426 ft length bounded by Front St, Mulberry St & Second St (Book A vol 1 pg 42), and the sd THOMAS HOLMS on 24 Oct 1693 for 10 pounds sold pt/o the lott facing Mulberry St unto JOHN FARMAR of Phila watchmaker ... and whereas the granted lott (together with other lotts of the sd THOMAS HOLMS) was afterwards taken in execution for the payment of some of his debts & was by JOHN CLAYPOOLE then high sheriff on 25 Mar 1690 conveyed unto ANDREW ROBISON then of Phila merchant, and whereas SILAS CRISPEN, PATRICK ROBISON & ROBERT LONGSHORE attys of sd THOMAS HOLMS on 11 Jul 1691 confirmed the same lott unto ANDREW ROBISON, and whereas SAMUEL ROBISON son & heir of sd ANDREW ROBISON on 24 Jun 1697 for 50 pounds sold unto the afsd JOHN FARMAR two other pieces of the afsd great lott one fronting Mulberry St 42 ft & 102 ft length and the other fronting Second St 51 ft & 42 ft depth, the sd two pieces bounded by THOMAS PEARL & the remaining pt/o the great lott in possession of sd SAMUEL ROBISON ... and the sd JOHN FARMAR on 3 Mar 1701 for 153 pounds conveyed the afsd lott to the sd JOHN WEBB .... Wit: SAMUEL HARRIOTT, JOSEPH REDMAN. Ackn 11 Oct 1707 before THOMAS MASTERS justice of the peace. THOMAS STORY recorder of deeds. (E3:pg 240)

11 Sep 1707. Quit Claim. HERRIOTT ROCKFORD of Phila carpenter son & heir of DEINUS[?] ROCKFORD late sd city merchant decd for 4 shillings quit claim unto THOMAS SHUTE of Phila Co yeoman a messuage and tr of land ... whereas the sd DEINUS ROCKFORD became in his life time seised in a messuage & tr of land e side of River Skoolkill adj JOHN MIFFIN ... 200 a. and the sd DEINUS ROCKFORD being so seised died intestate and MARY ROCKFORD his relict & adminrx (to enable her to pay his debts & bring up his children) on 1 Mar 1693/4 conveyed the sd messuage & tr of land unto the sd THOMAS SHUTE (Book A no 1 pg 57) .... Wit: NICHOLAS WALN, RICHARD HEATH, FRANCIS COOK. Ackn 13 Oct 1707 before DAVID LLOYD justice of the peace. THOMAS STORY recorder of deeds. (E3:pg 243)

12 Sep 1707. Deed of Release. SAMUEL CARPENTER of Phila merchant & JAMES LOGAN of sd city gent attys to DANIEL WHARLEY of Chalfont St. Giles Bucks Co gent, SAMUEL WALDENFIELD & HENRY GOLDNEY of London linnen drapers release unto JOHN HUGHES 257 a. ... whereas [same as E3:pg 226] ... among the lands included by mistake in the patent is one tr which by warrant dated 4 Aug 1684 was granted & surveyed to PETER YOCUM renter for 500 a. (wrongfully included in the patent of 7800 a. of LATITIA PENN) which the sd PETER YOCUM granted 1/2 to JOHN HUGHES of Chester Co yeoman adj widow YOCUM, GUNNER RAMBOE & WILLIAM DAVID .... Wit: EDWARD SHIPPEN, SAMUEL CART. Ackn 13 Oct 1707 before WILLIAM TRENT justice of the peace. THOMAS STORY recorder of deeds. (E3:pg 244)

15 Sep 1707. Deed of Release. SAMUEL CARPENTER & JAMES LOGAN both of Phila, attys to DANIEL WHARLEY of Chalfont St. Giles Bucks Co gent, SAMUEL WALDENFIELD & HENRY GOLDNEY of London linen drapers, release unto CHARLES YOCUM of Phila Co yeoman 100 a. adj River Skuylkill & JOHN HUGHES ... among the lands included by mistake in the 7800 a. patent of LATITIA PENN is one tr which by warrant dated 4 Aug 1684 was granted & surveyed to PETER YOCUM renter for 500 a. which the sd PETER YOCUM in his lifetime sold 1/2 pt to JOHN HUGHES & by his will granted 100 a. more being pt/o the remaining 250 a. to his son the sd CHARLES YOCUM .... Wit: EDWARD SHIPPEN, SAMUEL CART. Ackn 14 Oct 1707 before WILLIAM TRENT justice of the peace. THOMAS STORY recorder of deeds. (E3:pg 247)

6 May 1707. Deed of Release. SAMUEL CARPENTER of Phila merchant for 5 shillings release unto HENRY BADCOKE of sd city brewer free & undisturbed use of a House of Office ... whereas on 25 Apr 1704 the sd SAMUEL CARPENTER conveyed unto the sd HENRY BADCOKE a

messuage and ground in Phila bounded by DE Front St, King St, JAMES CLAYPOOLE & Wallnutt St . . . and whereas the sd SAMUEL CARPENTER & HENRY BADCOKE have since erected a new House of Office upon the s side of the wharf . . . . Wit: ROWLAND RICE, DAVID LLOYD, RICHARD HEATH. Ackn 16 Oct 1707 before WILLIAM CARTER justice of the peeace. JOSEPH SHIPPEN dep recorder of deeds. (E3:pg 251)

10 Oct 1707. Deed. THOMAS FAIRMAN of Shaskamapim Phila Co gent & JOHN HART of Bucks Co yeoman (only surviving executors of the will of ANNA SALTER late of Taconey of sd co widow decd) for 200 pounds sold to JACOB HALL of Taconey yeoman a messuage with 100 a. & 3 a. & 1/2 of a meadow . . . whereas by virtue of a deed poll executed by OLLE NELSON late of Taconey decd on 24 Nov -- the sd ANNA SALTER became in her lifetime seized in a messuage with 100 a. in Taconey adj THOMAS ASSON, JOHN WORRALL, Kings Rd & JACOB HALL . . . and also sd ANNA SALTER became in her lifetime seized in 3 a. ne side of Taconey Cr called "Erricks Lott" bounded by SAMUEL FURNEY, and 1/2 of a piece of meadow near Pennapeck Cr which formerly belonged to her afsd plantation in Taconey, and she being so seized made her will dated 7 Nov 1688 and did devise "all her estate which I do enjoy or shall enjoy in my own right or in the right of my sd son decd be leased & rented or sold & disposed of to the best advantage at the descretion of my executors RICHARD WHITFIELD, ROBERT STACY, CHARLES PICKERING & PATRICK ROBISON (all since decd) & sd THOMAS FAIRMAN & JOHN HART" (will proved Book A pg 91) . . . Wit: SAMUEL WALKER, DAVID LLOYD, RICHARD HEATH. Ackn 22 Oct 1707 before GEORGE ROACH justice of the peace. JOSEPH SHIPPEN dep recorder of deeds. (E3:pg 252)

1 Oct 1707. Deed. THOMAS CHALKLEY of Phila lawyer for 300 pounds sold to JOSEPH BROWN late of Cohansie w NJ but now of Phila merchant a remaining pt/o a piece of ground . . . whereas the sd THOMAS CHALKLEY was seized of a parcell of land on the bank of DE in Phila bounded by DE Front St, JOHN KINSEY & land which was purch by BENJAMIN CHAMBERS of sd city yeoman of one JAMES KINGSBURY . . . whereas WILLIAM MARKHAM, ROBERT TURNER & JOHN GOODSON commissioners of property of WILLIAM PENN proprietary & governour of PA by patent dated 16 May 1684 and another patent dated 12 Feb 1690 granted unto the sd BENJAMIN CHAMBERS 2 trs of land, paying yearly for 51 years from 15 Mar 1689/90 unto the sd proprietary 2 shillings 6 pence, and at the expiration of sd term the lots and improvements to be appraised and sd BENJAMIN CHAMBERS to pay to sd WILLIAM PENN the residue . . . and whereas sd BENJAMIN CHAMBERS on 24 Jun 1701 did convey unto the sd THOMAS CHALKLEY all the afsd land (Patent Book A vol 7 pg 345 & pg

339 and sd indenture Book E3 vol 5 pg 442) and THOMAS CHALKLEY on 12 Feb 1705 conveyed unto the sd JOSEPH BROWN the s pt/o the afsd ground (Book E3 vol 5 pg 514) on 13 Feb 1705 . . . . Wit: SAMUEL CARPENTER, GEORGE PAINTER. Ackn 23 Oct 1707 before NATHAN STANBERY justice of the peace. THOMAS STORY recorder of deeds. (E3:pg 254)

13 Sep 1707. Deed. LIONELL BRITTON of Phila shopkeeper for naturall love & affection which he beareth to his only surviving dau REBECCA KEARNEY w/o PHILIP KEARNEY gave to DANIEL RIDGE of same city weaver a brick messuage in Phila with a lott of ground bounded by High St, Second St, bank of DE, JOHN MIFFLAN & WILLIAM TILL for the use of REBECCA during the term of her naturall life and after her decease to the use of SUSANNAH KEARNEY one of the grandchildren of sd LIONELL BRITTON & dau of the sd PHILIP & REBECCA & to her heirs and for default of such issue to the heirs of REBECCA KEARNEY & for default of such issue to the use of PHILIP KEARNEY another grandchild of sd LIONELL BRITTON & son of MICHAEL KEARNEY by his late wife JOANNA the other dau of sd LIONEL BRITTON & to his heirs & for default of such issue to the use of sd LIONELL BRITTON & his heirs . . . . Wit: SAMUEL RICHARDSON, EDWARD EVANS, RICHARD HEATH. Ackn 5 Nov 1707 before EDWARD SHIPPEN justice of the peace. THOMAS STORY recorder of deeds. (E3:pg 258)

15 May 1707. Deed. CALET RANSTED of Phila chairmaker for 100 pounds sold to RICHARD HILL of sd city merchant a piece of ground in Phila 25 ft 6 inches breadth 152 ft length bounded by Second St, lott late of CRISTOPHER SIBTHORP, CASPAR HOODT & lott late of ABRAHAM HARDIMAN . . . paying yearly unto HENRY FLOWER of sd city barber the yearly rent of 4 pounds 16 shillings . . . . Wit: SAMUEL JENNINGS, CHARITY JONES. Ackn 12 Nov 1707 before WILLIAM CARTER justice of the peace. THOMAS STORY recorder of deeds. (E3:pg 261)

20 Oct 1707. Deed. GRIFFITH JONES of Phila merchant sold to THOMAS MILLER of same city butcher a piece of ground in Phila bounded by HARBERT CORRIER, JOHN JONES, JOHN COLLINS & THOMAS SHUTE, pt/o a DE front lott which WILLIAM PENN proprietary & governour of PA by a patent 27 Jun 1684 confirmed unto the sd GRIFFITH JONES (Patent Book A pg 62) . . . . Wit: FRANCIS RAWLE, DAVID LLOYD, RICHARD HEATH. Ackn 13 Nov 1707 before DAVID LLOYD justice of the peace. THOMAS STORY recorder of deeds. (E3:pg 263)

17 Sep 1707. Deed. ANDREW MULLIKIN of Gloucester Co w NJ yeoman son & heir of ERRICK MULLIKIN late of same place yeoman decd for 5 pounds sold to JACOB HALL a parcell of meadow . . . whereas the sd ERRICK MULLIKIN became in his life time seized in a parcell of meadow near Taconey bounded by the DE River, Taconey Cr, piece of ground called the "Tanyards" now in the tenure of Captain SAMUEL FENNEY & a meadow now in the tenure of JACOB HALL of Phila Co . . . which parcell descended to the sd ANDREW MULLIKIN his son . . . . Wit: HENRY MALLOWS, FRANCIS BRANIN. Ackn 15 Nov 1707 before DAVID LLOYD justice of the peace. THOMAS STORY recorder of deeds. (E3:pg 265)

12 Nov 1707. Deed. THOMAS MILLER of Phila Co butcher for 30 pounds sold to JOHN THOMAS of sd city taylor & SARAH his wife a messuage on Second St in Phila 30 ft length 18 ft breadth bounded by JONES's Alley, JAMES PORTUES & other tenements of sd THOMAS MILLER . . . . Wit: JOHN JONES, EDWARD EVANS. Ackn 15 Nov 1707 before WILLIAM TRENT justice of the peace. THOMAS STORY recorder of deeds. (E3:pg 266)

24 May 1707. Deed. JOB BATE of Phila Co yeoman for 12 pounds sold to JOSEPH BATE of same co husbandman a tr of land bounded by HUMPHREY BATE & ROBERT FAIRMAN . . . 103 a. pt/o 440 a. which ALEXANDER EDWARDS of Phila Co yeoman & THOMAS FAIRMAN of sd co gent on 5 Feb 1702/3 sold to JOB BATE . . . . Wit: JOHN EVANS, PHILIP DAVIES, DAVID LLOYD. Ackn 17 Nov 1707 before DAVID LLOYD justice of the peace. THOMAS STORY recorder of deeds. (E3:pg 268)

24 May 1707. Deed. JOB BATE of Phila Co yeoman for 12 pounds sold to HUMPHREY BATE of same co husbandman a tr of land adj JOB BATE, JOSEPH BATE, ROBERT FAIRMAN & ALEXANDER EDWARD . . . 102 3/4 a. pt/o 440 a. which ALEXANDER EDWARDS of sd co yeoman & THOMAS FAIRMAN of sd co gent on 5 Feb 1702/3 sold to sd JOB BATE . . . . Wit: JOHN EVANS, PHILIP DAVIES. Ackn 18 Nov 1707 before DAVID LLOYD justice of the peace. THOMAS STORY recorder of deeds. (E3:pg 270)

19 May 1703. Deed. SAMUEL FINNEY of Oxford Twp Phila Co merchant for 20 pounds sold to JACOB HALL of same place yeoman a parcell of land near Taconey adj SAMUEL FINNEY & other land of sd JACOB HALL . . . 59 a. pt/o 104 a. which WILLIAM PENN proprietary & governour of PA by patent dated 29 Oct 1701 did confirm unto sd SAMUEL FINNEY (Patent Book A vol 2 pg 219) and another parcel of land near Taconey . . . 30 a. pt/o the land EDWARD SHIPPEN, GRIFFITH OWEN, THOMAS STORY &

JAMES LOGAN commissioners of property by a patent dated 8 Dec 1702 confirmed unto the sd SAMUEL FINNEY (Patent Book A vol 2 pg 413) . . . . Wit: ANDREW BLANEY, REBECCA FINNEY. Ackn 20 Nov 1707 before DAVID LLOYD justice of the peace. THOMAS STORY recorder of deeds. (E3:pg 271)

8 Oct 1707. Deed. THOMAS TOMSON of Taconey Phila Co yeoman son & heir of CHIEFTAN THOMAS late of same place yeoman decd for 4 pounds sold to JACOB HALL a piece of meadow . . . whereas the sd CHIEFTAN THOMAS became in his life time seised in a piece of meadow in Taconey bounded by the DE River & a meadow lately sold by ANDREW MULLIKIN to JACOB HALL of sd co yeoman . . . and after his decease the meadow descended to sd THOMAS TOMSON his son . . . . Wit: HENRY MALLOWS, JOSEPH FINNEY. Ackn 21 Nov 1707 before DAVID LLOYD justice of the peace. THOMAS STORY recorder of deeds. (E3:pg 275)

15 Nov 1707. Deed of Release. HENRY MORRIS of Phila fishmunger brother & heir of JOSHUA MORRIS late of same place decd for 70 pounds release unto JOSHUA CARPENTER 200 a. . . . whereas WILLIAM POWELL on 2 Sep 1686 conveyed unto the afsd JOSHUA MORRIS a 200 a. tr of land adj EDGAR HILL & ISRAEL HOBBS . . . pt/o the sd WILLIAM POWELL's purch of 500 a. (Book E1 vol 5 pg 416), and the sd JOSHUA MORRIS on 18 Nov 1686 conveyed unto the sd WILLIAM POWELL the 200 a. upon condition that the sd JOSHUA MORRIS on 2 Sep 1688 should pay to the sd WILLIAM POWELL 6 pounds then the sd sale would be void, and the sd WILLIAM POWELL 27 Nov 1697 sett over unto JOSHUA CARPENTER of Phila merchant the sd 200 a. . . . . Wit: JOHN PLUMLY, CHARLES PLUMLEY, SAMUEL CARPENTER Junr. Ackn 22 Nov 1707 before DAVID LLOYD justice of the peace. THOMAS STORY recorder of deeds. (E3:pg 276)

8 Nov 1707. Deed. HUGH GRIFFITH & EVAN GRIFFITH both of Gwynedd Twp Phila Co yeoman for 52 pounds sold to ROBERT HUMPHREY of same place yeoman 115 a. pt/o a 376 a. parcell of land in the sd twp which the commissioners of WILLIAM PENN proprietary & governour by patent dated 22 Mar 1702 (Patent Book A vol 2 pg 496-497) granted unto sd HUGH GRIFFITH & EVAN GRIFFITH adj HUGH ROBERTS, JOHN HUGHES, JOHN HUMPHREY & ROBERT EVAN PRYTHRY . . . . Wit: EDWARD CADWALLADER, EVAN OWEN, JOHN CADWALLADER. Ackn 22 Nov 1707 before DAVID LLOYD justice of the peace. THOMAS STORY recorder of deeds. (E3:pg 278)

8 Nov 1707. Deed. HUGH GRIFFITH & EVAN GRIFFITH both of Gwynedd Twp Phila Co yeomen for 84 pounds sold to JOHN HUMPHREY of same place yeoman 50 a. pt/o [above patent] . . . adj ROBERT EVAN PRYTHRY, ROBERT HUMPHREY, JOHN HUGHS & other land of HUGH & EVAN GRIFFITH . . . . Wit: EDWARD CADWALLADER, EVAN OWEN, JOHN CADWALLADER. Ackn 27 Nov 1707 before DAVID LLOYD justice of the peace. THOMAS STORY recorder of deeds. (E3:pg 281)

7 Aug 1703. Quit Claim. JOHN FINCHOR only surviving son of FRANCIS FINCHOR decd release all my claim in the premises that was my fathers and now in possession of WILLIAM LAWRENCE for a valuable consideration. (E3:pg 283)

-- Sep 1707. Deed. MATHIAS WELLIS of Phila esqr carpenter for 29 pounds sold to PATRICK OGILBY of Phila bricklayer a lot on Chesnut St in Phila 35 ft breadth 178 ft length bounded by lot late of THOMAS ENGLAND & lot formerly of JOHN COUNTIS . . . granted by the commissioners of WILLIAM PENN proprietary & governour 7 Jun 1690 and surveyed by warrant unto JOHN COUNTIS who on 13 May 1695 assigned it unto JOHN WELLIS and by warrant dated 7 Jan 1701 was resurveyed 13 Feb following (Book A vol 2 pg 300-302) . . . and JOHN WELLIS on 25 Feb afsd sold it unto MATHIAS WELLIS . . . . Wit: JOHN JONES, BENJAMIN PRICHARD. Ackn 16 Jan 1707 before ANTHONY MORRIS justice of the peace. THOMAS STORY recorder of deeds. (E4:pg 1)

23 Jan 1707. Deed. ISAAC WATERMAN son & heir of HUMPHREY WATERMAN decd for 56 pounds 1 shilling sold to EDMUND MCVEAGH (MCVAUGH) of Phila Co a tr of land adj WALTER KING . . . 95 a. granted by patent to the sd HUMPHREY WATERMAN dated 26 Sep 1689 . . . . Wit: PETER TAYLOR, FRANCIS COOKE. Ackn before THOMAS WALTERS justice of the peace. THOMAS STORY recorder of deeds. (E4:pg 3)

24 Jan 1707/8. Quit Claim. MARGARET JONES w/o JOHN JONES the elder of Phila merchant formerly the w/o HUMPHREY WATERMAN decd quit claims unto EDMUND MCVEAGH of Phila Co the [above] tr of land . . . according to a power to her reserved by indenture dated 14 Dec 1696 between sd JOHN JONES of the first part, SAMUEL CARPENTER of sd city merchant and EDWARD [illegible] of Phila Co yeoman of the second part & sd MARGARET JONES by the name of MARGARET WATERMAN of the third part . . . . Wit: PETER EVANS, JOHN BLANEY. Ackn 27 Jan 1707 before THOMAS WALTERS justice of the peace. THOMAS STORY recorder of deeds. (E4:pg 4)

29 Sep 1707. Deed. SAMUEL RICHARDSON of Phila sold to NATHANIEL EDGECOME boulter a tr of land . . . whereas SAMUEL RICHARDSON by his indenture dated 25 Mar 1693 granted, for a certain number of years, unto EVAN GRIFFITH pt/o his DE front lot 20 ft breadth 102 ft length bounded by GRIFFITH JONES' lot (now NATHANIEL EDGECOME's), JAMES BORKUS, High St, HOWELL GRIFFITH & ROBERT HUTCHESON, which was sold by EVAN unto sd SAMUEL EDGECOME, which lot the sd SAMUEL RICHARDSON purch of one THOMAS BOWMAN 3 Jul 1686 (Vol 5 Book E fol 356) . . . . Wit: FRANCIS COOKE, RICHARD HITCHINGS, MARY COOKE, MARY FITS RANDOLPH. Ackn 31 Jan 1707 before NATHAN STANBURY justice of the peace. THOMAS STORY recorder of deeds. (E4:pg 5)

25 May 1705. Deed of Mortgage. WILLIAM WILLS of Phila glover for the security of payment of 73 pounds sold to GEORGE GRAY of sd city merchant a parcel of land n side of Vine St bounded by Second St & JOSEPH WILCOX . . . whereas the sd WILLIAM WILLS is indebted unto the sd GEORGE GRAY in the sum of 30 pounds 8 shillings 8 pence and also indebted unto BENJAMIN WRIGHT of sd city merchant for 18 pounds, THOMAS STORY of sd city gent for 8 pounds 11 shillings 4 pence, ALEXANDER PAXTON of sd city merchant for 7 pounds, MARGARET [illgible] of sd city for 5 pounds & GRIFFITH JONES of sd city merchant for 4 pounds, which the whole sum is 73 pounds and the sd GEORGE GRAY has paid unto the sd several persons the sums of money due unto them . . . if WILLIAM WILLS pays the 73 pounds with interest unto GEORGE GRAY on or before 25 May 1708 then this indenture to be utterly void . . . . Wit: JOHN SONGBURST, MAURICE SISK. Ackn 2 Feb 1707/8 before DAVID LLOYD justice of the peace. THOMAS STORY recorder of deeds. (E4:pg 7)

31 Jan 1707. Deed. JOHN HART of Phila bricklayer for 190 pounds sold to FRANCIS RICHARDSON of sd city goldsmith a messuage lot s side of Chesnut St in Phila 15 ft breadth 63 ft 1 inch 1/2 length bounded by sd FRANCIS RICHARDSON, sd JOHN HART, lot late in the tenure of RICHARD HALL & NATHANIEL SIKES . . . pt/o sd lot lately purch by the sd JOHN HART of sd NATHANIEL SIKES and pt/o sd lot purch 3 Mar 1703 by JOHN HART of HUMPHREY MORREY of sd city merchant . . . . Wit: SAMUEL POWELL, THOMAS STAPLEFORD. Ackn 3 Feb 1707 before NATHAN STANBURY justice of the peace. THOMAS STORY recorder of deeds. (E4:pg 9)

25 Dec 1707. Deed. EDWARD EVANS of Abington Twp Phila Co yeoman for 55 pounds sold to MORRIS MORRIS of same twp yeoman 51 a. pt/o a 250 a. tr of land bounded by sd EVANS & MORRIS' land, Susquehannah Rd &

JOSEPH PHIPPS . . . whereas on 12 Oct 1636 JOSEPH PHIPPS of sd co yeoman for 50 pounds sold to sd EDWARD EVANS a 250 a. tr of land in sd twp (Book E3 vol [?] pg 219) . . . . Wit: EDWARD CADWALLADER, EVAN ROBERTS. Ackn 4 Feb 1707 before DAVID LLOYD justice of the peace. THOMAS STORY recorder of deeds. (E4:pg 11)

14 Aug 1707. Deed. WILLIAM HOWELL of Phila Co yeoman, EDWARD JONES of Merrian Twp sd co, JOHN ROBERTS of same twp, GRIFFITH OWEN of Phila practitioner of physick and DANIEL HUMPHREYS of Haverford in Welsh Grant yeoman [trustees] release unto JOHN WILLIAM of Merion yeoman the remaining pt/o a tr of land bounded by ROWLAND ELLIS & JOHN EVANS . . . whereas THOMAS ELLIS late of Haverford yeoman was in his life time seized of a 600 a. tr of land bounded by ROWLAND ELLIS & CHRISTOPHER PERMOCK in Merion Twp, and being so seized made his will 1 Jan 1688 saying the sd 600 a., 30 a. with his dwelling plantation between DANIEL HUMPHREY & LEWIS DAVID in the town of Haverford, his house at Schuylkill & City Liberty, all his lots in Phila, and land beyond Darby Cr in Chester Co to be sold at the direction of his trustees to pay his debts & funeral expenses . . . the executor, having refused the executorship, of sd will administration was committed to ELLEN ELLIS widow & relict of sd testator and sd ELLEN having made sd DANIEL HUMPHREYS her executor died leaving the sd testators debts unpaid, and whereas the sd DANIEL HUMPHREYS for 96 pounds 4 shillings 8 pence sold the above tr of land unto sd JOHN WILLIAM 5 Sep 1698, the tr found to be 819 a. and the sd JOHN WILLIAM having sold unto JOHN EVANS 200 a. and unto ROBERT LLOYD 409 1/2 a. . . . . Wit: HERVEY PAUL, RICHARD HEATH. Ackn 5 Feb 1707 before DAVID LLOYD justice of the peace. THOMAS STORY recorder of deeds. (E4:pg 13)

14 Aug 1707. Deed of Release. WILLIAM HOWELL of Phila Co yeoman, EDWARD JONES of Merion Twp Phila Co practitioner of physick and DANIEL HAVERFORD HUMPHREYS of Haverford in the Welsh Tr yeoman release unto ROBERT LLOYD of Merion Twp Phila Co yeoman [illegible] . . . whereas THOMAS ELLIS late of Haverford yeoman [same as above] . . . . Wit: HERVEY PAUL, DAVID LLOYD, RICHARD HEATH. Ackn 6 Feb 1707/8 before DAVID LLOYD justice of the peace. THOMAS STORY recorder of deeds. (E4:pg 15)

14 Aug 1707. Deed of Release. WILLIAM HOWELL of Phila Co yeoman, EDWARD JONES of Merion Twp Phila Co practitioner of physick, JOHN ROBERTS of same twp malster, GRIFFITH OWEN of Phila practitioner of physick and DANIEL HUMPHREYS of Haverford in the Welsh Tr yeoman release unto JOHN EVANS a tr of land adj ROWLAND ELLIS, JOHN

WILLIAMS & EDWARD GRIFFITH . . . 200 a. . . . whereas THOMAS ELLIS late of Haverford yeoman [same as E4:pg 13] . . . . Wit: HENRY PAUL, DAVID LLOYD, RICHARD HEATH. Ackn 6 Feb 1707/8 before DAVID LLOYD justice of the peace. THOMAS STORY recorder of deeds. (E4:pg 17)

17 Feb 1707. Deed of Mortgage. RICHARD HILL of Phila merchant sold to CALEB RANSTED of sd city chairmaker a parcel of ground . . . whereas on 15 May last past sd CALEB RANSTED for 100 pounds sold unto sd RICHARD HILL a parcel of ground in Phila 25 6/10 ft breadth 152 ft length bounded by Second St, lot late of CHRISTOPHER SIBTHORP, CASPER HOODF & lot late of ABRAHAM HARDIMAN . . . paying yearly unto HENRY FLOWER of sd city 4 pounds 16 shillings (Book E3 vol 6 pg 261) . . . if the sd CALEB RANSTED shall pay unto the sd RICHARD HILL the sum of 100 pounds with interest of 8 pounds on 14 May next ensueing then 108 pounds residue before 15 May 1709 then sd RICHARD HILL shall convey unto CALEB RANSTED the parcel of ground . . . . Wit: JOSEPH AUTROLAY, CHARITY JONES. Ackn 18 Feb 1707/8 before WILLIAM CARTER justice of the peace. THOMAS STORY recorder of deeds. 30 Aug 1713 before CHARLES BROCKDEN dep recorder of deeds RICHARD HILL ackn [illegible] . . . . (E4:pg 18)

18 Feb 1707. Deed. WYNLIE (WEYNLIE) COLLETT of Phila widow for 320 pounds sold to MORDICAI HOWELL of Chester Borrough gent a piece of land on the bank of DE . . . whereas by patent dated 25 Aug 1690 granted unto THOMAS HOLMES surveyor general a lot on the bank of the DE and sd WYNLIE COLLETT is seized in pt/o the sd lot bounded by Front St, King St, JOHN GOODSON & Chesnut St as by indenture dated 10 Sep last past between JEREMIAH COLLETT of Chester gent and the sd WYNLIE COLLETT (Book E3 vol 6 pg 257) . . . . Wit: PETER STRETCH, THOMAS GOODFELLOW. Ackn 19 Feb 1707/8 before NATHAN STANBURY justice of the peace. THOMAS STORY recorder of deeds. (E4:pg 21)

7 Nov 1707. Deed. RICHARD HILL of Phila merchant for 100 pounds sold to ABELL COLLEY of sd city watchmaker a parcel of ground . . . whereas DANIEL ZACHERY late of Boston in New England merchant decd in his life time was seized in a parcel of ground in Phila 50 ft breadth 132 ft length bounded by Second St, THOMAS LLOYD, Strawbery Alley & WILLIAM HARWOOD, which sd lot DANIEL ZACHERY did direct in his will be sold for the payment of his debts, and whereas THOMAS FITCH of Boston & WALTER NEWBERRY of same place merchants executors of the will on 28 Jul last past made the sd RICHARD HILL their atty to sell the piece

of ground .... Wit: CALEB PUSEY, NATHAN STANBURY. Ackn 21 Feb 1707/8 before EDWARD SHIPPEN justice of the peace. THOMAS STORY recorder of deeds. (E4:pg 23)

6 Jan 1707. Deed. ABELL COLLEY of Phila watchmaker for 108 pounds sold to RICHARD HILL of sd city merchant a parcel of ground [same as above] . ... Wit: CALEB PUSEY, NATHAN STANBURY. Ackn 27 Feb 1707/8 before EDWARD SHIPPEN justice of the peace. THOMAS STORY recorder of deeds. (E4:pg 25)

13 Feb 1707/8. Deed. DANIEL PRICHARD of Bucks Co taylor for 100 pounds sold to SIMON ANDREWS of Phila Co yeoman and ESTHER his wife a messuage & 80 a. tr of land ... whereas on 8 Sep 1705 JOSEPH WEBB of Bucks Co yeoman and SARAH his wife relict of JOHN BURLING late of Phila Co wheelwright her late husband decd sold to the sd DANIEL PRICHARD a messuage plantation & 80 a. in Bristol Twp bounded by WILLIAM WILKINS, DAVID POTTS & THOMAS RUTTER .... Wit: ROBERT HEATH, DAVID EVANS, RICHARD HEATH. Ackn 26 Feb 1707 before DAVID LLOYD justice of the peace. THOMAS STORY recorder of deeds. (E4:pg 27)

6 Jul 1695. Deed of Mortgage. PETER KENELIS of Germantown baker for 40 pounds sold to ELIZABETH KNOWLES of Oxford Twp Phila Co widow a lot of land in Germantown where he now liveth 50 a. ... provided that if the sd PETER KENELIS shall pay unto the sd ELIZABETH KNOWLES the sum of 40 pounds with interest on 6 Jul 1696 then these presents to be void .... Wit: MARY PHILLIPS, ROBERT EWER. SAMUEL HOWELL & CHARLES PLUMLY both of Phila on 21 Feb 1707/8 before NATHAN STANBURY justice of the peace declared they were present & heard the sd PETER KENELIS ackn the within indenture. THOMAS STORY recorder of deeds. (E4:pg 28)

25 Feb 1707. Deed. THOMAS GRIFFITH of Phila cordwainer & ELIZABETH his wife (formerly ELIZABETH KNOWLES widow) for 48 pounds sold to GEORGE GRAY of sd city merchant a lot of land ... whereas PETER KENELIS of Germantown Phila Co baker by his indenture [see above] ... whereas the sd 40 pounds with interest was not paid on the day and time sd & remaineth unpaid by means whereof the sd lot forfeited unto the sd ELIZABETH .... Wit: FRANCIS KNOWLES, RICHARD NEWCOMBE, RICHARD HEATH. Ackn 22 Feb 1707/8 before NATHAN STANBURY justice of the peace. THOMAS STORY recorder of deeds. (E4:pg 29)

28 Feb --. Deed. ALEXANDER EDWARDS of North Wales Phila Co yeoman for 34 pounds sold to CADWALADER MORRIS of near North Wales afsd yeoman a parcel of ground adj RICHARD SMYTH . . . 100 a. pt/o 996 a. . . . whereas THOMAS FAIRMAN of Shaxamaxon sd co gent on 28 Dec 1702 released unto the sd ALEXANDER EDWARDS a 996 a. tr of land bounded by sd THOMAS FAIRMAN, THOMAS EVAN, JOB BATES & ROBERT FAIRMAN, being the same land granted unto the sd ALEXANDER EDWARDS by patent 12 Oct 1702 (Patent Book A vol 2 pg 19) . . . . Wit: HENRY PAULL, ROBERT ADAMS. Ackn 28 -- 1707 before NATHAN STANBURY justice of the peace. THOMAS STORY recorder of deeds. (E4:pg 31)

28 Feb 1707/8. Quit Claim. JOHN HUGHES of Phila Co yeoman for natural love & affection quit claim unto his only dau MARY HUGHES a parcel of land adj widow YOCUM & WILLIAM [?] . . . 557 a. . . . sd JOHN HUGHES reserved out of the afsd land the occupation of the sd land & premises unto my wife from the time of my decease during her natural life . . . . Wit: HENRY PAULL, RICHD NEWCOMBE. Ackn 2 Mar 1707/8 before NATHAN STANBURY justice of the peace. THOMAS STORY recorder of deeds. (E4:pg 33)

11 Feb 1707/8. Deed. JOHN MORGAN of Abbington Twp Phila Co taylor for 150 pounds sold to DAVID MARPLE of the Mannor of Moreland co afsd yeoman a tr of land upon the sd Mannor of Moreland adj Perrapecka Cr, ROBERT FITCH, REBECCA WOOD & SAMUEL [?] . . . 120 a. pt/o a 200 a. tr of land purch from ELIAS REACH & MARY his wife 28 Feb 1691 by WILLIAM HUNTLEY, and the sd HUNTLEY conveyed it unto JOHN MORGAN CALLOW 1 Apr 1697, and sd CALLOW conveyed the same unto the sd JOHN MORGAN 16 May 1699 . . . . Wit: JOSEPH EATON, HENRY STIRKE. Ackn 3 Mar 1707/8 before SAMUEL FINNEY justice of the peace. JOSEPH SHIPPEN dep recorder of deeds. (E4:pg 35)

21 Feb 1707/8. Quit Claim. THOMAS JONES executor of the will of GRIFFITH JOHNS decd have received of EVAN OWENS order to wit by security from JONATHAN JONES to the use of ROBERT OWENS' younger children for 150 pounds by one bond and 97 pounds by another bond and 50 pounds by ROBERT WILLIAMS bond and 48 pounds 12 shillings of CAYNOR one of the sd ROBERT OWENS daus in pt/o her portion and by security from the sd JONATHAN JONES to the use afsd for 1 years interest which several sums are in full discharge of the mortgage and interest (see Book B vol 3 pg 67) . . . the sd THOMAS JONES quit claims unto sd EVAN OWENS the mortgaged lands . . . . Wit: RICHARD HEATH, EDWARD

EVANS, DAVID LLOYD. Ackn 5 Mar 1707/8 before DAVID LLOYD justice of the peace. THOMAS STORY recorder of deeds. (E4:pg 38)

2 Mar 1704/5. Deed. GERHARD TIBBEN of Germantown Phila Co yeoman for 42 pounds sold to SAMUEL SAVAGE & ANNA RUTTER of sd co a tr of land at Summerhouse in the Germantownship between KREISHEIM and WIGARD SEVERING 100 a. in the tenure of GERHARD TIBBEN by virtue of a deed of sale from HERMAN VAN BON dated 29 Nov 1703 to whom the land was granted from DANIEL FATHUIRE[?] & JOHANNES JANERL attys of Frankford Company dated 23 Mar 1702/3 . . . 50 a. pt/o the 100 a., and the other 50 a. to the sd SAMUEL SAVAGE until the expiration of all the descent of the sd HERMAN VAN BON . . . . Wit: FRANCIS DANIEL PASTORRAY, JANE DORDEN. Ackn 6 Mar 1707/8 before EDWARD SHIPPEN justice of the peace. THOMAS STORY recorder of deeds. (E4:pg 38)

31 Dec 1707. Deed. EVAN OWEN of Merion Twp Phila Co yeoman son & heir of ROBERT OWEN late of same place decd for 420 pounds sold to JONATHAN JONES of Merion yeoman two trs of land . . . whereas by deed poll on 5 Aug 1691 THOMAS LLOYD late of PA gent decd conveyed unto the sd ROBERT OWEN a 450 a. tr of land in Merion Twp adj JAMES THOMAS, JOHN ROBERTS, THOMAS JONES & Co, ROBERT ROBERTS, EDWARD REESE & MARY HAVARCH[?] . . . and whereas HUGH ROBERTS of Merion on 16 Nov -- conveyed unto the sd ROBERT OWEN a tr of land in Merion adj EDWARD REESE . . . 7 a. and the sd ROBERT OWEN died seized of the sd trs of land and the same descended unto the sd EVAN OWEN his son & heir . . . and whereas on 8 Feb 1705 a patent was granted unto the sd EVAN OWEN on the 450 a. (Patent Book A vol 3 pg 29) . . . . Wit: ROWLAND ELLIS, ROBERT JONES, JOHN ROBERTS, THOMAS JONES. Ackn 9 Mar 1707/8 before DAVID LLOYD justice of the peace. THOMAS STORY recorder of deeds. (E4:pg 40)

1 Dec 1707. Deed. ROBERT ADAMS of Oxford Twp Phila Co yeoman for 100 pounds sold to JOSEPH PAULL Junr of sd twp a tr of land in sd twp adj JOSEPH PAULL Senr, JOHN HARPER, RICHARD TOMLINSON & MARY FLETCHER . . . by Dublin Twp . . . 95 a. pt/o land sold by THOMAS DUCKETT unto the sd ROBERT ADAMS 11 Jun 1692 . . . . Wit: JOHN COOKE, WILLIAM PRESTON, SARAH FLETCHER. Ackn 13 Mar 1707/8 before DAVID LLOYD justice of the peace. THOMAS STORY recorder of deeds. (E4:pg 42)

5 Mar 1707/8. Deed of Lease. WILLIAM HALL of Phila for 135 pounds sold to JOHN GILBERT of sd city boulter a water lott . . . whereas EDWARD SMOUT of same city on 24 Aug 1704 sold to the sd WILLIAM HALL a water

lott being in three pieces under the bank of the DE in Phila next to sd EDWARD SMOUT's other ground adj King Street and was originally granted by ROBERT TURNER unto one FRANCIS JARVIS for 44 years from 24 Aug 1694 and by the sd FRANCIS conveyed unto one SUSANNA ELTON by whose executors the same was conveyed unto the sd EDWARD SMOUT . . . during the term of the first grant . . . . Wit: JOSHUA GILBERT, JAMES STEEL. Ackn 13 Mar 1707/8 before DAVID LLOYD justice of the peace. THOMAS STORY recorder of deeds. (E4:pg 43)

10 Feb 1707/8. Deed. JOHN SIMES of Phila innkeeper for 80 pounds sold to RICHARD HALL of Cheltenham Twp Phila Co blacksmith a messuage & lot of land . . . whereas on 1 Apr 1696 ROBERT TURNER of Phila merchant sold to JOHN GIBBS of same place boat builder a lot of land n side of Garden Ally in Phila 30 ft breadth 52 ft back bounded by EDWARD WILLIAMS & FRANCIS JERVIS, paying unto the sd ROBERT TURNER 30 shillings on 1 Apr yearly forever, and the sd JOHN GIBBS having built a messuage on the sd lot died intestate after whose decease SARAH GIBBS his widow & relict (the better to enable her to pay the sd JOHN GIBBS debts & bring up his children) did on 20 Jul 1700 convey the sd messuage and lot unto THOMAS TRESSE of Phila merchant, and the sd THOMAS TRESSE on 5 Sep 1701 conveyed the lot unto the sd JOHN SIMES . . . . Wit: SAMUEL NICHOLAS, DAVID LLOYD, WILLIAM BLACKLEDGE, RICHARD HEATH. Ackn 15 Mar 1707/8 before DAVID LLOYD justice of the peace. THOMAS STORY recorder of deeds. (E4:pg 45)

10 Mar 1707/8. Deed. JOHN WALKER late of Phila rope maker but now of NJ for 200 pounds sold to WILLIAM TRENT & THOMAS MASTERS both of sd city merchants pt/o a piece of ground 15 ft breadth 213 ft length with the residue of the whole lot now in the tenure of MORDICAI HOWELL . . . whereas WILLIAM SOUTHBY of sd city boat builder on 27 Jan 1701/2 granted unto sd JOHN WALKER a piece of ground in Phila 45 ft breadth 213 ft length bounded by Front St, WILLIAM FISHER, JOSHUA TITTERY & THOMAS BRISTOW . . . . Wit: HENRY LEWIS, DAVID LLOYD, RICHARD HEATH. Ackn 20 Mar 1707/8 before DAVID LLOYD justice of the peace. THOMAS STORY recorder of deeds. (E4:pg 47)

9 Mar 1707/8. Deed. JOHN WALKER of Phila rope maker but now of NJ for 400 pounds sold to MORDICAI HOWELL of Chichester Twp Chester Co gent pt/o a piece of ground . . . whereas [same as above] . . . . Wit: HENRY LEWIS, DAVID LLOYD, RICHARD HEATH. Ackn 22 Mar 1707/8 before DAVID LLOYD justice of the peace. THOMAS STORY recorder of deeds. (E4:pg 49)

24 Dec 1707. Deed. JACOB HALL of Phila Co yeoman for 350 pounds sold to EDWARD SHIPPEN the younger of Phila merchant a messuage & several trs of land . . . whereas on 10 Oct last past THOMAS FAIRMAN of Shaxamaxon sd co gent & JOHN HART of Bucks Co yeoman only surviving executors of the will of ANNA SALTER late of Tacony sd co widow decd conveyed unto sd JACOB HALL a messuage with 100 a. in Tacony adj THOMAS ASSON & JOHN WORRELL, Kings Rd & other land of sd JACOB HALL (Book E3 vol 6 pg 252) and on 19 May 1703 SAMUEL FINNEY of Oxford Twp sd co merchant conveyed unto sd JACOB HALL a tr of land in Tacony adj sd SAMUEL FINNEY, sd JACOB HALL & Tacony Cr . . . 59 a., and also a parcel of land in Tacony . . . 30 a. [illegible] . . . a meadow 15 a. part whereof ANDREW MULLIKEN of Gloucester Co w NJ on 17 Sep last past conveyed unto the sd JACOB HALL (Book E3 vol 6 pg 265) and the residue of sd meadow THOMAS THOMSON of Tacony yeoman on 8 Oct last past conveyed unto the sd JACOB HALL (Book E3 vol 6 pg 275) . . . . Wit: MORDICAI HOWELL, DANIEL STREET, ARNOLD CAPELL, DAVID LLOYD, RICHARD HEATH. Ackn 23 Mar 1707/8 before DAVID LLOYD justice of the peace. THOMAS STORY recorder of deeds. (E4:pg 51)

6 Jan 1707. Deed of Mortgage. ARNOLD CASSELL of Phila Co yeoman for 40 pounds sold to PAUL (PAULL) WULF of Germantown sd co yeoman a parcel of land in the Liberties of Phila adj Goodson Cr & an Indian Tribe . . . 20 a. . . . provided that if the sd ARNOLD CASSELL shall pay unto the sd PAUL WULF 40 pounds with interest on 1 May next ensueing then this present indenture shall cease . . . . Wit: DANIEL RADLEY, RICHD HEATH, DAVID LLOYD. Ackn 27 Mar 1707 before DAVID LLOYD justice of the peace. THOMAS STORY recorder of deeds. On 1 Dec 1720 before CHARLES BROCKDEN recorder of deeds came PETER SHOEMAKER of Germantown yeoman surviving executor of the will of PAUL WULF and ackn that the sd PETER SHOEMAKER had received of EDWARD COLLINS of the Northern Liberties of Phila garderner 40 pounds and all interest in full satisfaction of the mortgage. (E4:pg 55)

1 Nov 1707. Deed. ABRAHAM CARPENTER of Phila merchant for 600 pounds sold to HENRY FLOWER of same city barber a messuage w side of Front St in Phila called "White Warf Inn" and stable with a parcel of ground 31 ft breadth 198 ft length bounded by the sd HENRY FLOWER, JOHN GOODSON, JOHN HAYWOOD, THOMAS MARLE & PHILIP RICHARDS, and also another piece of ground for a passage to the afsd lot n side of Chesnut St . . . . Wit: THOMAS HARDING, SAMUEL CARPENTER Junr, RICHARD HEATH. Ackn 29 Mar 1708 before THOMAS MASTERS justice of the peace. THOMAS STORY recorder of deeds. (E4:pg 57)

5 Nov 1707. Deed of Mortgage. HENRY FLOWER of Phila barber for 500 pounds sold to ABRAHAM CARPENTER of same city merchant a messuage w side of Front St in Phila called "White Hart Inn" and stable with a parcel of ground 31 ft breadth 198 ft length bounded by the sd HENRY FLOWER, ELIAS HUGG, JOHN HOWARD, THOMAS MARLE & lot late of PHILIP RICHARDS and also a piece of ground for a passage to the afsd lot n side of Chesnut St . . . provided that if the sd HENRY FLOWER shall pay unto the sd ABRAHAM CARPENTER 500 pounds with interest . . . then this present indenture shall cease . . . . Wit: H GRAHAM, THOMAS HARDING, SAMUEL CARPENTER Junr, RICHARD HEATH. Ackn 31 Mar 1708 before THOMAS MASTERS justice of the peace. THOMAS STORY recorder of deeds. (E4:pg 59)

30 Mar 1708. Deed. JOHN AM WEGG of Phila Co husbandman sold & exchanged unto SAMUEL SAVAGE & ANNA his wife a piece of land pt/o 100 a. adj Springfield Manner, sd SAMUEL SAVAGE, sd JOHN AM WEGG & GEORGE MILLER . . . 23 1/4 a. . . . whereas SAMUEL SAVAGE of Germantwp sd co stone cutter & ANNA his wife, her maiden name ANNA RUTTER, by virtue of a deed of sale executed by GERHARD TIBBEN of sd twp yeoman on 22 Mar 1704/5 (Book E4 vol 7 pg 46) became sezied of 100 a. in Summerhousen in sd twp between KRESHEM and land formerly of WIGGARD SEVERING now of JOHN AM WEGG, and whereas by a deed of sale executed by WIGGARD SEVERING of sd co carpenter on 19 Oct 1706 ackn before NATHAN STANBURY justice of the peace (Book B vol 2 pg 207) JOHN AM WEGG became seized of 100 a. in Sumerhousen between sd SAMUEL SAVAGE and GEORGE MILLER . . . the sd JOHN AM WEGG for the better improvement of his land and for a tr which the sd SAMUEL SAVAGE & ANN his wife on even date with these presents have sold unto the sd JOHN AM WEGG being pt/o the afsd 100 a. reaching from Plymouth Rd to Roxberry Twp . . . . Wit: ARNOLL CUSTER, FRANCIS DANIEL PASTORIUS. Ackn 1 Apr 1708 before JOSEPH PIDGEON justice of the peace. THOMAS STORY recorder of deeds. (E4:pg 61)

30 Mar 1708. Deed. SAMUEL SAVAGE of Germantownship Phila Co stone cutter and ANNA his wife, her maiden name ANNA RUTTER, for 6 pounds & a tr of land [see above] sold & exchanged unto JOHN AM WEGG a tr of land reaching from Plymouth Rd down to Roxberry Twp . . . 72 a. pt/o 100 a. . . . whereas the sd SAMUEL & ANNA SAVAGE by virtue of a deed executed by GERHARD TIBBEN of sd twp on 22 Mar 1704/5 ackn before EDWARD SHIPPEN justice of the peace (Book E4 vol 7 pg 46) became seized in 100 a. in Summerhousen sd twp between KRISHEIM and land formerly of WIGARD SEVERING now of JOHN AM WEGG, and whereas also JOHN AM WEGG by a deed of sale executed by WIGARD SEVERING

of sd co carpenter dated 19 Oct 1706 ackn before NATHAN STANBURY justice of the peace (Book B vol 2 pg 207) became seized of 100 a. in Sumerhousen between SAMUEL SAVAGE & GEORGE MILLER .... Wit: ARNOLL CUSTER, FRANCIS DANIEL PASTORIUS. Ackn 3 Apr 1708 before JOSEPH PIDGEON justice of the peace. THOMAS STORY recorder of deeds. (E4:pg 63)

10 Apr 1708. Deed. PETER KENZLIN of Germantown Phila Co yeoman for the ending of suits & differences & GEORGE GRAY of Phila merchant for 600 pounds bound themselves together to stand to the award & final judgement of arbitrators EDWARD SHIPPEN Senr of sd city merchant, RICHARD HILL of same place merchant, WILLIAM CARTER, SAMUEL CART of Abington same co yeoman & CASPER HOODT of sd city tailor . . . under their award dated 27 Mar last past have ordered & awarded that the sd PETER KENZLIN shall convey the land unto the sd GEORGE GRAY . . . whereas the sd GEORGE GRAY at Co Court of Common Pleas held 5 Jun 1707 by the consideration of sd Court did recover against the sd PETER KENZLIN a debt of 471 pounds 8 shillings & 62 shillings damages . . . PETER EVANS heigh sheriff by deed poll on 30 Aug 1707 for 214 pounds sold to WILLIAM CARTER of sd city block maker towards satisfaction of sd debt & damages a messuage of PETER KENZLIN having been seized by the sheriff for the debt afsd with a tr of land near Liberty of Phila adj DERICK SIPMAN & JOHN MOON . . . 80 a. . . . and whereas the sd WILLIAM CARTER on 20 Sep 1707 for 214 pounds sold unto the sd GEORGE GRAY the afsd messuage & land (Book B vol 3 pg 307) . . . PETER KENZLIN conveys the afsd tr of land unto GEORGE GRAY .... Wit: SAMUEL CART, CASPAR HOODT. Ackn 12 Apr 1708 before EDWARD SHIPPEN justice of the peace. THOMAS STORY recorder of deeds. (E4:pg 65)

9 Mar 1707/8. Deed. DANIEL JONES of Phila taylor & DOROTHY his wife in pursuance of an agreement and 10 shillings sold unto JAMES BINGHAM of Phila yeoman a piece of ground & premises upon special trust that WILLIAM HEWLING of Everham Burlington Co w NJ esqr shall have a yearly annuity during his natural life . . . whereas JOHN DENSEY of sd city carpenter & SAMUEL CARPENTER of same city merchant on 3 Sep last past for 121 pounds 13 shillings 5 pence sold unto the sd DANIEL JONES a lot of ground in Phila 20 1/2 ft breadth 80 ft length bounded by High St, SILAS CRISPIN, JOHN JAMES & GEORGE HARMER . . . and whereas the 121 pounds 13 shillings 5 pence was the money of sd WILLIAM HEWLING and it was agreed between the parties that the sd WILLIAM HEWLING shall receive a yearly annuity of 8 pounds out of sd premises during his natural life and the sd DANIEL JONES & DOROTHY his wife (she being one of the daus of the sd WILLIAM) shall have the residue .... Wit: WILLIAM HUDSON,

DAVID MARPLE, THOMAS STORY, HENRY BUCKHOLTS. Ackn 16 Apr 1707 before DAVID LLOYD justice of the peace. THOMAS STORY recorder of deeds. (E4:pg 69)

17 Apr 1708. Deed. SAMUEL SCOTT son of THOMAS SCOTT of Bucks Co batchelour for 40 pounds sold to JOSEPH HALL of the Manor of Mooreland Phila Co yeoman a tr of land upon the sd Manor of Mooreland being the proportion of NICHOLAS younger son of NICHOLAS MOORE decd and is among the lands granted on 3 Jun 1697 executed under the name of JOHN HOLM who married MARY relict of the sd NICHOLAS MOORE & became qualified to sell the land for the bringing up the sd NICHOLAS, adj sd JOSEPH HALL, WILLIAM MARSHALL & PATRICK KELLY . . . 100 a. . . . the sd THOMAS SCOTT purch the land from THOMAS GROVIN who purch from the afsd JOHN HOLM, and the sd THOMAS SCOTT bequeathed it by his will (probated 7 Jan 1703/4) unto sd SAMUEL SCOTT . . . . Wit: THOMAS SHELLY, HARBERT CORRIE, SAML WEAVER. Ackn 17 Apr 1708 before DAVID LLOYD justice of the peace. THOMAS STORY recorder of deeds. (E4:pg 72)

10 Apr 1708. Deed. JOHN GUEST of Phila for 50 pounds sold to THOMAS COLEMAN of sd city cordwainer the back pt/o a lot of ground whereon he now lives 10 ft front 165 ft backward with a new tenement thereon erected already in the tenure of the sd THOMAS COLEMAN for 6 years by virtue of a former contract . . . whereas PHILIP JAMES on 10 Dec 1687 (Book E vol 5 pg 680) granted unto ALCE GUEST (mother of sd JOHN GUEST) a piece of land in Phila 20 ft breadth 396 ft length bounded by JOHN AP JOHNS, DE Front St, sd PHILIP JAMES & Second St, pt/o a lot sold by THOMAS WYNNE to the sd PHILIP JAMES 9 Dec instant (Book E vol 5 pg --) . . . the sd ALCE GUEST by her will devised unto her son JOHN GUEST her brick messuage & lot of ground adj WILLIAM SAY . . . . Wit: HUGH LOWDEN, JOHN STACY, FRANCIS COOKE. Ackn 20 Apr 1708 before DAVID LLOYD justice of the peace. THOMAS STORY recorder of deeds. (E4:pg 73)

13 Apr 1708. Deed. JOSEPH TAYLOR of Phila cordwainer for 125 pounds sold to JACOB KOLLUCK of Sussex Co DE cooper all the yearly rent issueing out of a messuage piece of ground . . . whereas on 16 Aug 1705 the sd JOSEPH TAYLOR conveyed unto THOMAS COATES of Phila shopkeeper a messuage & piece of ground in Phila 20 ft breadth 62 ft length bounded by Second St, High St, ANDREW BIRD & HENRY PRESTON, paying unto JOSEPH TAYLOR the rent of 1 pepper corn yearly for 5 years 3 months and also paying unto the sd JOSEPH TAYLOR, at the end of 5 years 3 months, 5 pounds on 16 Nov & 5 pounds 16 May 1711 . . . . Wit: DAVID LLOYD, EDWARD EVANS, RICHARD HEATH. Ackn 27 Apr 1708 before

DAVID LLOYD justice of the peace. THOMAS STORY recorder of deeds. On 14 Nov 1710 before RICHARD HEATH dep recorder of deeds came JACOB KOLLUCK & ackn that he had received of JOSEPH TAYLOR 130 pounds in discharge of the indenture & the sd JACOB quit claims unto sd JOSEPH TAYLOR the yearly rent. (E4:pg 75)

2 Jan 1705/6. Deed. ROBERT ROBERTS late of Phila Co but now of MD yeoman son & heir & one of the executors of the will of HUGH ROBERTS late of Merion sd co yeoman, OWEN ROBERTS & EDWARD ROBERTS both of sd co yeoman the other sons & executors of sd HUGH ROBERTS decd for 160 pounds sold to GEORGE EVANS of sd co yeoman a 400 a. tr of land adj RICHARD TOWNSEND . . . whereas there was a patent granted 14 Nov 1685 unto JAMES CLAYPOOLE for a 500 a. tr of land between Germantown and the River Schuylkill (Book A fol 135), and whereas FRANCIS COOKE of Phila adminr of the estate of sd JAMES CLAYPOOLE unadministered by HELIONAH CLAYPOOLE widow & sole executor of the will of sd JAMES, together with NATHANIEL CLAYPOOLE & GEORGE CLAYPOOLE two of the sons of sd JAMES CLAYPOOLE on the last day of Jan 1695/6 conveyed the sd tr of land unto the sd HUGH ROBERTS (Book E2 vol 5 pg 303) . . . and sd HUGH ROBERTS being seized of the land (having disposed of 100 a.) made his will 25 Jul 1702 and did will that the 400 a. should pay his debts . . . . Wit: REECE THOMAS, JOHN REECE, EVAN OWEN, LEWIS REECE. Ackn 3 May 1708 before DAVID LLOYD justice of the peace. THOMAS STORY recorder of deeds. (E4:pg 79)

9 Mar 1707/8. Deed. EDWARD LANE of Phila Co planter for 16 pounds sold to PHILIP CHRISTIAN ZIMMERMAN of same co turner a tr of land bounded by DAVID POYLE, EDWARD WHITE, JOHN RUSSELL & land formerly JOHN BOWERS . . . 50 a. pt/o 500 a. sold unto WILLIAM LANE (father of the afsd EDWARD LANE) by WILLIAM PENN proprietary & governor of PA 27 Sep 1681 & conveyed unto the sd EDWARD LANE by sd WILLIAM LANE 24 Oct 1689 . . . . Wit: EDWARD BOLTON, MATHEW ZIMMERMAN, RICHARD HEATH. Ackn 5 May 1708 before DAVID LLOYD justice of the peace. THOMAS STORY recorder of deeds. (E4:pg 81)

10 May 1707. Assignment. JOHN PARRY of Dunhintley in the Parish of Kenabin Druby Co son & heir of OWEN PARRY decd for 3 pounds assigned unto OWEN ROBERTS of Merion Twp Phila Co his proportionable pt/o 5000 a. . . . whereas JOHN AP JOHN & THOMAS WYNN on 17 Jul 1682 covenanted that they, as soon as 5000 a. are laid out & appointed, shall release unto OWEN PARRY their due proportion being 150 a. . . . . Wit: ROWLAND ELLIS Junr, ELLIS PUGH, ELLEN EDWARDS, SUSANNA THOMAS, RICHARD DAVID, JAMES CLEAST. Ackn 6 May 1708 before DAVID LLOYD justice of the peace. THOMAS STORY recorder of deeds. (E4:pg 83)

23 Apr 1708. Deed. JOHN PIGGOTT of Birmingham Chester Co yeoman & REBECCAH his wife sole executrix of the will of ABRAHAM HARDIMAN late of Phila weaver her former husband decd for 120 pounds sold unto SAMUEL CARPENTER of Phila merchant on behalf of GEORGE FITZWATER of Phila merchant & MARY his wife one of the daus of sd ABRAHAM HARDIMAN decd, HANNAH HARDIMAN of Phila spinster & DEBORAH HARDIMAN of Phila spinster (until she shall attain 21 or is married which shall first happen) also daus of ABRAHAM HARDIMAN decd each 1/3 pt/o a 1/2 pt/o a messuage and lot of land . . . whereas by virtue of a deed poll under the hands of GRIFFITH OWEN, HUGH ROBERTS & JOHN ROBERTS attys for JOHN AP JOHN late of the Parish of Khuabon in Dentighshire Wales 1 Jun 1691 (Book E2 vol 5 pg 158) the sd ABRAHAM HARDIMAN became in his life time seized in a messuage & lot of land in Phila 26 ft breadth 396 ft length bounded by CASPAR HOODT, DE Front St, JOHN GUEST, THOMAS COLEMAN & Second St . . . and being so seized the sd ABRAHAM HARDIMAN made his will dated 28 Aug 1699 and devised 1/2 of lot to his wife REBECCA & the other 1/2 of his estate to be divided among his 4 children MARY, HANNAH, DEBORAH & REBECCA HARDIMAN . . . . Wit: JANE STEEL, RICH HEATH. Ackn 6 May 1708 before DAVID LLOYD justice of the peace. THOMAS STORY recorder of deeds. (E4:pg 84)

13 Nov 1703. Deed. JOHN VAUGHAN of Phila carpenter for 90 pounds sold to THOMAS BROWN of sd city cordwainer a messuage & lot of land . . . whereas GRIFFITH JONES on 5 Jun 1699 sold to sd JOHN VAUGHAN a messuage & piece of ground called the "Old Prison" w side of Second St from DE Front St (Book E3 vol 5 pg 283-284) 32 ft breadth 132 ft length bounded by JOHN BUZBY, JOSEPH TAYLOR & Plymouth Friends Lot . . . . Ackn 8 May 1708 before DAVID LLOYD justice of the peace. THOMAS STORY recorder of deeds. (E4:pg 86)

8 May 1708. Deed. THOMAS BROWN of Phila cordwainer for 280 pounds sold to THOMAS DAVIDS of Phila Co yeoman a messuage & lot of land called "Old Prison" . . . whereas WILLIAM MARKHAM & JOHN GOODSON commissioners of WILLIAM PENN proprietor & governor of PA by patent dated 1 Dec 1688 granted unto LAURENCE COCK a lot of land in sd city 164 ft length 132 ft breadth bounded by WILLIAM CLARKE, Second St, ARTHUR COOKE & lot of Plymouth Friends (Patent Book A vol 3 pg 259-260) . . . and the sd LAURENCE COCK of Passynick Phila Co on 4 Dec 1688 sold the sd lot unto GRIFFITH JONES of Phila merchant (Book E2 vol 5 pg 45), and sd GRIFFITH JONES on 5 Jun 1699 sold it unto JOHN VAUGHAN of Phila carpenter then called the "Old Prison" 32 ft breadth 132 ft length bounded by JOHN BUSHBY, JOSEPH TAYLOR & Plymouth

Friends, and sd JOHN VAUGHAN sold the same unto sd THOMAS BROWN [see above] .... Wit: THOMAS STORY, DANIEL RADLEY. Ackn 11 May 1708 before THOMAS MASTERS justice of the peace. THOMAS STORY recorder of deeds. (E4:pg 87)

8 May 1708. Deed. THOMAS DAVIDS of Phila Co yeoman for 300 pounds sold to THOMAS BROWN of Phila cordwainer a 245 a. tr of land ... whereas WILLIAM PENN proprietary governor of Worminghurst Sussex Co esqr by indenture of lease & release dated 23&24 Sep 1681 granted unto JOEL JELSON of Barton Regis Glocester Co haberdasher of small wares 250 a. (Book B vol 2 pg 255), and whereas WILLIAM MARKHAM and JOHN GOODSON commissioners of sd proprietary by patent dated 10 Aug 1687 confirmed the sd land unto the sd JOEL JELSON in 2 parcels, the one bounded by NICHOLAS MOORE, Southampton Twp ... 245 a. and the other in Liberties of Phila adj GEORGE SHORE ... 5 a. (Patent Book A vol 1 pg 228) ... and whereas JANE JELSON of Phila Co spinster only surviving dau & heir of sd JOEL JELSON (together with WILLIAM DELWYN atty of sd JOEL) on 12 Dec 1700 conveyed the 250 a. unto REES PREES of Phila Co yeoman, and the sd REES PREES on 2 Jun 1702 conveyed it unto THOMAS MORRIS of Phila Co, and whereas JOHN PREES of Phila carpenter son & heir of sd REES PREES (after the decease of his father) on 30 Apr 1706 quit claimed unto the sd THOMAS MORRIS the 250 a. (Book B vol 2 pg 417), and whereas the sd THOMAS MORRIS on 19 Nov 1706 conveyed unto the sd THOMAS DAVIDS the 245 a. (Book E3 vol 6 pg 28) .... Wit: NATHANIEL WALTON, THOMAS STORY, RICHARD NEWCOMB. Ackn 12 May 1708 before NATHAN STANBURY justice of the peace. THOMAS STORY recorder of deeds. (E4:pg 91)

16 Oct 1707. Deed. ROBERT ROBERTS of MD yeoman son & heir of HUGH ROBERTS late of Phila Co yeoman decd for 300 pounds sold to EDWARD REES of Merion Twp Phila Co yeoman a 220 a. tr of land and a 10 a. tr of meadow ... whereas the sd HUGH ROBERTS in his lifetime became seized in a tr of land in Merion Twp bounded by the great Welsh Tr formerly laid out for 200 a. by warrant dated 13 Mar 1684 but since resurvey now 220 a. bounded by JONATHAN JONES, THOMAS JONES, OWEN ROBERTS & EDWARD JONES ... and whereas on 16 Nov -- by virtue of an indenture from ROBERT OWEN of Merion yeoman sd HUGH ROBERTS in his life time became seized in a piece of marsh in sd twp at the head of Mill Cr ... 10 a. and being so seized the sd HUGH ROBERTS made his will dated 25 Jul 1702 and did devise the 220 a. tr of land & the 10 a. meadow called "Clean John Meadow" unto his eldest son the sd ROBERT ROBERTS .... Wit: WILLIAM CLARKE, DANIEL RAWLINGS. Ackn 17 Apr 1708 before NATHAN STANBURY justice of the peace. THOMAS STORY recorder of

deeds. Memorandum 25 Apr 1708 came ROBERT ROBERTS before JOHN MACKALL & THOMAS HOWE justices of the peace of Calvert Co MD & did ackn the within deed to be the right of sd EDWARD REES. (E4:pg 93)

13 Apr 1708. Deed. THOMAS SISSOM (SISOM) of Phila brickmaker for 120 pounds sold to JACOB COLLUCK (KOLLACK) of Sussex Co DE cooper a messuage & lot of ground upon the DE River in Phila 25 ft breadth 250 ft length bounded by HENRY WOODS, Front St & WILLIAM DILLWIN, and also a lot of ground n side of afsd lot 30 ft breadth 250 ft length bounded by lot late of BARNABAS WILLCOX but now of SAMUEL POWELL . . . . Wit: DAVID EVANS, EVAN THOMAS, WILLIAM HALL, JOHN CROSWHIT. Ackn 17 May 1708 before DAVID LLOYD justice of the peace. THOMAS STORY recorder of deeds. (E4:pg 96)

13 Apr 1708. Deed of Mortgage. JACOB KOLLUCK of Sussex Co DE cooper sold to THOMAS SISOM of Phila brick maker the [above] messuage & lots of ground . . . if the sd THOMAS SISOM shall pay unto sd JACOB KOLLUCK 116 pounds, i.e. 8 pounds on 13 Apr next ensueing and 108 pounds residue on 13 Apr 1710 . . . then the [above] indenture to be void . . . . Wit: DAVID LLOYD, THOMAS TRESSE, THOMAS TRESSE Junr. Ackn 18 May 1708 before DAVID LLOYD justice of the peace. THOMAS STORY recorder of deeds. 17 Jun 1721 Memorandum whereas my husband JACOB KOLLUCK decd in his lifetime received full satisfaction for the afsd mortgage, MARY KOLLUCK hereby releases the sd mortgaged premises unto the sd THOMAS SISOM. Wit: JACOB KOLLUCK, CHAS OSBORNE. (E4:pg 98)

24 Apr 1708. Deed. DAVID POWELL of Phila yeoman for 146 pounds sold to EVERARD BOLTON of Abington Twp Phila Co glover a tr of land in Cheltenham Twp Phila Co bounded by RICE PETERS, RICHARD HALL & EVERARD BOLTON . . . 229 a. 40 perches . . . which land was granted unto the sd DAVID POWELL by JOHN HAVARD of Phila Co yeoman on 12 Apr 1707 . . . . Wit: THOMAS STORY, RICHARD NEWCOMB. Ackn 20 May 1708 before DAVID LLOYD justice of the peace. (E4:pg 100)

15 Nov 1707. Deed. THOMAS SISOM of Phila yeoman for 25 pounds sold to DANIEL HOWELL of White Marsh Phila Co yeoman a lot of land . . . whereas the sd THOMAS did purch of one THOMAS SANGSTONE a lot of land on the bank of DE in Phila 25 ft breadth 252 ft length on 4 Dec 1690 . . . . Wit: JOHN WATSON, SAMUEL WEAVER. Ackn 20 May 1708 before DAVID LLOYD justice of the peace. THOMAS STORY recorder of deeds. (E4:pg 101)

30 Oct 1707. Deed of Mortgage. GEORGE EVAN of Phila Co yeoman for 150 pounds sold to REES HINTON of Chester, Chester Co yeoman a tr of land adj Wessahickon Cr, OWEN ROBERTS' sons land, JOHN LINDERMAN & RICHARD TOWNSEND . . . 332 a. . . . provided that if GEORGE EVAN shall pay unto the sd REES HINTON 198 pounds, that is 12 pounds on 30 Oct 1708, 12 pounds on 30 Oct 1709, 12 pounds on 30 Oct 1710 and 162 pounds residue on 30 Oct 1711, then this indenture to be void . . . . Wit: JOHN HOOD, DAVID LLOYD, RICHARD HEATH. Ackn 20 May 1708 before DAVID LLOYD justice of the peace. THOMAS STORY recorder of deeds. (E4:pg 103)

23 Mar 1707/8. Deed. ALEXANDER EDWARDS of Phila Co yeoman for 10 pounds 18 shillings sold to HUMPHREY BATE of same co yeoman a parcel of land adj JOHN EVAN ap EDWARDS, sd HUMPHREY BATE, ALEXANDER EDWARDS the younger & sd ALEXANDER EDWARDS the elder . . . 28 a. 150 perches pt/o 996 a. which was granted by patent from EDWARD SHIPPEN, GRIFFITH OWEN & THOMAS STORY commissioners of property dated 12 Oct 1702 unto the sd ALEXANDER EDWARDS (Patent Book A vol 2 pg 379) . . . . Wit: DAVID LLOYD, JOSEPH BATE, RICHARD HEATH. Ackn 21 May 1708 before DAVID LLOYD justice of the peace. THOMAS STORY recorder of deeds. (E4:pg 105)

6 May 1704. Deed. ROBERT FLETCHER late of Pine Spring Plantation Abington Twp Phila Co but now of Aston Twp Chester Co yeoman for 360 pounds sold to his son ROBERT FLETCHER of Pine Spring Plantation yeoman a tr of land in Abington Twp called Pine Spring Plantation bounded by DANIEL HEAPLEY decd, land late of NICHOLAS MOORE & SAMUEL ALLEN . . . 500 a. the same was granted unto the sd ROBERT the father by SILAS CRISPIN of Dublin Twp Phila Co gent & ESTHER his wife on 16 Nov 1695, and a piece of land bounded by THOMAS CANBY, ABRAHAM RICHARDS & sd SILAS CRISPIN . . . 51 1/2 a. . . . . Wit: JOSEPH KORKBRIDE, ELLIS DAVID, EDWARD EVANS. Ackn 21 May 1708 before DAVID LLOYD justice of the peace. THOMAS STORY recorder of deeds. (E4:pg 106)

19 Jan 1707/8. Deed. HUGH JONES of Plymouth Twp Phila Co yeoman & ROWLAND RICHARD of Merion Twp sd co yeoman (son in law of the sd HUGH JONES) for 120 pounds sold to CADWALADER MORGAN of Merion yeoman a tr of land . . . whereas GRIFFITH OWEN, THOMAS STORY & JAMES LOGAN commissioners of property granted by patent dated 8 Nov 1703 (Patent Book A vol 2 pg 611) unto HUGH JONES a tr of land in Merion adj River Schuylkill, JOHN ROBERTS, GRIFFITH JONES &

sd CADWALADER MORGAN . . . 92 a. and the sd HUGH JONES did (for the love & affection he hath toward his son in law ROWLAND RICHARD) give 1/2 to him and afterwards for 40 pounds sold the other 1/2 to him . . . but the sd HUGH JONES hath not conveyed it to the sd ROWLAND RICHARD . . . . Wit: JOHN KADWALADER, RICHARD HEATH, HUGH EVANS. Ackn 22 May 1708 before DAVID LLOYD justice of the peace. THOMAS STORY recorder of deeds. (E4:pg 108)

18 May 1708. Deed. THOMAS FAIRMAN of Shaxamaxon Phila Co gent for 90 pounds sold to MAURICE (MANZIRE) EDWARDS of Phila Co a tr of land . . . whereas a 162 a. parcel of land adj Guynid Twp, RICHARD ADAMS, JONAS POTTS, EDWARD BOLTON & THOMAS LEWIS pt/o 1100 a. was granted by patent by EDWARD SHIPPEN, THOMAS STORY & JAMES LOGAN commissioners of property 23 Oct 1702 unto THOMAS FAIRMAN (Patent Book A vol 2 pg 398) . . . . Wit: HENRY PENNEBECKERS, GEORGE BEARD. Ackn 23 May 1708 before NATHAN STANBURY justice of the peace. THOMAS STORY recorder of deeds. (E4:pg 110)

5 Apr 1708. Deed of Release. THOMAS STORY of Phila & ANN his wife for 10 shillings release unto ANTHONY MORRIS of sd city merchant a tr of land . . . whereas on 29 Jul 1706 EDWARD SHIPPEN the elder of sd city merchant (father of the sd ANN) gave unto the sd THOMAS STORY and ANN his wife a parcel of ground bounded by ANDREW CRISCOM, DAVID LLOYD & Second St, 40 ft breadth 200 ft length . . . . Wit: GEORGE CLAYPOOLE, CLEMT PLUMSTEAD. Ackn 24 May 1708 before THOMAS MASTERS justice of the peace. THOMAS STORY recorder of deeds. (E4:pg 111)

6 Apr 1708. Deed. ANTHONY MORRIS of Phila merchant for 10 shillings regranted unto THOMAS STORY of sd city gent and ANN his wife the [above] piece of ground . . . . Wit: GEORGE CLAYPOOLE, CLEMT PLUMSTEAD. Ackn 24 May 1708 before THOMAS MASTERS justice of the peace. THOMAS STORY recorder of deeds. (E4:pg 114)

21 May 1708. Deed. WILLIAM WELLS of Moyamensing Phila Co yeoman for 30 pounds sold to ABELL NOBLE of Phila cooper a 50 a. tr of land . . . by virtue of an indenture dated 30 Apr last past between RICHARD HALLIWELL of New Castle town & co gent & SAMUEL LOWMAN of same place esqr & the sd WILLIAM WELLS, the sd WILLIAM WELLS became seized in a parcel of swamp adjacent to Wickacoo & Moyamensing lands bounded by Hollanders Cr, WILLIAM CARTER & Sweeds Marsh . . . 50 a. . . . . Wit: WALTER LONGER, DAVID LLOYD, RICHARD HEATH. Ackn 25 May 1708 before DAVID LLOYD justice of the peace. THOMAS STORY recorder of deeds. (E4:pg 116)

29 Sep 1693. Deed of Lease. SAMUEL RICHARDSON of Phila Co merchant farm lett unto JOHN JONES of sd city cordwainer a lott 17 ft breadth 102 ft length bounded by GRIFFITH JONES, JOHN ROBERTS, High St & THOMAS PRITCHARD in Phila . . . for 60 years paying yearly 30 shillings 8 pence . . . . Wit: YOUNG MORGAN, THOMAS ROBERTS, WILLIAM HUDSON. Ackn 23 May 1708 before THOMAS MASTERS justice of the peace. THOMAS STORY recorder of deeds. (E4:pg 118)

29 May 1708. Deed of Mortgage. JOHN GUEST of Phila sadler for 100 pounds sold to TOBY LEECH (LEICH) of Cheltenham Twp Phila Co gent a brick house with cellars shop on Front St in Phila adj WILLIAM SAY, THOMAS COLEMAN & Second St, 10 ft breadth 240 ft length . . . provided if the sd JOHN GUEST shall pay unto TOBY LEECH 108 pounds upon 29 May 1709 then this present indenture shall be utterly void . . . . Wit: EDWARD FARMAR, JOHN HURFORD. Ackn 29 May 1708 before EDWARD FARMAR justice of the peace. THOMAS STORY recorder of deeds. (E4:pg 119)

26 Dec 1707. Deed. HENRY BADCOKE of Phila brewer and MARY his wife for 160 pounds sold to JOHN CHEETAM of sd city tailor the residue of a lot of land bounded by the other pt/o the lot & ISAAC BLAND . . . whereas NATHANIEL WEBB late of Phila cooper on 7 Aug 1704 conveyed unto sd HENRY BADCOKE and MARY his wife a messuage & lot of land n side of Chesnut St in Phila between Third & Fourth Sts bounded by lot late of JOHN AUSTIN (but now of MARY BRADWAY) & High St, and whereas the sd HENRY BADCOKE & MARY his wife have sold unto sd JOHN CHEETAM a piece of the sd lot 20 ft breadth 100 ft length . . . . Wit: ROWLAND RICE, JOAM[?] FORREST, MARY BADCOKE Junr, RICHARD HEATH. Ackn 13 May 1708 before DAVID LLOYD justice of the peace. THOMAS STORY recorder of deeds. (E4:pg 122)

21 May 1708. Deed. REINIER HERMANS late of Germantown Twp Phila Co but now of MD yeoman for 140 pounds sold to ISAAC DEAVES of Germantown yeoman a messuage & 117 a. tr of land in the Village of Creshiun[?] within Germantown Twp bounded by THOMAS RUTTER, PETER KUNDERS & HENDRICK SELL . . . 42 a. of which adj the Germantown line was sold unto the sd REINIER HERMANS by JACOB TELNOR and is pt/o the sd TELNOR's purch of 5000 a., and 50 a. more of the tr next adj the 42 a. is pt/o 2000 a. which the sd JACOB TELNOR sold to HERMAN OPDEN GRAEF, DIRK OPDEN GRAEF & ABRAHAM OPDEN GRAEF, and the sd ABRAHAM OPDEN GRAEF sold 125 a. of the same land (whereof the sd 50 a. is part) unto JACOB SHUMAKER who sold the 50 a. unto the sd REINIER HERMANS, and 25 a. residue of the 117 a. is pt/o the

5000 a. which DIRK SIPMAN of Ceevelt of Menes Co in Germany merchant purch of WILLIAM PENN and the sd DIRK SIPMAN sold 200 a. (whereof the 25 a. is part) unto PETER SHUMAKER (decd), who conveyed the sd 25 a. unto his son in law the sd REINIER HERMANS . . . . Wit: EDWARD EVANS, DAVID LLOYD, RICHARD HEATH. Ackn 31 May 1708 before DAVID LLOYD justice of the peace. THOMAS STORY recorder of deeds. (E4:pg 124)

5 Aug 1703. Deed. PHILIP PRICE of Upper Merrion in the Welsh Tr yeoman for 46 pounds paid and 74 pounds to be paid sold to RICHARD MORRIS of Phila Co husbandman a parcel of land in Whitepain Twp Phila Co bounded by JOHN PALMER, the Plymouth Line & WILLIAM THOMAS . . . 417 a. pt/o 832 a. 156 perches sold by one WILLIAM PALMER to the sd PHILIP PRICE 7 Jul last past . . . . Ackn 9 Sep 1703. ROBERT ASSHETON prothonitary. 17 Feb 1706 REES THOMAS received 120 pounds of RICHARD MORRIS. Wit: PHILIP PRICE, THOMAS HOWELL, HUMPHREY ELLIS. Recorded 2 Jun 1708. (E4:pg 126)

20 May 1708. Deed of Lease. WILLIAM HALL of Phila chuirgeon for 39 pounds leased unto JOHN FROGG of sd city merchant a new brick tenement upon pt/o a water lot betwixt JOSEPH PIDGEON's grannery and a new building of the sd WILLIAM HALL, during the term of the first lease . . . whereas EDWARD SMOUT of same city on 24 Aug 1708 sold to sd WILLIAM HALL a water lot in three parcels under the bank of DE in Phila next to sd EDWARD SMOOT's other ground on King St and was originally granted by ROBERT TURNER unto one FRANCIS JARVIS for 44 years from 4 Aug 1694 & by the sd FRANCIS JARVIS sold unto one SUSANNA ELTON by whose executors the same was conveyed unto the sd EDWARD SMOUT . . . . Wit: JOHN CROSWHITE, JEROME PHILLIPS, DAVID EVANS, EVAN THOMAS. Ackn 8 Jun 1708 before WILLIAM CARTER justice of the peace. THOMAS STORY recorder of deeds. (E4:pg 127)

25 Feb 1707/8. Deed of Mortgage. BENJAMIN WRIGHT of Phila for 100 pounds sold to HENRY STEVENS of same city mariner and MARTHA his wife a messuage & lot n side of Chesnut St in Phila 24 ft breadth 50 ft length bounded by ground late of PATRICK ROBINSON & lot late of PHILIP RICHARDS, and also his granery or warehouse with a parcel of ground w side of afsd tr of land adj THOMAS SISOM & WILLIAM CARTER . . . provided that if the sd BENJAMIN WRIGHT pay unto the sd HENRY STEVENS 100 pounds with interest on 25 Feb next ensueing then this present indenture shall cease . . . . Wit: DAVID POWELL, RICHARD HEATH. Ackn 9 Jun 1708 before WILLIAM CARTER justice of the peace. THOMAS STORY recorder of deeds. 4 May 1716 before RICH HEATH dep recorder of deeds MARTHA

STEVENS by virtue of a letter of atty from her husband HENRY STEVENS states they received full satisfaction & discharges the mortgage. (E4:pg 128)

31 May 1708. Deed. CONVER (CAURE) BOON (BOONE) of Boughtown Salem Co w NJ widow & executrix of the will of her late husband PETER BOON decd and SWAN BOON of Calconhook Darby Twp Chester Co yeoman feoffees in trust for ANDREAS BOONE, MORTON BOONE & PETER BOONE orphans & heirs of sd PETER BOON decd for 150 pounds conveyed unto JOHN ELLOTT of Carcosshook Phila Co yeoman 150 a. pt/o 1040 a. . . . whereas ANDREW SWANSON BOON of Mincas Island Phila Co by his will dated 18 Apr 1694 bequeathed unto his son PETER BOONE husband of sd CONVER BOONE a 150 a. tr of land and plantation in Carcosshook, and whereas the sd PETER BOONE sold it for 150 pounds unto the sd JOHN ELLOTT on 12 May 1705, the sd PETER BOONE bound himself to the pennel sum of 300 pounds to the sd JOHN ELLOTT to make a legal deed of sale to the sd JOHN ELLOTT, the payment of 150 pounds to be paid to MATTHIAS STARK late of Boughtown w NJ being the purch money due from the sd PETER BOONE to the sd MATTHIAS STARK for the purch of 1/3 pt/o 1040 a. in Boughtown of which sd land the sd PETER BOONE died in peaceable possession yet had received no deed of conveyance . . . . Wit: JOHN HOOD, JONATHAN HOOD. Ackn 12 Jun 1708 before DAVID LLOYD justice of the peace. THOMAS STORY recorder of deeds. (E4:pg 131)

9 Jun 1708. Deed. MATTHIAS VAN BEBBER late of Phila merchant (but now of Cecil Co MD) & JOHN ROSTERS of Craven in Germantwp Phila Co yeoman for 32 pounds sold to JOHN UMSTAT of Bebber Twp Phila Co yeoman 204 a. . . . whereas the sd MATTHIAS VAN BEBBER on 25 Feb 1702 sold unto the sd JOHN ROSTERS a parcel of land bounded by EDWARD LANE, other land of sd MATTHIAS VAN BEBBER & HENRY PENNEBECKER . . . 204 a. pt/o 6166 a. granted unto the sd MATTHIAS VAN BEBBER by WILLIAM PENN proprietary & governor of PA by patent dated 22 Feb then current (Patent Book A vol 2 pg 463), whereas the sd JOHN ROSTERS by deed poll conveyed the 204 a. back to sd MATTHIAS VAN BEBBER provided the sd JOHN ROSTERS shall pay to the sd MATTHIAS VAN BEBBER 33 pounds 2 shillings 6 pence on 5 Jan 1707 with interest, then the deed poll would be utterly void . . . . Wit: RICHARD HEATH, RICHARD NEWCOMBE, PETER SHOEMAKER. Ackn 12 Jun 1708 before DAVID LLOYD justice of the peace. THOMAS STORY recorder of deeds. (E4:pg 133)

10 Jun 1708. Deed. MATTHIAS VAN BEBBER of Cecil Co MD merchant for 25 pounds sold to CHRISTOPHER ZIMMERMAN of Phila Co yeoman a tr of land in Bebber Twp adj DANIEL TILLEMAN & JOHN NEWBERRY ... 100 a. pt/o 6166 a. granted by patent 22 Feb 1702 unto the sd MATTHIAS VAN BEBBER (Book A vol 2 pg 463) . . . . Wit: HERMANS CUSTERS, RICHARD HEATH. Ackn 12 Jun 1708 before DAVID LLOYD justice of the peace. THOMAS STORY recorder of deeds. (E4:pg 136)

10 Jun 1707. Deed. MATTHIAS VAN BEBBER of Cecil Co MD merchant sold to JOHANNES SCHOLL of Phila Co yeoman a tr of land in Beebers Twp adj HERMANS KUSTER & CHRISTOPHER ZIMMERMAN . . . 200 a. pt/o 6166 a. granted by patent 22 Feb 1702 unto the sd MATTHIAS VAN BEBBER (Book A vol 2 pg 463) . . . . Wit: HERMANS KUSTERS, RICHARD HEATH. Ackn 13 Jun 1708 before DAVID LLOYD justice of the peace. THOMAS STORY recorder of deeds. (E4:pg 137)

10 Dec 1706. Deed. PETER SHUMAKER (SHOEMAKER) the younger of Germantown Phila Co turner for 15 pounds sold to MATTHIAS VAN BEBBER of Cecil Co MD merchant two parcels of land 300 a. . . . whereas PETER SHUMAKER the elder on 27 Aug 1694 conveyed unto his sd son PETER SHUMAKER the younger 150 a. pt/o 5000 a. which WILLIAM PENN proprietary & governor of PA conveyed to DERICK SIPMAN who sold it unto the sd PETER SHUMAKER the father, and whereas ISAAC SHOEMAKER of Germantown & SARAH his wife sole dau & heir of GERRAT HENDRICKS decd on 6 Dec 1699 conveyed unto the sd PETER SHUMAKER the younger a 150 a. also taken up in right of the sd DERRICK SIPMAN's purch who sold the same to the sd GERRAT HENDRICKS in his life time . . . . Wit: HENDRICK SELIN, HENDRICK PENNEBECKER, FRANCIS DANIEL PASTORIUS. Ackn 13 Jun 1708 before DAVID LLOYD justice of the peace. THOMAS STORY recorder of deeds. (E4:pg 139)

10 Dec 1706. Quit Claim. MATTHIAS VAN BEBBER of Cecil Co MD merchant for valuable considerations quit claim unto PETER SHOEMAKER Junr of Germantown Phila Co turner the rent . . . 50 a. pt/o 200 a. formerly granted to PETER SHOEMAKER Senr by DIRK SIPMAN now in the tenure of the sd PETER SHOEMAKER Junr & RENIER HERMANS VAN BURKLOW 25 a. at Germantown between ABRAHAM AP DEN GRAES & JACOB TELNOR and 25 a. at Kresheim in Germantownship between RENIER HERMANS & HENRY SELLEN, the sd PETER SHOEMAKER Junr & RENIER HERMANS VAN BURKLOW shall pay no rent at all unto MATTHIAS VAN BEBBER . . . whereas the sd PETER SHOEMAKER being seized of 200 a. by a deed under the hand of his father PETER SHOEMAKER Senr dated 27 Aug 1694 conveyed to sd PETER SHOEMAKER Senr by

DIRK SIPMAN of Crefeld Meurs Co Germany merchant on 16 Aug 1685, and whereas the sd PETER SHOEMAKER Junr being further seized of 150 a. by another deed of sale from ISAAC SHOEMAKER & SARAH his wife sole dau & heir of GERRARD HENDRICKS decd on 6 Dec 1699 which 150 a. pt/o 200 a. granted unto sd GERRARD HENDRICKS by DIRK SIPMAN 16 Aug 1685, and did sell 300 a. unto the sd MATTHIAS VAN BEBBER . . . . Wit: HENDRICK SULLEN, HENDRICK PANNEBECKERS, FRANCIS DANIEL PASTORIUS. Ackn 13 Jun 1708 before DAVID LLOYD justice of the peace. THOMAS STORY recorder of deeds. (E4:pg 140)

12 Jun 1708. Deed. MATTHIAS VAN BEBBER of Cecil Co MD merchant for 18 pounds sold to THOMAS WISEMAN of Phila Co yeoman a tr of land in Bebber Twp adj CLAUS JOHNSON, WILLIAM & CORNELIUS DEWEESE . . . 90 a. pt/o 6166 a. which by patent dated 22 Feb 1702 was granted unto the sd MATTHIAS VAN BEBBER (Patent Book A vol 2 pg 463) . . . . Wit: HERMANS KUSTERS, RICHARD HEATH. Ackn 13 Jun 1708 before DAVID LLOYD justice of the peace. THOMAS STORY recorder of deeds. (E4:pg 142)

12 Jun 1708. Deed. MATTHIAS VAN BEBBER of Cecil Co MD merchant for 37 pounds sold to DANIEL DESMONT of Phila Co yeoman a tr of land in Bebbers Twp adj JOHN NEWBERRY & GERRARD ENDEHOOF . . . 150 a. pt/o 6166 a. which by patent dated 22 Feb 1702 was granted unto the sd MATTHIAS VAN BEBBER (Patent Book A vol 2 pg 463) . . . . Wit: HERMANS KUSTERS, RICHARD HEATH. Ackn 14 Jun 1708 before DAVID LLOYD justice of the peace. THOMAS STORY recorder of deeds. (E4:pg 144)

12 Jun 1708. Deed. MATTHIAS VAN BEBBER of Cecil Co MD merchant for 58 pounds sold to WILLIAM DEEWEES & CORNELIUS DEEWEES of Germantown Twp Phila Co yeoman a tr of land adj JOHN NEWBERRY & THOMAS WISEMAN . . . 290 a. pt/o 6166 a. which by patent dated 22 Feb 1702 was granted unto the sd MATTHIAS VAN BEBBER (Patent Book A vol 2 pg 463) . . . . Wit: HERMANS KUSTERS, RICHARD HEATH. Ackn 14 Jun 1708 before DAVID LLOYD justice of the peace. THOMAS STORY recorder of deeds. (E4:pg 145)

12 Jun 1708. Deed. MATTHIAS VAN BEBBER of Cecil Co MD merchant for 60 pounds 15 shillings sold to HENRY PANNENBECKER of Bebbers Twp Phila Co a parcel of land in Bebbers Twp adj THOMAS KUSTERS, sd MATTHIAS VAN BEBBER & JOHN KREY . . . 204 a. pt/o 6166 a. which by patent dated 22 Feb 1702 was granted unto the sd MATTHIAS VAN BEBBER (Patent Book A vol 2 pg 463) . . . .

Wit: PETER SHOOMAKER, FRANCIS DANIEL PASTORIUS. Ackn 15 Jun 1708 before DAVID LLOYD justice of the peace. THOMAS STORY recorder of deeds. (E4:pg 147)

28 Jun 1708. Appointment. THOMAS STORY keeper of the great seal, master of the rolls, recorder of the inrollment office of PA . . . reposing special trust and confidence in thy ability, I have appointed thee RICHARD HEATH of Phila gent my lawful dep . . . . (E4:pg 149)

16 Sep 1694. Deed. HESTER ELFRETH widow & sole adminr of the estate of JOHN BOWYER late of Phila decd and her son JOHN BOWYER son & heir apparent of the sd JOHN BOWYER of Phila ship carpenter for 31 pounds sold to WILLIAM WILKINS of Phila Co husbandman 150 a. the remainder of 200 a. confirmed in a patent dated 30 Jul 1687 unto JOHN BOWYER in right of WALTER KING (Patent Book A pg 235) . . . and hath made FRANCIS COOKE their atty to deliver this deed in open court . . . . Wit: JAMES SHATTICK, JAMES WHITE, FRANCIS COOKE. Ackn 5 Mar 1695/6. JOHN CLAYPOOLE clerk. Recorded 29 Jun 1708. (E4:pg 150)

13 Aug 1701. Deed. JAMES DELAPLAINE and JOHANNES CUSTER of Germantown yeoman and THOMAS RUTTER of Phila Co blacksmith for 16 pounds sold to WILLIAM WILKINS of the sd co yeoman a parcel of land adj JOHN BOWYER & ROBERT LONGSHORE . . . 50 a. with other 50 a. granted by patent 7 Nov 1690 unto THOMAS FAIRMAN who by assignment did transfer the same to BENJAMIN CHAMBERS sheriff in execution for MARY JESTES whereupon the sd JAMES DELAPLAINE bought the same 10 Jul 1691 (Book E2 vol 5 pg 167) and the sd 50 a. hereby granted was made over to the sd CUSTERS by assignment 21 May 1694 and the sd JOHANNES CUSTERS sold same to the sd THOMAS RUTTER who sold the same to the sd WILLIAM WILKINS but no conveyance was made . . . the sd JAMES DELAPLAINE, JOHANNES CUSTER and THOMAS RUTTER appoint FRANCIS COOKE their atty to deliver these presents in open court . . . . Wit: THOMAS KUNDERS, ANTONA LEOCST. Ackn 19 Sep 1702 before ROBERT ASHTON prothonitary. Recorded 29 Jun 1708. (E4:pg 151)

15 Apr 1708. Deed. HANNAH HODGES of Phila Co widow & relict of her late husband THOMAS HODGES decd and NICHOLAS WALLN of same co executors of the will of sd THOMAS HODGES for 250 pounds sold to EDWARD GRAY of Phila Co husbandman a messuage and tr of land . . . whereas JAMES JAMES of Bristol Twp Phila Co on 29 Sep 1703 did grant unto the sd THOMAS HODGES a messuage & tr of land in Bristol Twp adj Tacony Cr, WILLIAM JAMES & land late of JOHN SONGHURST . . . 200 a. pt/o 500 a. confirmed by patent unto one JOHN BARNES and by some

good conveyance either from sd JOHN BARNES or some other under him the sd 500 a. was confirmed to one HOWELL JAMES and by him 200 a. was confirmed unto the sd JAMES JAMES to hold unto the sd THOMAS HODGES, and whereas the sd THOMAS HODGES being so seized made his will dated 21 Mar 1707/8 and did devise sundry goods to his wife HANNAH and all the rest of his estate should be sold, the 1/3 part thereof he gave to his sd wife and the remainder to be equally divided amongst his children, copy of the will to the probate under the hand of PETER EVANS 3 Apr 1708 . . . . Wit: JOHN WARDER, FRANCIS COOKE. Ackn 29 Jun 1708 before NATHAN STANBURY justice of the peace. THOMAS STORY recorder of deeds. (E4:pg 152)

16 Apr 1708. Deed of Mortgage. EDWARD GRAY of Phila Co husbandman sold to HANNAH HODGES and NICHOLAS WALN (WALLN) of same co the [above] messuage & 200 a. tr of land . . . provided that if the sd EDWARD GRAY shall pay unto the sd HANNAH HODGES and NICHOLAS WALN 162 pounds on 15 Apr 1710 then these presents to be void . . . . Wit: JOHN WARDER, FRANCIS COOKE. Ackn 13 Jun 1708 before NATHAN STANBURY justice of the peace. THOMAS STORY recorder of deed. (E4:pg 154)

19 Jun 1708. Deed. SAMUEL SPENCER of Phila mariner and HESTER his wife for 65 pounds sold to JOSEPH ASHTON two lots 102 ft fronting and 200 ft deep . . . whereas there is a lot in Phila 51 ft breadth 200 ft length bounded by Sasafras St, Second St, Front St & JOHN BURCHALL . . . which lot was confirmed by patent unto JOHN SONGHURST son and heir of JOHN SONGHURST who took up the same & seated it together with the lot next adj in right of JOHN BURCHALL which was also conveyed unto the sd JOHN SONGHURST by deed 10 Jul 1693 and sold to one WILLIAM FREEMAN, all the front pt/o both lots 102 ft breadth 150 ft deep being 1/2 of the whole and by sd WILLIAM FREEMAN sold unto JOHN JENNETT 14 Jan 1695/6 and the other 1/2 bounded by JOHN MACCONST[?] & JOHN JENNETT's other lot sold by the sd JOHN SONGHURST unto the sd JOHN JENNETT 10 Jul 1690 & by a release afterwards signed by the sd JOHN SONGHURST unto the sd SAMUEL SPENCER 200 ft from the front of both lots 21 Dec 1705, and whereas JOHN JENNETT by his will dated 10 Sep 1699 & proved by a probate under the hand of WILLIAM MARKHAM lieutenant governor dated 1 Nov next after the sd will where he did bequeath unto his dau HESTER (now the w/o SAMUEL SPENCER) all that house I purch of WILLIAM FREEMAN together with 200 ft from the end of the two lots I purch from sd FREEMAN and of JOHN SONGHURST, and the sd SAMUEL & HESTER SPENCER having sold the s 1/2 that was JOHN BURCHALL's unto one GEORGE FITZWATER for 39 pounds 26 Dec 1705, and by the sd GEORGE

the same was sold to JOSEPH ASHTON Junr of Phila carpenter, and he not liking the sd deed hath requested the sd SAMUEL & HESTER SPENCER to include and ratify the same in these presents having now purch the remaining 1/2 . . . . Wit: ABRAHAM BICKLEY, FRANCIS COOKE. Ackn 7 Jul 1708 before NATHAN STANBURY justice of the peace. THOMAS STORY recorder of deeds. (E4:pg 156)

27 Apr 1708. Deed. HENRY FLOWER of Phila barber for 100 pounds sold to WILLIAM ROBINSON of same city sadler a messuage & lot of land . . . whereas on 24 Dec 1702 LIONELL BRITTON of Phila blacksmith sold to FRANCIS RICHARDSON of Phila a messuage & lot of land in Phila 20 ft breadth 198 ft length bounded by lot late of PHILIP JAMES, Front St, lot formerly of PHILIP RICHARDS but now of sd HENRY FLOWER & lot late of PHILIP ALFORD (Book B vol 2 pg 310), and on 19 Nov 1703 sd FRANCIS RICHARDSON sold to sd HENRY FLOWER the afsd lot . . . . Wit: THOMAS HARDING, RICHARD HEATH, DAVID LLOYD. Ackn 9 Jul 1708 before DAVID LLOYD justice of the peace. THOMAS STORY recorder of deeds. (E4:pg 158)

7 Oct 1704. Deed. WILLIAM PENN Junr son & heir of WILLIAM PENN esqr proprietary & governor of PA for 850 pounds sold to WILLIAM TRENT & ISAAC NORRIS both of Phila merchants 7480 a. on River Schuylkill bounded by Plymouth Twp, Whiptains Twp & Manor of Bebberts . . . which was granted by patent dated 2 Oct 1704 unto the sd WILLIAM PENN the son . . . the sd WILLIAM PENN the son hath made JOHN MOORE his atty to ackn these presents in court . . . . Wit: URN MONINGTON MOORE, JOHN BOURCHUR. Ackn 26 Jul 1708 before JOSEPH PIDGEON justice of the peace. RICHARD HEATH dep recorder of deeds. WILLIAM PENN Junr received 100 pounds (together with several obligations signed by sd WILLIAM TRENT & ISAAC NORRIS the one for 400 pounds the other for 350 pounds) amounts to 850 pounds the consideration money afsd. Ackn 7 Dec 1704 before ROB ASHETON prothonitary. (E4:pg 161)

1 May 1708. Quit Claim. JONATHAN HAYES (HAYS) of Marple Chester Co yeoman for 1210 a. granted to him by the proprietary & 10 shillings quit claim unto WILLIAM TRENT and ISAAC NORRIS both of Phila merchants a 1100 a. tr of land . . . whereas WILLIAM PENN of Worminghurst Sussex Co England esqr proprietary & governor of PA on 24&25 Jan 1681 granted by patent unto BENJAMIN CHAMBERS of Bearst Parish Kent Co turner 1000 a. (Book A vol 1 pg 120-124), and by virtue of a warrant dated 7 Apr 1680 there was surveyed & laid out unto the sd BENJAMIN CHAMBERS as pt/o the sd purch a tr of land bounded ne side of Schoolkill near opposite of Barbadoes Island & land late of JOHN CHAMBERS . . . 610 a. and whereas

sd BENJAMIN CHAMBERS (of Phila yeoman) on 29 Jun 1699 did grant unto the sd JONATHAN HAYES the 610 a. (Book E3 vol 5 pg 303), and whereas the proprietary by like indentures on same date conveyed unto JOHN CHAMBERS of Thurnham Kent Co turner brother of BENJAMIN 500 a. (Book B vol 2 pg 222-223), and whereas the sd JOHN CHAMBERS died seized of the 500 a. and the same descended to ELIZABETH CHAMBERS his sole dau & heir, and ELIZABETH CHAMBERS of Phila spinster on 30 Oct 1686 conveyed unto the sd BENJAMIN CHAMBERS (resident of the Free Society of Traders of PA) 490 a. pt/o the 500 a. (Book E vol 5 pg 471), and whereas the sd BENJAMIN & ELIZABETH (by the name ELIZABETH CLEMSON of Phila widow) on 29 Jun 1699 conveyed the 490 a. unto the sd JONATHAN HAYES, and whereas the sd JONATHAN HAYES made application to the proprietary for a confirmation of the several trs of land by patent in one tr containing 1100 a. . . . the two trs or greatest pt/o the same were within the lines of the mannor of WILLIAM STADT which sd mannor had been surveyed & laid out unto WILLIAM PENN Junr esqr son & heir apparent of the proprietary . . . by order the sd proprietary granted to sd JONATHAN HAYES that there should be laid to him elsewhere a like quantity of valuable land to his satisfaction, by warrant dated 13 Apr 1703 there was surveyed unto the sd JONATHAN 1 Mar 1704 a tr of land in Hatfield Twp adj BENJAMIN FURLOW & JOHN MORRIS . . . 1210 a. patent dated 3 Dec 1705 (Patent Book A vol 3 pg 219), and whereas the proprietary by patent dated 2 Oct 1704 confirmed unto the sd WILLIAM PENN the son the afsd tr of land, and whereas the sd WILLIAM PENN Junr sold the 7480 a. [see above deed] . . . . Wit: JOSH TILTERY, SAMUEL CART, JAMES LOGAN. Ackn 27 Jul 1708 before NATHAN STANBURY justice of the peace. THOMAS STORY recorder of deeds. (E4:pg 163)

24 Dec 1702. Deed. CHRISTOPHER SIBTHORP of Phila for 25 pounds sold to ROBERT PARSONS of Phila weaver a lot of land . . . whereas EDWARD SHIPPEN, GRIFFITH OWEN, THOMAS STORY & JAMES LOGAN commissioners of property, by warrant dated 6 Oct last past granted to the sd CHRISTOPHER SIBTHORP in right of 500 a. the original purch of THOMAS SCOTT a lot of land 51 ft breadth 300 ft length bounded by Second St & HENRY WADY . . . . Wit: ABRA BICKLEY, THOS BROWN. Ackn 2 Aug 1708 before THOMAS MASTERS justice of the peace. RICHARD HEATH dep recorder of deeds. (E4:pg 168)

31 Aug 1708. Deed. SAMUEL MEALS of Phila cooper for 3 pounds sold to ROBERT BURROW of same city shopkeeper a piece of ground in Phila pt/o the sd SAMUEL's Chesnut St lot 106 ft length 14 ft breadth bounded by High St, sd ROBERT BURROW, sd SAMUEL MEALS & lot late of JOHN MILLS . . . . Wit: JOSEPH COLEMAN,

RICHARD HEATH. Ackn 31 Aug 1708 before WILLIAM CARTER justice of the peace. RICHARD HEATH dep recorder of deeds. (E4:pg 169)

24 Apr 1708. Deed. JOSEPH CLAYPOOLE of Phila joiner for 55 pounds sold to CHARLES PLUMLEY of same city joiner a parcel of ground s side of Walnut St in Phila 59 ft length 47 ft breadth bounded by THOMAS GRIFFITH & ground formerly of THOMAS DUCKET . . . . Wit: THOS STORY, RICHARD HEATH, CHARLES MOORE, RICHD NEWCOMB. Ackn 1 Sep 1708 before THOMAS MASTERS justice of the peace. RICHARD HEATH dep recorder of deeds. (E4:pg 170)

25 Sep 1708. Deed. HANNAH DAWSON of Phila widow & relict of EMANUEL DAWSON late of same city mason her former husband decd for 100 pounds sold to HENRY BADCOKE of Phila brewer and MARY his wife a messuage & lot of land . . . whereas by a deed poll ackn in court by JOHN SANDERS late of Phila bricklayer decd on 5 Mar 1695/6 the sd EMANUEL DAWSON became in his lifetime seized in a messuage & lot of land in Phila 26 ft breadth 300 ft length bounded by lot late of the sd JOHN SANDERS, Second St & EDWARD SHIPPEN . . . and the sd EMANUEL DAWSON being so seized made his will dated 31 Mar 1708 & devised unto his wife HANNAH DAWSON all his dwelling house . . . which lot is pt/o the 51 ft lot granted by warrant from WILLIAM PENN proprietary & governor of PA on 1 Sep 1683 unto GEORGE SIMCOCK who sold the same to the sd JOHN SANDERS 1 Sep 1693 (Book E3 vol 5 pg 393) . . . . Wit: WILLIAM COLEMAN, JACOB ISHER, ABRAHAM CARLILE, RICHD HEATH. Ackn 30 Sep 1708 before NATHAN STANBURY justice of the peace. RICHARD HEATH dep recorder of deeds. (E4:pg 171)

25 Apr 1708. Deed. ROWLAND POWELL of Haverford Twp Chester Co yeoman for 150 pounds sold to HUGH THOMAS of Merrion Twp Phila Co husbandman a messuage and 125 a. . . . whereas on 10 Jul 1704 ROBERT ROBERTS, OWEN ROBERTS & EDWARD ROBERTS all of Phila yeoman executors of the will of HUGH ROBERTS of Merion their late father decd sold to the sd ROWLAND POWELL a messuage & a 125 a. tr of land in Blockley Twp adj the proprietary's land, River Schoolkill, land late of sd HUGH ROBERTS & land late of CLEIN JOHNS & now of DAVID MERSG . . . . Wit: RICHARD HEATH, RICHD TAYLOR, RICHD NEWCOMB. Ackn 1 Oct 1708 before NATHAN STANBURY justice of the peace. RICHARD HEATH dep recorder of deeds. (E4:pg 173)

13 Oct 1708. Deed. PHILIP HOWELL of Phila taylor for 10 pounds sold to DAVID LLOYD of Phila gent all my estate right to 250 a. which by warrant dated 9 Nov 1702 were granted unto me . . . . Wit: JOSHUA LAURENCE,

RICHD HEATH. RICHD NEWCOMB. Ackn 25 Oct 1708 before THOMAS MASTERS justice of the peace. RICHARD HEATH recorder of deeds. (E4:pg 175)

29 Oct 1708. Agreement. MARGARET TUCKER (Junr) of Phila spinster for 5 shillings assigns unto JAMES TUCKER of same city butcher an Indian boy of the sd MARGARET TUCKER's named DON JOHN aged about 3 years for the term of 28 years for the use of sd MARGARET TUCKER during the sd term but in case the sd MARGARET shall happen to dye before the expiration of the term then to the use of NICHOLAS TUCKER the brother of the sd MARGARET during the residue of the sd term, but in case the sd NICHOLAS shall happen to depart this life before the end of the sd term then to the use of the sd JAMES TUCKER and MARGARET his wife during the residue of the sd term, and after the expiration of sd term, or after the decease of the sd MARGARET (in case they shall happen to survive the sd NICHOLAS & MARGARET their son and dau, and dye before the end of the sd term) then the sd MARGARET TUCKER the dau doth grant that the sd Indian Boy DON JOHN shall from thence forth forever be free . . . . Wit: JOSEPH EFORD, JOHN RICHMOND, RICHD HEATH, RICHD NEWCOMB. Recorded 2 Nov 1708. (E4:pg 176)

11 Oct 1708. Deed. EVERARD BOLTON of Phila Co yeoman for 180 pounds sold to HENRY WARD of Phila merchant a house & lot of land . . . whereas WILLIAM MARKHAM, ROBERT TURNER & JOHN GOODSOM late commissioners of WILLIAM PENN proprietary & governor of PA by a patent dated 3 Aug 1692 granted unto RICHARD DAVIS (purchaser of the 5000 a.) a lot of land n side of High St in Phila 132 ft breadth 306 ft length adj FRANCIS COOK (Patent Book A vol 1 pg 364), and whereas THOMAS LLOYD, WILLIAM POWELL, HUGH ROBERTS, JOHN HUMPHREYS & DAVID POWELL by virtue of a letter of atty executed by sd RICHARD DAVIS 20 Aug 1686 (Book A vol 4 pg 166) as attys for sd RICHARD DAVIS by their deed poll on 16 Aug 1692 did grant same unto JEREMIAH POWELL of Phila (Book E3 vol 5 pg 326), and whereas the sd JEREMIAH POWELL on 1 Dec 1692 did amongst other lands convey unto ROBERT SONGSHORE of Phila Co yeoman a lot of ground (being pt/o the afsd High St lot) 26 ft breadth 306 ft length adj JOHN SAUNDERS, and on 18 Sep 1693 the sd ROBERT SONGSHORE conveyed unto NEHEMIAH ALLEN of Phila cooper the last mentioned piece of ground, and whereas the sd NEHEMIAH ALLEN on 20 Apr 1694 conveyed the same unto JOHN SANDERS of Phila bricklayer, and whereas the sd JOHN SANDERS on 19 May 1694 conveyed the same unto EDWARD BURCH of Phila shoemaker, and whereas the sd EDWARD BURCH on 8 Dec 1697 conveyed the same unto STEPHEN COLEMAN of Phila merchant taylor, sd STEPHEN COLEMAN being seized

of the sd messuage and lot of ground made his will and devised unto wife SARAH COLEMAN all his land and made her sole executrix, after the sd STEPHEN died 21 Aug 1699, the sd SARAH COLEMAN on 15 May 1700 conveyed the sd messuage and lot of land unto HENRY ELDERSLEY of Cecil Co MD planter (Book E3 vol 5 pg 398), and whereas CASPAR HOODT of Phila taylor and SARAH his wife at Court of Common Pleas held 17 Sep 1702 did recover against JAMES RODGERS & PERNELL his wife executrix of the will of sd HENRY ELDERSLEY then decd a debt of 155 pounds and 50 shillings damages, whereupon by a writ of execution THOMAS FARMAR sheriff seized the lands of sd HENRY and sold the house & lot on High St in Phila adj THOMAS MARLE, JOHN HART & GEORGE WALKER 26 ft breadth 306 ft length unto EVERARD BOLTON for 132 pounds 10 shillings, and whereas sd THOMAS FARMER sheriff on 10 Apr 1703 conveyed the same unto the sd EVERARD BOLTON . . . . Wit: THOMAS STORY, ABADIAH BONSALL, RICHD HEATH, RICHD NEWCOMB. Ackn 6 Nov 1708 before WILLIAM CARTER justice of the peace. THOMAS STORY recorder of deeds. (E4:pg 177)

13 Nov 1708. Deed. THOMAS TRESSE of Phila ironmonger sold to THOMAS ASHTON of sd city shipwright a messuage & lot of land . . . whereas by a patent dated 28 Oct 1701 granted unto WILLIAM FISHER of Phila carpenter & BRIDGET his wife a lot of land upon the bank of DE in Phila adj ROBERT EWINER & WM GOULDING . . . provided that the sd WM FISHER & BRIDGET his wife leave 30 ft of ground pt/o sd lot for a cartway (Patent Book A vol 2 pg 177) . . . and whereas the sd WILLIAM FISHER and BRIDGET his wife on 2 Dec 1701 conveyed the bank lot unto ROBERT PROSSMALE (PRESMALE) of Phila, and whereas the sd ROBERT PROSSMALE on 19 Jul 1704 conveyed the same unto the sd THOMAS TRESSE . . . . Wit: JOHN RICHMOND, JOSHUA LAURENCE, RICHARD NEWCOMB. Ackn 17 Nov 1708 before NATHAN STANBURY justice of the peace. RICHARD HEATH dep recorder of deeds. (E4:pg 181)

16 Nov 1708. Deed. BARTHOLOMEW SONGSTROTH of Phila Co yeoman and RICHARD TAYLOR of Cheltenham Twp Phila Co yeoman for 350 pounds sold to THOMAS WALTON of Byberry Twp Phila Co yeoman a messuage and tr of land adj JOHN BROCK, JOHN JONES, JOHN SWIFT, THOMAS PERRY, GEORGE BURSON & the Mannor of Morrland . . . 300 a. which was purch of THOMAS FAIRMAN of Phila Co gent by the sd RICHARD TAYLOR 25 Feb 1695 . . . . Wit: ROBERT HEATON Senr, HEN STIRKE. Ackn 17 Nov 1708 before NATHAN STANBURY justice of the peace. RICHARD HEATH dep recorder of deeds. (E4:pg 184)

20 Nov 1708. Deed. DANIEL FALCONER (FALCKNER) & JOHANNES JAWERT both of Germantown Phila Co attys (letter of atty dated 24 Jan 1700 Book D2 vol 4 pg 104) of CATHARINE ELIZABETH SCHUTZEN widow of JACOB VAND WALLON decd the heirs of DANIEL BEHAGELL decd, JOHANNES KEMBLER, BALTHAZAR JAWERT (JANHERT), JOHAN WILHELM PETERSON, GERHARDT VAN MASTRICH, JOHAN LEBRUN, MARIA VANDWALL widow of Doctor THOMAS VAN WILLING & the rest of the Frankfort Company in Germantown sold to ABRAHAM TUNIS of Germantown yeoman a parcel of land adj Mannor of Springfield, ABRAHAM TUNIS, WILLIAM STREPER & CHARLES JONES & Company ... 75 a. (pt/o 5700 a. granted to sd Frankfort Company by patent 3 Apr 1689 Patent Book A pg 245) ... paying the rent of three rix dollars or pieces of eight on 1 Mar yearly forever .... Wit: JOHN HENRY SPROGELL. Ackn 27 Nov 1708 before NATHAN STANBURY justice of the peace. RICHARD HEATH dep recorder of deeds. (E4:pg 185)

22 Nov 1701. Writ of Execution. WILLIAM PENN proprietary & governor of PA at a Court of Commmon Pleas on 5 Jun last recovered against RANDLE SPIKMAN (SPECKMAN) (SPAKMAN) adminr of the estate of DANIEL SMITH a debt of 200 pounds & 45 shillings 3 pence damages ... THOMAS FARMAR sheriff of Phila Co in pursuance of a writ 13 Sep 1701 seized in execution a messuage & lot of land of sd DANIEL SMITH bounded by JOHN JENNETT, ROBERT EWER & Second St, also another lot 88 ft length 36 ft breadth bounded by JOHN JENNETT, ground which did belong to SOMEREY ADAMS & the Governors lot, and another lot 55 ft breadth 195 ft length bounded by HENRY SAXTON & Third St ... and for 124 pounds sold same to sd RANDLE SPIKMAN .... Wit: NATHANIEL EDGCOME, HENRY ELFRETH. Ackn 4 Dec 1701 before ROBT ASHETON prothonatary. Recorded 27 Nov 1708. (E4:pg 187)

20 Nov 1708. Deed. HENRY PANNENBECKER of Bebbers Twp Phila Co yeoman for 37 pounds 10 shillings sold to PETER BON of same twp planter a tr of land in Bebbers Twp adj JOHANNES UMSTAT & JOHN REY ... 100 a. pt/o 204 a. sold unto sd HENRY PANNENBECKER by MATTHIAS VAN BEBBER 12 Jun last past (Book E vol 7 pg 188) .... Wit: THOMAS KUNDERS Junr. Ackn 27 Nov 1708 before NATHAN STANBURY justice of the peace. RICHARD HEATH dep recorder of deeds. (E4:pg 189)

19 Jun 1708. Deed. RICHARD RHODES of Passyunk Phila Co yeoman & KATHERINE his wife for 24 pounds sold to HENRY TREGENY of Phila merchant a tr of land in Passyunk adj River Schuylkill, MARTHA COCK, land late of JOSEPH KIELL decd, HENRY BADCOKE & PETER COCK's widow ... 39 a. .... Wit: THEODORNS LORD, JOHN V TOURCHIER[?],

CHARLES MOORE, JOHN B BIRD. Ackn 7 Dec 1708 before NATHAN STANBURY justice of the peace. RICHARD HEATH dep recorder of deeds. (E4:pg 190)

18 Dec 1708. Deed. GRACE PARSONS of Phila widow & sole executrix of the will of ROBERT PARSONS late of sd city weaver decd for 90 pounds sold to WILLIAM WAITE of Phila shopkeeper a lot of land . . . whereas by virtue of a deed from CHRISTOPHER SIBTHORP of Phila brasier on 24 Dec 1702 (Book E4 vol 7 pg 211) ROBERT PARSONS in his life time became seized in a lot of land s side of Second St [illegible] adj THOMAS STORY, and being so seized made his will dated 2 Aug last past and did devise unto his wife GRACE "all my house & lot on Second St", and also the residue of his estate . . . . Wit: THOMAS STORY, THOMAS BROWN. Ackn 27 Dec 1708 before NATHAN STANBURY justice of the peace. RICHARD HEATH dep recorder of deeds. (E4:pg 192)

19 Dec 1708. Deed. JONAS POTTS of Germantown Phila Co husbandman for 60 pounds sold to HERMAN CASDORP of Phila ship carpenter a tr of land in Germantown bounded by ISAAC VAN SINTERN & JACOB GATTSCHALK BROAD . . . 20 3/4 a. pt/o 50 a. which JOHN LUCKEN, out of his 200 a. granted to him by BENJAMIN FURLY ACENT of the Frankfort Company at Rotterdam by deed of inrollment dated 8 Jun 1683 (Book E vol 5 pg 80-82), conveyed unto EVE BELLONGE 8 May 1697 (pg 105) and the sd EVE BELLONGE did sell the sd 50 a. unto PAUL ENGELL 1 Feb 1697/8, and the sd PAUL ENGEL sold to ARNOLD CUSTER 13 May 1699, and sd ARNOLD CUSTER 2 Oct 1705 sold to sd JONAS POTTS (Book B vol 2 pg 301) . . . . Wit: ISAAC VAN SINTERN, FRANCIS DANIEL PASTORIUS. Ackn 28 Dec 1708 before NATHAN STANBURY justice of the peace. RICHARD HEATH dep recorder of deeds. (E4:pg 194)

24 Dec 1708. Deed of Mortgage. THOMAS BROWN of Phila cordwainer for 50 pounds sold to GRACE PARSONS of same city widow a tr of land adj NICHOLAS MOORE & Southampton Twp . . . 245 a. provided that if the sd THOMAS BROWN shall truly pay to the sd GRACE PARSONS 70 pounds (4 pounds on 24 Dec 1709, 4 pounds 24 Dec 1710, 4 pounds 24 Dec 1711, 4 pounds 24 Dec 1712 & 54 pounds residue on 24 Dec 1713) then this present indenture shall cease . . . . Wit: THOMAS STORY, WM WAIT. Ackn 25 Dec 1708 before NATHAN STANBURY justice of the peace. RICHARD HEATH dep recorder of deeds. 23 Mar 1713 before CHARLES BROCKDEN dep recorder of deeds came GRACE PARSONS & ackn that she had received of THOMAS BROWN 70 pounds & interest in full satisfaction of afsd mortgage and releases same. (E4:pg 195)

4 Dec 1708. Deed. MARY FLETCHER of Oxford Twp Phila Co widow & relict of JOHN FLETCHER decd for 200 pounds sold to JOHN SHALLCROSS of sd twp yeoman a messuage & 265 a. adj JOSEPH ASHTON, ATTWELL WILMOTE, land late of THOMAS SEARIES, br of Tacomy Cr, ROBERT ADAMS & JOSEPH PAUL . . . also 112 1/2 a. . . . whereas by virtue of a patent dated 14 Dec 1702 (Patent Book A vol 2 pg 240) the sd MARY FLETCHER is seized in a messuage & 265 a. where she now dwells in the sd twp, and by virtue of a deed by JOHN HART of Phila bricklayer and MARY his wife dated 25 Apr 1705 the sd MARY FLETCHER is also seized in 112 1/2 a. in sd twp . . . . Wit: DAVID LLOYD, JOSHUA LAURENCE. Ackn 25 Dec 1708 before WILLIAM CARTER justice of the peace. RICHARD HEATH dep recorder of deeds. (E4:pg 197)

19 Dec 1708. Deed. JAMES JACOBS of Phila cordwiner for 230 pounds sold to LIONEL BRITTEN of sd city shopkeeper a messuage n side of High St in Phila formerly in the tenure of WILLIAM SALLWAY (SALWAY) decd but now in the possession of the widow BIRCH 30 ft breadth 254 ft length adj Front St, King St & lot late of JOHN WHITE now in the tenure of CHARLES READ . . . subject to the proprotionable pt/o a certain rent provision mentioned in the original patent granted to one SAMUEL RICHARDSON, paying 30 shillings to the sd SAMUEL RICHARDSON for the same . . . . Wit: DAVID LLOYD, JOSHUA LAURENCE. Ackn 31 Dec 1708 before NATHAN STANBURY justice of the peace. RICHARD HEATH dep recorder of deeds. Memorandum: Full & peaceable possession was granted by sd JAMES JACOBS to sd LIONEL BRITTEN. Wit: ABEL COTTEY, SAMUEL JACOB. (E4:pg 200)

17 Oct 1708. Deed of Gift. JOSEPH PHIPPS of Abington Twp Phila Co yeoman for natural love & affection gives to JOHN PHIPPS of same twp yeoman, one of the sons of sd JOSEPH PHIPPS, and ANN PHIPPS w/o JOHN PHIPPS a messuage whereon the sd JOSEPH now dwells in Abington Twp adj ISAIAH PHIPPS, DANIEL THOMAS, TOBY LEECH, GEORGE SHOEMAKER & EDWARD EATON . . . 174 a. pt/o 2 trs of 250 a. each, the one granted by patent from JAMES CLAYPOOLE & ROBERT TURNER late commissioners of property dated 22 Sep 1686 unto the sd JOSEPH PHIPPS (Book A pg 167), and the other tr granted by patent dated 22 Sep 1686 unto ROBERT EWER (pg 168), and the sd ROBERT EWER sold it to sd JOSEPH PHIPPS 7 Oct 1690 . . . . Wit: WILLIAM ROUTLIGE, HENRY BENNETT. Ackn 25 Dec 1708 before JOSEPH GROWDON chief justice. RICHARD HEATH dep recorder of deeds. (E4:pg 202)

25 Mar 1700. Deed. PATRICK (PAT) ROBINSON of Phila gent for 220 pounds sold to JOHN FISHER of same place blacksmith his remaining 1/2 pt/o his DE Front St lot in Phila bounded by ENOCH (now HENRY)

FLOWERS & other 1/2 of lot formerly sold to sd JOHN FISHER . . . also 1/2 pt/o low ground in sd town adj afsd lot . . . the first lot was granted by patent (for the whole lot) to WILLIAM HAIG 6 Jun 1684, & he sold it to the sd PATRICK ROBINSON 2 Oct 1684 (Vol 5 fol 48-50) the other piece of low land was granted to sd PATRICK ROBINSON by patent (for the whole lot) 28 Jan 1690 . . . sd PATRICK ROBINSON appoints SAMUEL WEAVER to be his atty to ackn these presents . . . . Wit: JEREMIAH ALLEN, JOHN JAMES, WM HOUSTON. Ackn 14 Jan 1708/9 before NATHAN STANBURY justice of the peace. RICHARD HEATH dep recorder of deeds. (E4:pg 204)

4 Dec 1708. Quit Claim. JOSEPH JONES of Phila Co gent son and heir apparent of GRIFFITH JONES of same place merchant for 40 pounds quit claims unto JOHN COLLEE of Phila hatter the yearly rent of 40 shillings . . . whereas on 20 Oct 1693 GRIFFITH JONES conveyed unto WILLIAM SAYCOCK of Phila taylor a piece of his lot in sd city 20 ft breadth 100 ft length bounded by Second St & WILLIAM KELLEY, paying 40 shillings rent yearly forever unto sd GRIFFITH JONES . . . and whereas the sd piece of ground by virtue of sundry conveyances is now in the tenure of sd JOHN COLLEE, and whereas on 5 Aug 1704 the sd GRIFFITH JONES did grant unto the sd JOSEPH JONES the yearly rent of 40 shillings . . . the sd JOHN COLLEE to pay rent of 1 pepper corn on 4 Dec every year forever . . . . Wit: DAVID LLOYD, RICHD HEATH, ROWLAND RICE. Ackn 8 Jan 1708/9 before ANTHONY MORRIS justice of the peace. THOMAS STORY recorder of deeds. (E4:pg 206)

20 Dec 1708. Deed. SAMUEL MEALES of Phila cooper for 31 pounds 10 shillings sold to HENRY STEVENS of same city marriner and MARTHA his wife a messuage & piece of ground n side of Chestnut St in Phila 14 ft breadth 72 ft length bounded by sd HENRY STEVENS & lot late of JOHN MILLES, which is pt/o a lot granted by patent dated 21 Sep 1685 unto one WILLIAM NICHOLLS, and the sd WILLIAM NICHOLLS on 28 Sep 1685 (Book E vol 5 pg 125) conveyed the whole lot to WILLIAM HUDSON of Chester Co mason, and he on 6 Jan 1689 conveyed a piece of the whole lot unto CHRISTOPHER HARRISON of Phila lawyer, and he on 27 May 1695 conveyed the piece unto the sd SAMUEL MEALES . . . . Wit: EDWARD EVANS, ROBERT VJARROW, RICHD HEATH. Ackn 20 Jan 1708 before NATHAN STANBURY justice of the peace. RICHARD HEATH dep recorder of deeds. (E4:pg 208)

16 Dec 1708. Deed. DANIEL FALKNER of Germantown Phila Co gent for 300 pounds sold to JOHN HENRY SPROGELL of Phila merchant a 535 a. tr of land lately belonging to JACOB VANDEWALLER and one other 428 a. tr

of land lately belonging to JOHAN JACOB SCHUTE in Germantown, and one other 107 a. tr of land lately belonging to WILHELM UBERFELD in Germantown, and one other 356 2/3 a. tr of land lately belonging to DANIEL BEHAGILL in Germantown, and one other 178 1/3 a. tr of land lately belonging to GEORGE STRAUSS in Germantown, and one other 535 a. tr of land lately belonging to IAN[?] LAURENSS in Germantown, and one other 535 a. tr of land lately belonging to ABRAHAM HASENOELL in Germantown, and also two other trs in the Liberties in Phila (excepting 50 a. which the sd DANIEL FALKNER conveyed to ANDREW ROBINSON), one tr adj BENJAMIN MORGAN, WISSAHOCKEN MILLS & River Schuylkill . . . 100 a., the other adj WILLIAM PALMER, [illegible] VACKRIS & BENJAMIN MORGAN . . . 80 a. together with the city lots lately belonging to JOHANNA ELEANORA PETERSON and CASPAR MERIAN as in a patent dated 28 Jul 1684 together with 100 a. near Phila . . . . Wit: JOSHUA LAURENCE, THOMAS OWEN, RICHARD NEWCOMB. Ackn 20 Jan 1708 before NATHAN STANBURY justice of the peace. RICHARD HEATH dep recorder of deeds. (E4:pg 210)

13 Aug 1708. Deed. DANIEL FALKNER of Germantown Phila Co yeoman in the name of BENJAMIN FURLY of Rotterdam, Holland merchant for 133 pounds confirmed unto JOHN HENRY SPROGETT of Phila merchant a 1000 a. tr of land in Bucks Co between NATHAN STANBURY and JAMES BOYDEN in lieu of 1000 a. surveyed by CHARLES ASHCOM together with 50 a. being the remaining pt/o 5000 a. . . . whereas WILLIAM PENN proprietary & governor of PA by his indenture of lease & release dated 11&12 Aug 1682 did convey unto the sd BENJAMIN FURLY 5000 a., and the sd WILLIAM PENN on 9 Jan 1682 released unto the sd BENJAMIN FURLY the yearly rent of 45 shillings pt/o the quit rent to the end the yearly rent of 5 shillings and no more, and whereas 1000 a. was surveyed by sd CHARLES ASHCOM to the sd BENJAMIN FURLY in pt/o sd purch between the brs of Brandywine Cr and Chester Cr in Chester Co adj THOMAS BARKER, RICHARD WHITEPAINE & JOHN BEAZOR, and whereas the 1000 a. or part thereof before the same was surveyed to the sd BENJAMIN FURLY was taken into the survey of the 30,000 a. called ye Welsh Tr & appropriated to one of the Welsh purchasers under whom THOMAS LLOYD in his life claimed which since his decease was confirmed by patent unto sd THOMAS LLOYD's executors who have since sold the same, and sd BENJAMIN by a letter of atty dated 23 Apr 1700 stile of Holland in Rotterdam authorized the sd DANIEL FALCKNER and JUSTUS his brother to survey his land (that was not then surveyed) and set out to him the same to dispose of (Book D2 vol 5 pg 17), and whereas the sd DANIEL FALCKNER did obtain surveys & patents for 3900 a. and because he could not have quiet possession of the 1000 a. nor obtain a patent he released ye sd BENJAMIN FURLY's right therein .

... Wit: DAVID LLOYD, JOSHUA LAURENCE. Ackn 26 Jan 1708 before JOSEPH GROWDON chief justice. RICHARD HEATH dep recorder of deeds. (E4:pg 213)

20 Jan 1708. Deed. RICHARD JONES of Phila cooper son & heir of RACHEL JONES late of same city decd for 58 pounds sold to EDWARD JAMES of same city bricklayer a messuage & lot of land ... whereas by virtue of a patent under the hands of WILLIAM MARKHAM & JOHN GOODSON commissioners of property dated 29 Jan 1688 the sd RACHEL JONES became in her life time seized of a messuage & lot n side of Chesnut St in Phila 40 ft breadth 178 ft length bounded by High St, lot formerly of HENRY PATRICK but now of ABEL NOBEL & lot formerly of WILLIAM NICHOLLS but now of HENRY STEVENS, and the sd RACHEL JONES being so seized died intestate after whose decease the same descended to the sd RICHARD JONES her son and heir .... Wit: WILLIAM POWELL, ROWLAND RICE, JOSHUA LAURENCE. Ackn 27 Jan 1708 before NATHAN STANBURY justice of the peace. RICHARD HEATH dep recorder of deeds. (E4:pg 215)

26 Nov 1708. Deed. HUMPHREY EDWARDS of Germantown Phila Co husbandman for 58 pounds sold to DIRK JANSEN of same place weaver & JOHN DOEDEN of same place a 100 a. tr of land whereof 76 1/2 a. are in Germantown adj HERMANN VAN BON & lot formerly of ISAAC SHEFER and now returned to the Frankfort Company, and the residue 23 1/2 a. lying in [illegible] ... conveyed to sd HUMPHREY EDWARDS by JOHANNES UMSTAT 28 Apr 1704 .... Wit: ANDW ROBESON, DAVID EVANS. Ackn 28 Jan 1708 before NATHAN STANBURY justice of the peace. RICHARD HEATH dep recorder of deeds. (E4:pg 217)

29 Jan 1708. Quit Claim. NICHOLAS MOORE of Phila gent surviving son of NICHOLAS MOORE late of Phila Co doctor in physick decd & WILLIAM SHUBEY of Phila merchant and SARAH his wife surviving dau of the sd NICHOLAS MOORE decd for 5 shillings quit claim unto BENJAMIN DUFFILD of Phila Co yeoman a 600 a. lot of land called "Irregular Slip" ... whereas the afsd NICHOLAS MOORE died intestate and at the time of his death indeted to sundry persons in England and in these parts in great sums of money over and above the value of his personal estate and by reason of the great maintenance and necessary subsistance of his young and sickly children and of great losses in stock in husbandry & tillage since his decease, his relict and adminr with one JOHN HOLME late of Salem Co w NJ yeoman decd with whom she intermarried after the death of the afsd NICHOLAS MOORE were reduced to such straits that they were necessitaded to sell several parcels of the lands of sd NICHOLAS MOORE, among which was a 600 a. tr of land called "Irregular Slip" ... whereas SAMUEL MOORE son & heir of sd NICHOLAS

MOORE after he attained the age of 21 on 6 Nov 1694, did make his will & named his father in law the sd JOHN HOLME his executor, and whereas the sd SAMUEL MOORE & the afsd MARY w/o the sd JOHN HOLME soon after died and after whose decease the sd JOHN HOLME on 1 Jan 1694 sold the afsd tr of land bounded by Southampton Rd, RICHARD COLLET, JOHN HART, Potquissing Cr, Dublin Twp & Mannor of Moorland to the afsd BENJAMIN DUFFILD . . . . Wit: WILLIAM TRENT, RICHARD WALKER, JOHN BUDD. Ackn 13 Feb 1708 before EDWARD SHIPPEN justice of the peace. RICHARD HEATH dep recorder of deeds. (E4:pg 219)

3 Feb 1708. Deed. DANIEL FLOWER of Phila in discharge of the rent of 1 pound 15 shillings yearly and for 5 shillings sold to JACOB USHER of same place carpenter pt/o a lot of ground 30 ft breadth 178 ft length . . . whereas WILLIAM MARKHAM and JOHN GOODSON commissioners of property by a patent dated 25 Apr 1688 did grant unto BENJAMIN ROBERTS a lot of ground in Phila 44 ft breadth 178 ft length bounded by High St, JOSEPH AMBLER, Chestnut St & JOHN MOODY . . . by virtue of the patent the sd BENJAMIN ROBERTS became in his life time seized in the sd lot after whose decease the same descended to his sister MARY CROW of Saint Buttolph Parish Without Aldersgate London, and whereas HUMPHREY MORREY and JOHN GOODSON by letter of atty by sd MARY CROW (Book D2 vol 4 pg 45) dated 29 Jul 1699 conveyed the sd lot unto JOHN BITTLE of Phila merchant, and the sd JOHN BITTLE on 10 Nov 1699 conveyed the lot unto THOMAS ENGLAND of Phila baker, and the sd THOMAS ENGLAND on 1 Mar 1701/2 conveyed the lot with 1/2 of a well unto JACOB USHER, and on 1 Jun 1703 the sd JOHN USHER conveyed the same unto the sd DANIEL FLOWER, paying unto sd JACOB USHER rent of 1 pound 15 shillings on 24 Dec & 24 Jun yearly forever, and whereas the sd JACOB USHER had conveyed the annual rent unto HENRY FLOWER . . . . Wit: JOHN RICHMOND, WM COLEMAN, JOSHUA LAURENCE. Ackn 14 Feb 1708 before NATHAN STANBURY justice of the peace. RICHARD HEATH dep recorder of deeds. (E4:pg 221)

3 Feb 1707. Deed. FRANCIS PLUMSTED of Menorys London ironmonger for 11 pounds sold to RICHARD HILL of Phila merchant 2500 a. . . . whereas by indenture of lease & release the lease dated 24 & release 25 Oct 1681 WILLIAM PENN of Wormingham Sussex Co esqr sold to the sd FRANCIS PLUMSTED 2500 a. . . . the sd FRANCIS PLUMSTED hath made JOHN MOORE, DAVID LLOYD & SAMUEL PRESTON his attys to deliver these presents in Court . . . . Wit: ISAAC NORRIS, JAMES THOMAS, ISAAC WILLISON, JNO CARPENTER, JOHN PAGE. Ackn 14 Feb 1708 before JOSEPH GROWDON judge. THOMAS STORY recorder of deeds. (E4:pg 225)

19&20 Jun 1683. Deed of Lease. WILLIAM PENN late of Worminghurst Sussex Co esqr for 5 shillings leased unto NATHANIEL BRANSON of Sining Parish Berks Co shoemaker 1250 a. to be set out in such places as by concessions bearing date 11 Jul 1681 for the term of 1 year . . . paying unto the sd WILLIAM PENN the rent of 1 pepper corn only upon the last day of sd term . . . these premises to be sold to sd NATHANIEL BRANSON the next day . . . . Wit: HARTEL SPRINGETT, THOS COX, SELL CRASHE. Recorded 24 Feb 1708/9. (E4:pg 227)

30 Jun 1683. Deed of Release. WILLIAM PENN late of Worminghurst Sussex Co esqr for 25 pounds sold to NATHANIEL BRANSON of Berks Co shoemaker a 1250 a. tr of land [see above] . . . . Wit: HARTEL SPRINGETT, THO COXE, SELL CRASH. Recorded 24 Feb 1708/9. (E4:pg 228)

30 Jun 1683. Receipt. WM PENN late of Worminghurst Sussex Co esqr received of NATHANIEL BRANSON of Sining Parrish Berks Co shoemaker 25 pounds it being for the purch of 1250 a. [see above] . . . . Wit: HARLT SPRINGETT, THOS COXE, SELL CRASHE. (E4:pg 230)

6 Aug 1707. Deed of Release. NATHANIEL BRANSON (BRANSTONE) of Soning Berks Co shoemaker for natural love & affection & 5 shillings release unto his son WILLIAM BRANSON 1250 a. [same as above] . . . . Wit: JOHN BRANSTONE, JAMES GATFIELD, WILLIAM BRANSTONE. (E4:pg 230)

1 Mar 1708. Deed. THOMAS SHELLY of Phila cooper for 350 pounds sold to WILLIAM YARD of same city bricklayer a messuage & 2 pieces of ground . . . whereas GRIFFITH JONES of Phila merchant on 1 Oct 1705 conveyed to ROBERT TATE of Phila yeoman a piece of ground in Phila 30 ft breadth 50 ft length bounded by JOSEPH CLAYPOOLE, Walnut St, remaining pt/o sd GRIFFITH JONES' lot & RICHARD HILL . . . the sd ROBERT TATE on 3 Jan 1705 conveyed the same to JESSEY POLLARD of Phila merchant, and the sd JESSEY POLLARD on 12 Jul 1706 conveyed the same to the sd THOMAS SHELLY (Book B vol 2 pg 16), and the sd THOMAS SHELLY hath since erected a brick dwelling house upon the lot . . . and whereas the sd GRIFFITH JONES on 25 Mar 1704 conveyed unto JOSEPH CROSS of Phila joyner a piece of ground w side of afsd lot 18 1/2 ft breadth 50 ft length bounded with [illegible], lot late of CHARLES PLUMLY & RICHARD HILL . . . and whereas on 25 Aug last past the sd JOSEPH CROSS conveyed the last sd lot to sd THOMAS SHELLY (Book E4or5 vol 7 pg 14) . . . . Wit: ROBERT YELDALL, SARAH MORREY. Ackn 5 Mar 1708 before NATHAN STANBURY justice of the peace. RICHARD HEATH dep recorder of deeds. (E4:pg 232)

4 -- 1687. Deed. JOSEPH JONES ye older of Southampton Town & Co blacksmith for 15 pounds sold to PETER CHAMBERLAINE of Bristleton in sd co husbandman & LUCY his wife 500 a. which the sd JOSEPH JONES purch about 4 yrs ago of WILLIAM PENN of Worminghurst Sussex Co esqr governor of PA by one deed which the sd JOSEPH delivered here in England unto the hands of my loving friend JOHN SWIFT formerly GLAZIER and now an inhabitant in Southampton PA as to a friend in trust . . . and also the sd JOSEPH JONES for 15 pounds give my right unto 1/2 a. in Phila unto sd PETER CHAMBERLAINE & LUCY his wife which 1/2 a. was a gift to sd JOSEPH upon consideration of his purch of sd 500 a. of WILLIAM PENN . . . furthermore sd JOSEPH JONES appoints his loving friend sd JOHN SWIFT my atty to deliver sd two trs of land to sd PETER CHAMBERLAINE & LUCY his wife . . . sd JOSEPH JONES appoints my loving friend MARK RITTERIS of Southampton husbandman to be my atty to ask & receive sd deed under the hand of sd WILLIAM PENN out of the hand & uses of the heirs & executors of sd JOHN SWIFT . . . . Wit: JAMES HAWKINS, ABRAHAM JONES, WM JENNINGS Junr. Recorded 18 Mar 1708/9. (E4:pg 235)

28 Feb 1708/9. Deed. FRANCIS RICHARDSON of Phila goldsmith for 30 pounds sold to SARAH ARROWSMITH of same city widow a piece of ground 20 ft breadth 35 ft length . . . whereas WILLIAM MARKHAM, ROBERT TURNER & JOHN GOODSON commissioners of property by patent dated 13 May 1691 did grant unto SAMUEL LEVIS and WILLIAM GARRETT both of Chester Co a lot of land in Phila 20 ft breadth 396 ft length bounded by HUMPHREY MORREY, DE Front St, NATHANIEL ALLEN & Second St . . . and they on 24 Oct 1691 conveyed the same to NATHANIEL SYKES of Phila carpenter (Book E2 vol 5 pg 255), and on 29 Jan last past the sd NATHANIEL SYKES conveyed a piece off the w end of the lot to JOHN HART of Phila bricklayer (Book E5 vol 7 pg 153), and on 31 Jan last past the sd JOHN HART conveyed the same unto the sd FRANCIS RICHARDSON (Book E5 vol 7 pg 158) . . . . Wit: ROWLAND RICE, JOSHUA LAURENCE. Ackn 18 Mar 1708 before NATHAN STANBURY justice of the peace. RICHARD HEATH dep recorder of deeds. (E4:pg 237)

23 Dec 1708. Deed. ISAAC MORRIS (NORRIS) of Phila merchant for 125 pounds sold to WILLIAM FISHBOURN of sd city merchant a lot of land . . . on 20 Jul 1705 WILLIAM REED then of Stepney[?] Middlesex Co England marriner & ANN his wife one of the daus & heirs of ANN MOORE widow decd, JOHN ASKEW of London merchant & ELIZABETH his wife another dau, RACHEL MOORE spinster another dau, NAOMI MOORE spinster another dau & JOHN TIZACK of London merchant conveyed unto sd ISAAC MORRIS a lot of land 51 ft breadth 250 ft length bounded by DE Front St,

SUSANNAH [illegible] & JOHN CLAYPOOLE.... Wit: DAVID LLOYD, RICHARD HEATH, JOSHUA LAURENCE. Ackn 21 Mar 1708/9 before NATHAN STANBURY justice of the peace. RICHARD HEATH dep recorder of deeds. (E4:pg 239)

17 Jun 1703. Deed. DANIEL FALKNER & JUSTUS FALKNER both of Phila Co gent for 160 pounds sold to ABRAHAM DENNIS & JOHN LUCKEN (LUCKENS) (LURCKENS) both of sd co yeoman 1000 a. . . . whereas WILLIAM PENN proprietary & governor of PA by his indenture of lease & release dated 11&12 Aug 1682 granted 5000 a. to BENJAMIN FURLEY (HURLEY) of Rotterdam, Holland merchant, and whereas the sd BENJAMIN FURLEY by letter of atty dated 23 Apr 1700 (Book D2 vol 5 pg 17-19) appointed the sd DANIEL FALKNER & JUSTUS FALKNER to dispose of his 5000 a., and sd BENJAMIN FURLEY's letter on 28 Jul 1701 was proved here by JACOB CLASSEN ARENTS[?] & MATTHEW VANBEBBER wits to the same before NATHAN STANBURY justice of the peace . . . on 8 May 1703 a patent was granted by EDWARD SHIPPEN, GRIFFITH OWEN & JAMES LOGAN commissioners of property for 1000 a. adj JOHN HOLLAND & JAMES CLAYPOOLE pt/o the sd 5000 a. (Patent Book A vol 2 pg 534-535) . . . . Wit: ARNOLD CASSEL, THOMAS KUNDERS, MAURICE LISTE[?]. Ackn 9 Sep 1703 before ROBERT ASHETON prothonotary. Recorded 25 Mar 1709. (E4:pg 241)

12 Feb 1701/2. Deed. JOHN GREENE of Phila taylor for 75 pounds sold to THOMAS SHUTE of Phila Co yeoman 300 a. . . . whereas WILLIAM PENN proprietary & governor of PA by patent dated 17 Sep last past (Book A vol 2 pg 76-77) granted unto sd JOHN GREENE a 300 a. tr of land adj WILLIAM MARKHAM, FRANKLIN FARMAR, Plymouth Twp, land formerly of GEORGE KEETHE & EDWARD FARMAR . . . . Wit: NATHANIEL EDGECOME, FRANCIS COOKE. Ackn 11 Jan 1703 before ROBERT ASHETON prothonotary. Recorded 26 Mar 1709. (E4:pg 243)

9 Mar 1703/4. Deed. JOHN REDWITZER of Plymouth Twp Phila Co taylor for 12 pounds sold to WILLIAM DICKINSON of same place husbandman a tr of land in Plymouth Twp bounded by land of sd WILLIAM DICKINSON in right of THOMAS SHUTE & sd JOHN REDWITZER's other land, surveyed & laid out to the sd WILLIAM DICKINSON 25 Dec 1702 . . . 28 a. pt/o 228 1/2 a. sold to sd JOHN REDWITZER by FRANCIS RAWLE & ELIZABETH FOX 26 Mar 1702, which 228 1/2 a. are pt/o 5327 a. 79 perches called Plymouth Twp, and also pt/o 2500 a. that WILLIAM PENN proprietary & governor of PA by his indenture of lease & release dated 12&13 Mar 1685 granted unto JAMES FOX late husband of sd ELIZABETH FOX, the sd JAMES FOX on 22 Oct 1690 sold 212 a. to JAMES SHALLICK for 6 pounds,

and the sd JAMES SHALLICK on 1 Mar 1696/7 sold the same to the sd JOHN REDWITZER for 46 pounds, and sd JOHN REDWITZER sold 12 a. to one PHILIP PRICE and purch of sd ELIZABETH FOX 28 1/2 a. which by a late survey is found to have 212 a. . . . [illegible] . . . . Wit: THOMAS SHUTE, FRANCIS COOKE. Ackn 9 Mar 1703 before ROB ASHETON prothonotary. Recorded 20 Mar 1709. (E4:pg 245)

6 Jan 1703/4. Deed. THOMAS SHUTE of Phila Co yeoman for 70 pounds sold to WILLIAM DICKINSON of Plymouth Twp Phila Co yeoman a tr of land in Plymouth Twp adj DAVID MORRIS, PHILIP WALLES, DAVID WILLIAMS & DAVID HARRIS . . . 200 a. pt/o 300 a. granted by WILLIAM PENN proprietary & governor of PA to JOHN GREEN of Phila taylor as by his warrant of 29 Feb 1683 & laid out 18 May 1688 & confirmed by patent 17 Sep 1701 (Patent Book A vol 2 pg 76&77), and JOHN GREENE sold to sd THOMAS SHUTE 21 Jan 1701/2 . . . . Wit: EDWARD MIFFLIN, FRANCIS COOKE. Ackn 8 Mar 1704 before ROBERT ASHETON prothonotary. Recorded 28 Mar 1709. (E4:pg 247)

30 Dec 1700. Deed. ANN DILWORTH (DILLWORTH) of Phila widow & sole executrix of the will of JAMES DILWORTH late of Bristol Twp Phila Co yeoman decd with the advice of NICHOLAS WALLN and EDMOND ORPWOOD trustees of sd will for 600 pounds sold to ROBERT HEATH late of Payne, Chickley Parish, Stafford Co, England but now of Phila Co yeoman two trs of land . . . whereas JOSEPH WILCOX of Phila rope maker & ANN his wife on 4 Nov 1696 sold to sd JAMES DILWORTH for 310 pounds two trs of land in Bristol Twp, the first adj Tacony Cr & sd JOSEPH WILCOX . . . 300 a., the other tr adj Tacony Cr & GEORGE WILCOX decd . . . 200 a. (Book E2 vol 5 pg 64), and sd JAMES DILWORTH being seized of the two trs of land made his will 8 Sep 1699 & devised all his estate to be sold . . . and sd ANN DILWORTH hath made DAVID LLOYD her atty to deliver this deed in Court . . . . Wit: JOHN DILWORTH, CASPAR HOODT, RICHARD ARNETT, NICHOLAS WALN, EDMOND ORPWOOD. Ackn 9 Jan 1700 before ROBERT ASSHETON, clk cur. 30 Dec 1700 ANN DILWORTH received of ROBERT HEATH 600 pounds in full discharge of the afsd deed. Wit: NICHOLAS WALN, JOSEPH PAUL. Recorded 30 Mar 1709. (E4:pg 248)

30 Mar 1709. Deed. WILLIAM TRENT of Phila merchant for 900 pounds sold to ISAAC NORRIS of same place merchant a messuage & lot of land 57 ft breadth 69 ft length . . . whereas by patent dated 24 Jun 1684 granted unto SAMUEL CARPENTER of Phila merchant a lot of land in Phila 107 ft breadth 396 ft length bounded by CHRISTOPHER TAYLOR, DE Front, ROBERT PREENAWAY (or TREENAWAY) & Second St (Patent recorded

2 Aug 1684 fol 17) . . . and whereas THOMAS HOOTON of Phila cordwainer on 22 Jun 1692 sold to SAMUEL CARPENTER a piece of ground 8 1/2 ft breadth 396 ft length to be taken out of the sd THOMAS HOOTON's DE Front St lot . . . and the sd SAMUEL CARPENTER on 19 1704 conveyed unto the sd WILLIAM TRENT a messuage & lot of land on Second St in Phila 57 1/2 ft breadth 269 ft length bounded by ISAAC MORRIS & HOOTEN's alley pt/o the first mentioned lot . . . . Wit: JOHN BOURCHIER, JOHN MOORE, CHARLES MOORE. Ackn 30 Mar 1709 before NATHAN STANBURY justice of the peace. RICHARD HEATH dep recorder of deeds. (E4:pg 251)

29 Jan 1708/9. Deed. WILLIAM CARTER of Phila brickmaker for 70 pounds sold to MOSES EDWARDS of Phila weaver three lots of land . . . whereas by patent dated 24 Jul 1684 granted unto JOHN BURGE a lot of land in Phila between Sasafras St & Mulberry St 60 ft breadth 247 1/2 ft length bounded by REES REDRANE[?], LEWIS DAVID & Second St from Skhuylkill, which sd lot the sd JOHN BURGE by his will gave unto SARAH his wife, who after intermarrying with JOHN ECKLEY since also decd, the sd lot was by him sold but not conveyed to LEWIS THOMAS of Phila since likewise decd, and whereas SAMUEL CARPENTER merchant only surviving executor of sd SARAH sole executrix of will of sd husband JOHN ECKLEY on 3 Jun 1697 sold it to sd LEWIS THOMAS, and whereas the sd LEWIS THOMAS some time before his decease by deed on 25 Mar 1701 conveyed the same unto sd WILLIAM CARTER . . . and whereas by patent dated 24 Jul 1684 granted unto HENRY LEWIS a lot in Phila between Sassafras St and Mulberry St 60 ft breadth 147 1/2 ft length bounded by LEWIS DAVID, JAMES CLAYTON & Second St from Schuylkill, which sd lot HENRY LEWIS Junr & SAMUEL LEWIS sons of HENRY LEWIS sometime after their father's decease by deed on 7 Mar 1701 granted unto sd WILLIAM CARTER . . . and whereas by patent dated 24 Jul 1684 unto JOSHUA FEARN a lot in Phila between Sassafras St & Mulberry St bounded by Third St from Schuylkill 60 ft breadth 247 1/2 ft length and the sd FEARN on 17 Nov 1684 granted unto HENRY LEWIS Senr since decd, & sd HENRY LEWIS Junr & SAMUEL LEWIS sons of sd HENRY LEWIS Senr on 7 Mar 1701 granted the same unto sd WILLIAM CARTER . . . . Wit: FRANCIS ELLIS, JOHN CADWALADER. Ackn 30 Mar 1709 before NATHAN STANBURY justice of the peace. RICHARD HEATH dep recorder of deeds. (E4:pg 254)

1 Apr 1709. Deed of Mortgage. WILLIAM DICKINSON of Plymouth Twp Phila Co yeoman for 70 pounds sold to SAMUEL CART of Abington sd co yeoman and JOB GOODSONN of sd co chyrurgeon a messuage & 2 trs of land, one tr adj DAVID MORRIS, PHILIP WALLIS, DAVID WILLIAMS & DAVID HARDIE . . . 200 a., the other tr adj Plymouth Twp & JOHN REDWITZER . . . 28 a. . . . provided that if sd WILLIAM DICKINSON shall

pay to sd SAMUEL CART & JOB GOODSONN 109 pounds 4 shillings to the several intents mentioned in an indenture dated 8 Dec 1705 between JOHN COLLEY of Phila hatter & SUSANNA his wife, ANN w/o JOHN NASH of Phila Co yeoman (dau of sd JOHN & SUSANNA) & sd SAMUEL CART & JOB GOODSONN, that is 5 pounds 12 shillings on 1 Apr next ensueing, 5 pounds 12 shillings on 1 Apr 1811, 5 pounds 12 shillings on 1 Apr 1712, 5 pounds 12 shillings on 1 Apr 1713, 5 pounds 12 shillings on 1 Apr 1714, 5 pounds 12 shillings on 1 Apr 1715 & 75 pounds 12 shillings residue on 1 Apr 1716, then this present indenture shall cease . . . . Wit: THOMAS SHUTE, JOHN BLUNSTON. Ackn 2 Apr 1709 before NATHAN STANBURY justice of the peace. RICHARD HEATH dep recorder of deeds. (E4:pg 256)

20 May 1695. Bond. GEORGE JAFFREY (JAFFERY) of Portsmouth in New England am firmly bound unto Mr JOHN DEPLOURYS of Phila in the sum of 2000 pounds to be paid unto sd JOHN DEPLOURYS . . . the condition of this obligation is such that BENJAMIN BLACKLIDGE master of brigantine & the sd GEORGE shall carry in his brigantine a seeding of tobacco now intended to send in PA on DE to some pt/o England, Wales or Lower of Barwick upon [?] . . . . Wit: JOHN WEST or NEFF, ALEXANDER GRANT. Ackn 21 May 1695 before ANTHONY MORRIS justice of the peace. Recorded 20 May 1709. (E4:pg 259)

22 Aug 1706. Deed. JOHN WILLIAMSON for securing the payment of 30 pounds to be paid in a deed of feossment made by sd RANDALL SPEAKMAN unto sd JOHN WILLIAMSON dated 16 Nov 1703 sold to RANDALL SPEAKMAN of Phila 2 pieces of land in Northern Liberties in Phila [illegible] . . . . Wit: JOSHUA TILLERY, FRANCIS COOKE, MARY COOKE. Ackn 28 May 1709 before NATHAN STANBURY justice of the peace. RICHARD HEATH dep recorder of deeds. (E4:pg 259)

30 Dec 1708. Deed. EDWARD FARMER of Farmars Town Phila Co gent for 50 pounds sold to SEBIS BARTLESON of same place yeoman a 170 a. piece of land adj PAUL CLEMFRESS[?] & JOHN ROADS [illegible] . . . whereas Major JASPER FARMAR decd late father of sd EDWARD FARMER by virtue of a patent dated 30 Jan 1683 (Book A pg 300) was in his lifetime seized of 2500 a. in Farmers Town and being so seized the sd Major JASPER FARMAR left his estate between his wife MARY FARMAR & the sd EDWARD FARMAR his son after whose decease the sd MARY became seized in 1/2 of the 2500 a., and the sd EDWARD FARMER became seized in the other 1/2, and whereas the sd MARY FARMAR afterwards purch 1250 a. adj her land of one THOMAS WEBB who had purch the same of RICHARD FARMAR (Book E1 vol 5 pg 156 & 174) and the sd MARY FARMAR being seized of the 1250 a. and 1/2 of the 2500 a. made her will

dated 21 Oct 1686 & did give the land to her son the sd EDWARD FARMER and soon after died . . . . Wit: HENRY BURKHOLDER, HENRY CASTLEBERRY, DAVID LLOYD. Ackn 18 Jun 1709 before NATHAN STANBURY justice of the peace. RICHARD HEATH dep recorder of deeds. (E4:pg 261)

31 Jan 1708. Deed of Mortgage. EDWARD JAMES of Phila bricklayer for 70 pounds sold to SAMUEL MEALES of same city cooper a messuage n side of Chesnut St in Phila with a lot 40 ft breadth 178 ft length bounded by High St, ABEL NOBLE & HENRY STE[?] . . . provided that sd EDWARD JAMES pay to the sd SAMUEL MEALES 70 pounds with interest on 14 Jan next ensueing then this present indenture shall cease [illegible] . . . . Wit: RICHD JONES. Ackn 18 Jun 1709 before NATHAN STANBURY justice of the peace. RICHARD HEATH dep recorder of deeds. (E4:pg 263)

14 Feb 1704/5. Deed of Exchange. THOMAS SISOM of Phila brickmaker give unto HENRY CARTER of Phila Co brickmaker a lot of ground on Second St in Phila 30 ft breadth 40 ft length bounded by THOMAS MORRIS, PHILIP RICHARDS & lot originally RICHARD CROSLEY's but now of sd HENRY CARTER being pt/o 2 pieces of land granted by patent unto ALEXANDER PARKER 24 Mar 1693/4, and after sd PARKER's decease conveyed to JOHN GOODSON who on 3 Dec 1698 granted it unto ANTHONY MORRIS who on 21 May 1700 conveyed it unto THOMAS MORRIS, and he conveyed the same to sd THOMAS SISOM 21 May 1700 . . . in exchange the sd HENRY CARTER shall give unto THOMAS SISOM his back lot in Phila 30 ft breadth 250 ft length . . . . Wit: JOHN SPERING, THOMAS MAHER. Ackn 22 Mar 1704 before ROBERT ASHETON prothonotary. Recorded 19 Jun 1709. (E4:pg 265)

10 Feb 1708 at Shackamaxon. Deed. THOMAS FAIRMAN of Phila Co yeoman for 25 pounds sold to HUMPHREY BATE near Gwyned Phila Co husbandman a parcel of land adj JOSEPH BATE, land late of DENNIS RACHFORD, HUGH EDWARDS, sd HUMPHREY BATE . . . 100 a. pt/o 666 a. which sd FAIRMAN purch from ELIZABETH WEBB 4 May 1705 & also original deeds of lease & release from WILLIAM PENN proprietary & governor of PA 12&13 Jul 1681 pursuant to which the land was surveyed & laid out to sd THOMAS FAIRMAN by warrant dated 8 Sep 1708 . . . . THOMAS FAIRMAN consitutes JOHN CADWALADER his atty to ackn this deed in Court. Wit: NICHOLAS STEIGLEET, JOSEPH BATE, ELIZABETH FAIRMAN. Ackn 20 Aug 1709 before NATHAN STANBURY justice of the peace. RICHARD HEATH dep recorder of deeds. (E4:pg 266)

10 Feb 1708/9 at Shackamaxon. Deed. THOMAS FAIRMAN of Phila Co yeoman for 25 pounds sold to JOSEPH BATE near Germantown Phila Co husbandman a piece of ground [illegible] . . . THOMAS FAIRMAN constitutes JOHN CADWALADER his atty to ackn this deed in Court. . Wit: NICHOLAS STEIGLEET, HUMPHREY BATE, ELIZABETH FAIRMAN. Ackn 20 Aug 1709 before NATHAN STANBURY justice of the peace. RICHARD HEATH dep recorder of deeds. (E4:pg 268)

6 Sep 1709. Deed. JOSHUA TITTERY of Phila sadler[?] sold to JOSEPH KIRKBRIDE of Bucks Co merchant [illegible] . . . whereas on 19 Jun 1708 THOMAS STORY of Phila gent, SAMUEL CART of Abington Phila Co yeoman, ROBERT FLETCHER Junr of Pine Spring, Abington yeoman, THOMAS CAULEY of Abington yeoman sold to sd JOSHUA TITTERY a parcel of land adj sd ROBERT FLETCHER, Mannor of Moorland, sd THOMAS CAULEY & LEWIS JONES . . . 50 a., and also a parcel of land adj sd THOMAS CAULEY, land late of ABRAHAM RICHARDS & land late of SILAS CRISPIN . . . 51 1/2 a. [illegible] . . . . Wit: SAMUEL BAKER, BALDWIN [?]. Ackn 7 Sep 1709 before NATHAN STANBURY justice of the peace. RICHARD HEATH dep recorder of deeds. (E4:pg 269)

1 May 1709. Deed. PETER MATSON sold to JUSTA JUSTASON . . . [illegible] . . . by name of Sayamensing Island w side of Skoolkill adj sd JUSTA JUSTASON . . . 10 a. of fast land, 31 a. of marsh, lands formerly in the tenure of sd PETER MATSON the father by virtue of a patent dated 1 May 1671 granted by FRANCIS LOVELAGE then governor of NY to LAVRS PETERSON but now in the possession of sd JUSTA JUSTASON [illegible] . . . . Wit: DAVID LLOYD, JOSHUA LAURENCE. [signed by] PETER & KATHARIN (CATRIN) MATSON. Wit: JOHN R[?], JOHN R[?] Junr. (E4:pg 272)

17 Oct 1709. Deed. THOMAS FAIRMAN of Shackamaxon Phila Co gent for 5 shillings [?] to EDWARD FARMAR of same co gent [illegible] . . . will of THOMAS MADOX late of same co decd & HANS MICHAEL TRUMP late of [?] on River Rhyne in Germany but now of sd co husbandman . . . a tr of land in upper Dublin Twp adj JOHN SOUTHWORTH & RICHARD MARTIN . . . 150 a. pt/o 511 a. which by patent on 11 Jan 1705 was granted unto the sd THOMAS FAIRMAN [illegible] . . . . [signed also by JOHN ROADES]. Wit: ARNOLD CASSELL, JOHANNES NICHOLAUS STEIGLEET, HENRY KINGSTON, RICHARD HEATH. Ackn 22 Oct 1709 before [?] justice of the peace. (E4:pg 274)

27 Apr 1709. Deed. JOHN WEBB of Phila taylor surrender unto GEORGE GUEST of Phila cooper all his right in a messuage . . . whereas the sd GEORGE GUEST on 24 Dec 1706 did demise unto the sd JOHN WEBB a

messuage e side of Front St & w side of King St in Phila called "Crooked Billet" bounded by JOHN CRAPP & lot late of PHILIP JAMES under special trust . . . . Wit: ANTHONY MORRIS, DAVID LLOYD, JOSHUA LAURENCE. Ackn 7 Nov 1706 before NATHAN STANBURY justice of the peace. RICHARD HEATH dep recorder of deeds. (E4:pg 276)

28 Apr 1709. Deed. GEORGE GUEST late of Phila but now of Bristol Bucks Co cooper sold to ANTHONY MORRIS Junr brewer a messuage between DE Front St & King St in Phila called "Crooked Billet" formerly in the tenure of ALICE GUEST decd the late mother of sd GEORGE GUEST, 24 ft breadth bounded by JOHN CRAPP, lot late of PHILIP JAMES now of HENRY CARTER [illegible] . . . . Wit: ROBERT FLETCHER, WILLIAM CORKER, JOHN BILES, MARY KIRKBRIDE. Ackn -- Nov 1709 before NATHAN STANBURY justice of the peace. RICHARD HEATH dep recorder of deeds. (E4:pg 278)

11 Jul 1709. Deed. GEORGE HEATHCOLE of Bucks Co merchant for 108 pounds sold to WILLIAM POOLE two trs of land . . . whereas by patent dated 1 Oct 1694 granted unto THOMAS JENNER of Phila carpenter a lot of land on the bank of DE in Phila 75 ft breadth 250 ft length bounded by SEEMERCY ADAMS & PHILIP HOWELL paying yearly for 51 years from 29 Mar 1689 unto WILLIAM PENN 1 English half crown . . . provided that sd THOMAS JENNER shall regularly leave 30 ft clear for a cartway . . . and by patent granted 1 Oct 1699 unto SEEMERCY ADAMS of Phila glover a tr of land on the bank of DE in Phila 25 ft breadth 250 ft length bounded by sd JENNER's lot paying yearly for 51 years unto sd WILLIAM PENN 1 English half crown, and at the end of the terms, value of the lots would be appraised by 2 men mutally chosen . . . and whereas on 27 Dec 1689 the sd SEEMERCY ADAMS sold to THOMAS JENNER the last mentioned lot of land . . . whereas on 10 Oct 1690 the sd THOMAS JENNER sold to THOMAS PASCHALL of Phila pewterer both bank lots, excepting 20 ft w side of cartway sold by the sd THOMAS JENNER to ELIZABETH IBLE [illegible] . . . . Wit: WILLIAM MORNINGTON, JOHN WEBB. Ackn 8 Nov 1709 before NATHAN STANBURY justice of the peace. RICHARD HEATH dep recorder of deeds. (E4:pg 280)

20 Dec 1708. Deed of Release. SAMUEL CARPENTER & JAMES LOGAN of Phila attys to DANIEL WHARLEY of Chalfont St Giles Bucks Co gent, SAMUEL WALDENFIELD and HENRY GOULDING (GOLDNEY) of London linnen drapers release unto PETER COCK of Phila Co yeoman 404 3/4 a. pt/o 7800 a. . . . whereas WILLIAM PENN proprietary & governor of PA by deeds of lease & release dated 27 Oct 1681 did grant unto his dau LETITIA PENN 5000 a. which by virtue of a warrant was surveyed and laid

out in about 1683 w side of River Skulkill which tr by virtue of another warrant resurveyed in 1701 was found to contain 7800 a. included by mistake of the surveyor which had been surveyed & laid in the possession of other purchasers many years before, the 7000 a. confirmed by patent 24 Oct 1701 . . . and whereas the sd LETITIA having since the date of the patent intermarried with WILLIAM AUBRY of London and by their deeds of lease & release dated 3&4 May 1703 (Book A vol 1 pg 265&266) conveyed to the sd DANIEL WHARLEY, SAMUEL WALDENFIELD & HENRY GOULDING the 5000 a., whereas they on 21 Sep 1703 (Book A vol 1 pg 268) appointed the sd SAMUEL CARPENTER & JAMES LOGAN their attys to convey the afsd 5000 a. . . . and whereas among other land included by mistake in the afsd patent there is one tr which by warrant dated in 1684 was laid out unto SASSE COCK & Company for 1000 a. which the sd SASSE having in his lifetime granted 500 a. to GUNNER RAMBO & he by his will, devised 250 a. to his son JOHN COCK and 250 a. unto his son PETER COCK which last mentioned 250 a. was resurveyed by virtue of a warrant dated 26 May 1701 & is bounded by River Skoolkill, GUNNER RAMBO & JOHN RAMBO . . . [illegible] . . . . Wit: CALEB PUSEY, JOHN CARPENTER, JOSHUA GRANGE. Ackn 15 Apr 1709 before NATHAN STANBURY justice of the peace. RICHARD HEATH dep recorder of deeds. (E4:pg 284)

14 Oct 1709. Deed. THOMAS WALTON of Phila Co yeoman for 140 pounds sold unto DANIEL WALTON of same co yeoman a parcel of land . . . whereas THOMAS FAIRMAN of sd co on 1 Dec 1688 conveyed unto the sd THOMAS WALTON a piece of land adj ANDREW GRISCOM, RICHARD COLLETT, NATHANIEL WALTON & sd DANIEL WALTON . . . 100 a. (Book E vol 5 pg 88) . . . . Wit: HENRY HOLLINGSWORTH, JOHN B[?], DAVID LLOYD. Ackn 26 Nov 1709 before NATHAN STANBURY justice of the peace. RICHARD HEATH dep recorder of deeds. (E4:pg 288)

5 Nov 1709. Deed. JOHN HOLME of Dublin Twp Phila Co yeoman for 75 pounds sold to ANTHONY YERCAS of same place yeoman a tr of land upon the Manor of Moreland adj THOMAS WOOD & THOMAS PERRY . . . 300 a. which was located in 2 trs of land seized upon for certain just debts due from NICHOLAS MOORE decd unto BENJAMIN CHAMBERS President of the Free Society of PA . . . seized by BENJAMIN WRIGHT high sheriff & sold unto sd JOHN HOLME 26 Nov 1705 . . . . Wit: ALEXANDER [?], JOSHUA LAURENCE. Ackn 27 Nov 1709 before NATHAN STANBURY justice of the peace. RICHARD HEATH dep recorder of deeds. (E4:pg 290)

19 Dec 1709. Deed. JOHN PRICHARD and JAMES JACOB both of Phila cordwiners for 50 pounds sold to GEORGE SIMES of same city hatter a messuage & lot of land . . . whereas on 7 Jun 1690 GRIFFITH JONES of Phila

merchant sold to sd JOHN PRICHARD his DE front lot 20 ft breadth 42 ft length bounded by ROBERT WALLIS & sd GRIFFITH JONES . . . and the sd JOHN PRICHARD sold the same to the sd GEORGE SIMES but did not convey . . . . Wit: EVAN THOMAS, JOSHUA LAURENCE. Ackn 23 Dec 1709 before NATHAN STANBURY justice of the peace. RICHARD HEATH dep recorder of deeds. (E4:pg 292)

18 Dec 1709. Deed of Gift. HENRY JOHNSON of Phila carpenter, for natural love & affection he hath for his nephew HENRY JOHNSON the younger of Stainmon Parrish, Westmoreland Co, Great Brittain yeoman only son of THOMAS JOHNSON late of sd parrish yeoman decd and brother of the sd HENRY JOHNSON ye elder, gives unto JOHN GUY of same city mariner, MICHAEL WALTON of same city shopkeeper and WALTER LONG of same city mariner a messuage with the lot of land n end of Phila on the bank of DE River 40 ft breadth 250 ft length bounded by lot late of WILLIAM SALWAY & lot late of NICHOLAS PEARCE, & all the rest of sd HENRY's messuages & lots in PA . . . for the use of sd HENRY JOHNSON the elder during the term of his natural life and to the use of sd JOHN GUY, MICHAEL WALTON and WALTER LONG during the life of sd HENRY JOHNSON the elder upon trust, & after his decease to the use of the sd HENRY JOHNSON the younger during his natural life . . . provided that the sd HENRY JOHNSON the elder shall have full authority to revoke or alter all the uses herein . . . . Wit: JEREMIAH LONGHORN, JOSHUA LAURENCE. Ackn 23 Dec 1709 before NATHAN STANBURY justice of the peace. RICHARD HEATH dep recorder of deeds. (E4:pg 294)

10 Feb 1707/8. Deed of Mortgage. FRANCIS JARVICE of Phila carpenter for 33 pounds sold to THOMAS TRESSE a parcel of land in Phila on DE Front St 16 ft breadth 78 ft length bounded by JOHN ORLON, JANE PARKER & lot formerly belonging to ROBERT TURNER . . . now in the tenure of sd FRANCIS JARVICE by virtue of an agreement given unto him by JAMES STANFIELD and WM WELLS on an indenture of lease between THOMAS BRISTOM and ROBERT TURNER dated 24 Sep 1689 . . . provided that if the sd FRANCIS JARVICE pays unto the sd THOMAS TREESE 33 pounds on or before 9 Feb 1709/10 with interest then this present indenture shall be voyd . . . . Wit: THOMAS TRESSE Junr, WILLIAM MALLETT, WILLIAM MALLETT. Ackn 24 Dec 1709 before NATHAN STANBURY justice of the peace. RICHARD HEATH dep recorder of deeds. (E4:pg 296)

29 Sep 1709. Deed. JOHN PARKER of Phila leather draper for 8 pounds sold to GEO SIMCOE of Phila hatter a parcel of land . . . whereas on 8 Sep 1704 JOSEPH JONES of Phila Co merchant conveyed to the sd JOHN PARKER a parcel of land in Phila adj EDMOND DAVIS, ROBERT WALLIS, Jones

Alley & JAMES JACOBS .... Wit: FRANCIS KNOWLES, JAMES JACOB, JOSHUA LAWRENCE. Ackn 29 Sep 1709 before NATHAN STANBURY justice of the peace. RICHARD HEATH dep recorder of deeds. (E6:pg 1)

13 Oct 1709. Deed. JOAN (JEAN) BYWAYTER widow & relict of GERVAS BYWATER late of Phila laborer decd for 40 pounds sold to SARAH SMITH of Darby Twp Chester Co widow a messuage & piece of ground s side of Jones Alley 20 ft breadth 30 ft length adj JAMES PORTNESS, WM BYWATER & THOMAS MILLER, pt/o a lot which GRIFFITH JONES of Phila gent on 5 Aug 1704 conveyed to JOSEPH JONES, and on 1 May 1707 the sd JOSEPH JONES conveyed same unto GERVAS BYWATER & JOAN his wife, whereby the sd GERVAS BYWATER & JOAN his wife became joyntly seized of the premises & after the sd GERVAS dying intestate the right converted to the sd JOAN .... Wit: JONATHAN JONES, JOHN CADWALADER. Ackn 9 Oct 1709 before NATHAN STANBURY justice of the peace. RICHARD HEATH dep recorder of deeds. (E6:pg 3)

9 Oct 1709. Deed. SAMUEL CARPENTER of Phila merchant & JOHN MAULE of same city merchant & CHARITY his wife, sole dau of ROBERT JONES late of same city blacksmith decd, for 36 pounds sold to GEO PAINTER of Phila cooper a shop called "The South Shop" & piece of ground e side of a 30 ft cartway on King St 15 ft breadth 20 ft length bounded by sd CARPENTER & sd GEORGE PAINTER ... pt/o a piece of a bank lot which ELIZABETH RICKETTS widow & sole executrix of the will of ISAAC RICKETTS her husband decd on 20 Jun 1695 conveyed to the sd SAMUEL CARPENTER paying 1/2 the yearly quit rent & the whole ground rent reserved in the identures made by GRIFFITH JONES & WM SALWAY & sd ISAAC RICKETTS in his lifetime for 2 banklots whereof the afsd lot is part (Book E2 vol 5 pg 339), and whereas the sd SAMUEL CARPENTER did heretofore sell but not convey the afsd lot to sd ROBERT JONES in his lifetime who built the shop, and the sd JOHN MAULE & CHARITY his wife have since sold the sd shop unto sd GEO PAINTER .... Wit: SAMUEL CARPENTER Junr, SAMUEL LADD. Ackn 17 Nov 1709 before NATHAN STANBURY justice of the peace. RICHARD HEATH dep recorder of deeds. (E6:pg 5)

8 Aug 1705. Deed. ABEL COTLEY of Phila watchmaker at the direction of JACOB COFFING (COFING) late of Phila but now of w NJ cloathier for 307 pounds sold to MARTYN JERVIS late of Gloucester Co but now of Phila cordwainer a messuage & tr of land 20 ft breadth 62 ft length bounded by lot late of HENRY CARTER now of LIONELL BRITTON, Second St & Strawberry Lane ... whereas on 4 Mar 1702/3 RICHARD HILL conveyed to sd ABEL COTLEY a piece of ground [illegible] ....

Wit: WM HOWARD, DAVID LLOYD. Ackn 17 Nov 1709 before NATHAN STANBURY justice of the peace. RICHARD HEATH dep recorder of deeds. (E6:pg 10)

[NOTE: Page numbers scratched out but used them anyway.]

29 Oct 1709. Deed. JOHN HENDRICKS of Phila carpenter for [illegible] sold to ABRAHAM PORTER now resident in w NJ timber merchant a tr of land . . . whereas CHRISTOPHER of Phila sadle tree maker on 12 Jul 1706 (Book B vol 3 pg 174) conveyed unto sd JOHN HENDRICKS a lot on the bank of DE in Phila 44 1/2 ft breadth 250 ft length adj SAMUEL ELPETH and another lot in Phila adj ANDREW RUDIMAN [illegible] . . . . Wit: THOMAS LACE, LEESON LOFTUS, FRANCIS COOKE. Ackn 29 Nov 1709 before NATHAN STANBURY justice of the peace. RICHARD HEATH dep recorder of deeds. (E6:pg ?)

10 Aug 1709. Deed. NICHOLAS BUSBY of Dublin Twp Phila Co yeoman for 52 pounds 10 shillings sold to ATTIWIL (ATTIWILL) WILMERTON of Oxford Twp Phila Co yeoman a plantation & parcel of land which the sd NICHOLAS BUSBY lately purch of WILLIAM DAVIS, in Oxford Twp adj MATTHIAS KOON, other land of sd ATTIWIL WILMERTON & JOHN WELLS . . . 50 a. pt/o 495 a. granted by patent to THOS LEARY decd dated 18 Jul 1684 (Book A fol 161) & was late in the possession of RICHD LEARY son & heir of the sd THOS LEARY who sold the same to WM DAVIS 1 Jun 1702, and by the sd DAVIS sold unto the sd NICHOLAS BUSBY 9 Aug 1709 . . . . Wit: JOHN SHALLCROSS, PETER TAYLOR. Ackn 10 Dec 1709 before NATHAN STANBURY justice of the peace. RICHARD HEATH dep recorder of deeds. (E6:pg ?)

9 Aug 1709. Deed. WILLIAM DAVIS of Oxford Twp Phila Co turner for 95 pounds sold to NICHO BUSBY of same place yeoman a tr of land [same as above] . . . . Wit: EDWARD BUSBY, RICHARD BUSBY, WM PRESTON. Ackn 10 Dec 1709 before NATHAN STANBURY justice of the peace. RICHARD HEATH dep recorder of deeds. (E6:pg 18)

12 Aug 1709. Deed of Gift. ATTIWELL WILMERTON & HANNAH his wife of Oxfrod Twp Phila Co yeoman for 20 pounds & love, good will & natural affection give to their son JOHN WILMERTON of the afsd place batchler a tr of land in Oxford Twp adj MATHIAS KEINS, NICHOLAS BUSBY & JOHN WELLS . . . 150 a. pt/o 495 a. granted by patent to THOMAS LEARY decd 18 Mar 1684 (Book A vol 101) late in possession of RICHD LEARY son of sd THOMAS LEARY who sold 157 1/2 a. to the sd ATTIWELL WILMERTON & HANNAH his wife 7 Dec 1703 (Book B vol 2 pg

351&352), also 50 a. pt/o 150 a. to be granted is pt/o the 495 a. sold by sd RICHD LEARY to WILLIAM DAVIS 1 Jun 1702, who conveyed unto NICHOLAS BUSBY 22 May 1706, who conveyed the same unto the sd ATTIWELL WILMERTON 10 Aug 1709 . . . . Wit: JOHN SHALLCROSS, NICHOLAS BUSBY, PETER TAYLOR. Ackn 10 Sep 1709 before NATHAN STANBURY justice of the peace. RICHARD HEATH dep recorder of deeds. (E6:pg 19)

7 Dec 1709. Deed. NICHOLAS MOORE of Phila gent surviving son of NICHOLAS MOORE late of Phila Co doctor of physic decd & WILLIAM SLUBY of Phila merchant & SARAH his wife dau of sd NICHOLAS MOORE decd for 9 pounds sold to JOSEPH HALL of Phila Co yeoman a tr of land adj HENRY COMELY, HUGH MORGAN, THOS WHITTON & THOMAS SCOTT . . . 65 a. pt/o a large tr called "Manor of Mooreland" the sd NICHOLAS MOORE the father died seized of and after his decease by virtue of divers conveyances JOHN TURNER of Bybary Twp yeoman became seized in 29 Jul 1707, and the sd JOHN TURNER conveyed the same unto sd JOSEPH HALL, and the sd WILLIAM SLUBY on 23 Jun 1709 appointed JOHN BUDD of Phila brewer his atty to convey the sd land . . . . Wit: SAMUEL JACOB, JOHN WOODWARD. Ackn 11 Dec 1709 before NATHAN STANBURY justice of the peace. RICHARD HEATH dep recorder of deeds. (E6:pg 22)

5 Dec 1709. Deed. SAMUEL HARRIOTT of Phila marriner for 105 pounds sold to GEORGE FITZWATER of same city merchant a lot of land called "Sign of the Globe" adj Front St & King St 17 ft 4 inches breadth 30 ft length bounded by JOSEPH PEDERSON, SAMUEL CARPENTER & lot conveyed by SAMUEL CARPENTER the elder of Phila merchant unto sd SAMUEL HARRIOTT, certified to him by patent 21 Jan 1705 . . . [illegible] . . . . Wit: JOHN WEBB, WILLIAM MORRINGTON, EDWARD SMOUT Junr, JOHN LAURENCE. Ackn 10 Dec 1709 before NATHAN STANBURY justice of the peace. RICHARD HEATH dep recorder of deeds. (E6:pg 26)

5 Dec 1709. Deed. GEORGE FITZWATER of Phila merchant for 116 pounds sold to SAMUEL CARPENTER of same city merchant son & heir apparent of JOSHUA CARPENTER of Phila brewer 1/4 pt/o a tr of land called "Sign of the Globe" . . . whereas on 5 Dec 1706 SAMUEL HARRIOTT of Phila marriner conveyed to sd GEORGE FITZWATER a lot of land now in the occupation of GONNSTONE BOND, bounded by JEFFERY PODDARDS & SAMUEL HARRIOTT (Book E3 vol 6 pg 22) . . . [illegible] . . . . Wit: JOSHUA LAURENCE. Ackn 10 Dec 1709 before NATHAN STANBURY justice of the peace. RICHARD HEATH dep recorder of deeds. (E6:pg 30)

16 Dec 1709. Quit Claim. THOS PRATT of Phila Co yeoman son & heir of ABRAHAM PRATT decd for 5 shillings release unto SAMUEL WAYNRIGHT & ELIZABETH his wife two messuages & lot of land . . . whereas the sd ABRAHAM PRATT was in his life time seized in two small messuages with a lot s side of Chestnut St in Phila 28 ft breadth 51 ft length bounded by lot formerly of SAMUEL ATKINS, lot formerly of CHAS PICKERING but late of HENRY TREGENY & lot late of PHILIP RICHARDS, & being so seized the sd ABRAHAM PRATT for the love of his dau ELIZABETH w/o SAMUEL WAYNRIGHT of Phila taylor did grant the two messuages & tr of land unto the sd SAMUEL WAINWRIGHT & ELIZABETH his wife . . . . Wit: DAVID LONG, JOSHUA LAWRENCE. Ackn 11 Jan 1709 before WILLIAM CARTER justice of the peace. RICHARD HEATH dep recorder of deeds. (E6:pg 33)

24 Jun 1709. Deed. ROWLAND ELLIS of Merrion Phila Co gent for 143 pounds sold to HENRY PUGH of Merrion yeoman a tr of land bounded by sd ROWLAND ELLIS, PETER JONES, CADWALADER WALKER & land late of JOHN EVANS . . . 100 a. . . . whereas EDWARD JONES late of Merrion glover on 11 Apr 1702 for 140 pounds granted unto the sd ROWLAND ELLIS a 100 a. tr of land in Merrion pt/o 881 a. which WILLIAM PENN proprietary & governor of PA by his commissioners EDWARD SHIPPEN, GRIFFITH OWEN & THOMAS STORY by patent dated 23 Aug 1703 granted unto the sd ROWLAND ELLIS (Patent Book A vol 3 pg 573) . . . . Wit: DAVID LLOYD, JOSHUA LAWRENCE. Ackn 12 Jan 1709 before NATHAN STANBURY justice of the peace. RICHARD HEATH dep recorder of deeds. (E6:pg 35)

23 Nov 1709. Deed. HERBERT CORRIE (HARBERT COURRIE) of Phila innholder for 100 pounds set over unto HUGH LONDON of same place merchant a parcel of land to farm let for the residue of 60 years . . . whereas on 29 Sep 1703 SAML RICHARDSON of Phila Co merchant farm let to HERBERT CORRIE a parcel of land in Phila 17 ft breadth 102 ft length bounded by GRIFFITH JONES, lot late in possession of JOHN GRIFFITH Junr & High St for the term of 60 years under the yearly rent of 30 shillings 8 pence . . . . Wit: WILLIAM ROBINSON, DANL JONES, JOHN MOORE, CHARLES MOORE. Ackn 12 Jan 1709 before NATHAN STANBURY justice of the peace. RICHARD HEATH dep recorder of deeds. (E6:pg 37)

23 Nov 1709. Deed. HERBERT CORRIE of Phila innholder for 50 pounds sold to HUGH LONDON of same city merchant a tr of land . . . whereas there is a piece of ground in Phila 20 ft breadth 60 ft length bounded by CATHERINE BLANY, sd HERBERT CORRIE & JOHN DAVIS . . . formerly sold by GRIFFITH JONES to DAVID LLOYD who sold the same

to KATHERINE BLANY who sold the same to sd HERBERT CORRIE 6 Apr 1705, which was granted by patent 27 Jun 1684 unto sd GRIFFITH JONES (Patent Book A pg 52) . . . . Wit: WM ROBINSON, DANIEL JONES, JOHN MOORE, CHARLES MOORE. Ackn 13 Jan 1709 before NATHAN STANBURY justice of the peace. RICHARD HEATH dep recorder of deeds. Received of HUGH LONDON 50 pounds in full. ROBERT CORRIE. (E6:pg 39)

4 Aug 1709. Deed. EDWARD CHURCH of Phila cordwainer & SUSANNA CARTER of same city widow executrix of the will of HENRY CARTER late of same city brickmaker decd for 270 pounds sold to WILLIAM BRANSON of Phila joyner a messuage & two trs of land . . . whereas THOMAS MARTIN[?] of Phila merchant by his deed dated 19 Oct 170- did convey unto the sd HENRY CARTER a messuage & piece of ground in Phila adj Chestnut St, Second St & THOMAS SISOM . . . and the sd HENRY CARTER conveyed the same unto ANTHONY MORRIS (Book E5 vol 7 pg 309) . . . and whereas THOMAS SISOM of Phila Co brickmaker on 14 Feb 1704/5 conveyed a lot unto the sd HENRY CARTER 30 ft breadth 40 ft length bounded by land then of THOMAS HARRIS but now of BENJAMIN WRIGHT, PHILIP RICHARDS & Second St . . . [illegible] . . . the sd HENRY CARTER made his will dated 5 Oct 1708 & did order the sd EDWARD CHURCH to sell the land . . . . Wit: W BITRIDGE[?], JOHN CADWALADER. Ackn 19 Jan 1709 before GRIFFITH JONES justice of the peace. RICHARD HEATH dep recorder of deeds. (E6:pg 42)

9 Feb 1709. Deed. ANDREW HAINES & JOHN HAINES both of Phila merchants executors of the will of HENRY WARD late of same city merchant decd for 135 pounds sold to THOMAS ELDRIDGE of Phila cordwinder a messuage & lot of land . . . whereas on 11 Oct 1708 EDWARD BOLTON of Phila Co yeoman conveyed to sd HENRY WARD a messuage & lot of land n side of High St in Phila 26 ft breadth 306 ft length adj THOMAS [?], JOHN HART & [?] (Book E4 vol 7, pg 222) . . . the sd HENRY WARD being seized in the messuage & lot of land made his will dated 9 Apr last past & did authorize his executors to sell his real & personal estate excepting his negro woman JUDITH to be reserved to the use of his children, and appointed EDWARD SHIPPEN Senr, ANDREW HAINES, JOHN HAINES merchants & DAVID GIFFIN & AUTHOR SMITH all of Phila joynt executors . . . . Wit: JOSEPH RICHARDS. Ackn 11 Feb 1709 before NATHAN STANBURY justice of the peace. RICHARD HEATH dep recorder of deeds. (E6:pg 45)

23 Jan 1709. Deed of Mortgage. THOMAS PALMER of Phila Co yeoman for 60 pounds sold to BENJAMIN DUFFIELD of same co tanner a messuage & tr of land adj NICHOLAS MOORE & JOSEPH FISHER . . . 500 a. . . .

provided that if the sd THOMAS PALMER shall pay unto the sd BENJAMIN DUFFIELD 93 pounds 12 shillings, to wit 10 pounds 16 shillings on 23 Jan next ensueing, 4 pounds 16 shillings on 23 Jan 1711, 5 pounds 16 shillings on 23 Jan 1712, 4 pounds 16 shillings on 23 Jan 1713, 4 pounds 16 shillings on 23 Jan 1714, 4 pounds 16 shillings on 23 Jan 1715, 64 pounds 16 shillings residue on 23 Jan 1716, then this present indenture shall cease . . . . Wit: DAVID POWELL, JOSHUA LAWRENCE. Ackn 11 Feb 1709 before NATHAN STANBURY justice of the peace. RICHARD HEATH dep recorder of deeds. 28 Mar 1718 before CHAS BROCKDEN recorder of deeds came BENJAMIN DUFFIELD & ackn he received from THOS PALMER the full sum of 93 pounds 12 shillings in full satisfaction of the mortgage. (E6:pg 47)

28 Jan 1709. Deed. NICHOLAS MOORE of Phila gent the surviving son of NICHOLAS MOORE late of Phila Co doctor of phisic decd & WILLIAM SLUBY of Phila merchant & SARAH his wife dau of sd NICHOLAS MOORE decd for 5 shillings & also 15 pounds paid by BENJAMIN DUFFIELD, the guardian & grandfather of THOS WHITTON, sold to THOMAS WHITTON of Phila Co only surviving child & son of THOS WHITTON of same co late decd two trs of land 163 a. . . . whereas HENRY COMELY of Phila Co yeoman on 6 Mar 1698 conveyed unto THOS WHITTON decd in his life time a tr of land in the Manor of Mooreland adj JOHN BOUCHER & HENRY COMELY (upon THOMAS KUNBER[?], PATRICK KELLY & land of THOS WHITTON) 150 a. . . . whereas JOHN BOUCHER on 8 Mar 1698/9 conveyed unto the sd THOS WHITTON decd in his life time a tr of land in the Manor of Mooreland adj PATRICK KELLY, sd WHITTON, JOHN BOUCHER & JOHN CATON . . . 13 a. . . . and the sd NICHOLAS MOORE the father died seized of the land and sd WM SLUBY by his letter of atty date 23 Jun 1709 appointed JOHN BUDD of Phila brewer his atty to sell & convey the land . . . . Wit: RICHD WALKER, CESAR GHIRELIN[?], JOSEPH YARD. Ackn 4 Mar 1709 before NATHAN STANBURY justice of the peace. RICHARD HEATH dep recorder of deeds. (E6:pg 51)

7 Feb 1709. Deed. ANTHONY MORRIS Senr of Phila merchant sold to NATHAN STANBURY & PENTECOST (PANTECROST) TEAGE both of same city merchants & ANTHONY MORRIS the younger of Phila brewer a tr of land . . . whereas ANTHONY MORRIS the elder for natural love & affection he hath for his son ANTHONY MORRIS the younger gave to NATHAN STANBURY & PENTECOST TEAGUE 1/2 pt/o a messuage in Phila . . . [illegible] . . . a lot late in the tenure of JOSEPH STIALL[?], lot late in the tenure of JACOB REIGNIER & Front St with 1/2 pt/o . . . [illegible] . . . after the decease of sd ANTHONY MORRIS the elder to the use of sd ANTHONY MORRIS the younger . . . . Wit: JOSEPH WILLCOX,

SARAH STUREY, THOMAS MITCHELL. Ackn 1 Mar 1709 before JOSEPH WILLCOX justice of the peace. RICHARD HEATH dep recorder of deeds. (E6:pg 53)

15 Jan 1709. Deed. PHILIP HOWELL of Phila taylor for 33 pounds 15 shillings sold to WILLIAM POOLE of same city brickmaker a piece of ground bounded by King St, Front St, lot late of THOMAS JENNER but now of sd WM POOLE & lot late of WM BRADFORD but now of ISAAC NORRIS . . . whereas WILLIAM PENN proprietary & governor of PA by his commissioners of property SAML CARPENTER, WM MARKHAM, ROBERT TURNER & JOHN GOODSON by patent dated 5 Mar 1690/1 granted unto the sd PHILIP HOWELL a lot of land on the bank of DE in Phila 25 ft breadth 250 ft length paying during the space of 51 years from 29 Mar 1689 unto the sd WM PENN 2 shillings 6 pence on 1 Mar every year and at the end of 51 years shall be appraised by two men mutually chosen, 1/3 pt/o the appraisal shall forever after be paid to the sd WM PENN on 1 Mar every year . . . provided that the sd PHILIP HOWELL shall leave 30 ft of ground in the clear for a cartway (Patent Book A vol 1 pg 319) . . . . Wit: ISAAC NORRIS, JOSHUA LAURENCE. Ackn 6 Mar 1709 before NATHAN STANBURY justice of the peace. RICHARD HEATH dep recorder of deeds. (E6:pg 58)

24 Nov 1709. Deed of Release. SAMUEL CARPENTER & JAMES LOGAN both of Phila attys to DANIEL WHARLEY of Chatfont St. Giles Bucks Co gent & SAML WALDENFIELD & HENRY GOULDNEY of London linnen drapers release unto JOHN RAMBO of Phila Co yeoman a 250 a. tr of land . . . whereas WM PENN proprietary & governor of PA by patent dated 22 Oct 1681 granted unto his dau LATITIA PENN 5000 a. surveyed & layed out in 1684 which by virtue of a resurvey in 1701 was found to contain 7800 a. including by mistate of the surveyor divers parcels which had been surveyed to other purchasers many years before, which tr was confirmed by patent 24 Oct 1701 . . . and also erected the "Manor of Mount Joy", and whereas LATITIA having since intermarried with WILLIAM AUBRY of London merchant, they by deed of lease & release dated 3 May 1703 (Book A vol 1 pg 265&266) conveyed unto the sd DANIEL WHARTON, SAML WALDENFIELD & HENRY GOULDNEY the 5000 a. . . . [illegible] . . . (Book A vol 1 pg 258) & did appoint the sd SAML CARPENTER & JAMES LOGAN their attys to sell & convey the 5000 a. . . . whereas among other lands included by mistake a tr which by virtue of a warrant in 1684 was a 1000 a. tr unto LAPE COOK and the sd LAPE in his life time granted 500 a. to GUNER RAMBO & also 250 a. to JOHN RAMBO both of Phila Co yeoman as by the sd LAPE's obligation dated 9 Jan 1696 to the sd GUNER & JOHN, the 250 a. being resurveyed by warrant dated 26 May 1701 bounded by River

Sckuylkill & PETER COOK . . . [illegible] . . . . Wit: DAVID POWELL, ISREAL PEMBERTON, NOAH LAWRENCE Junr, RICHARD NEWCOMBE. Ackn 6 Mar 1709 before NATHAN STANBURY justice of the peace. RICHARD HEATH dep recorder of deeds. (E6:pg 62)

8 Feb 1709. Deed. DANIEL FLOWER of Phila carpenter sold to JACOB COFING (COFFING) of same city weaver a messuage & piece of ground . . . whereas a messuage & piece of ground n side of Chesnut St in Phila 50 ft breadth 178 ft length bounded by High St, REBECCA TROTTER & JACOB USHER was granted unto the sd DANIEL FLOWER by patent 16 Dec 1704 (Patent Book A vol 3 pg 120) and the residue of the piece of ground which JOHN GOODSON & HUMPHREY MORREY attys of MARY CROW late of London on 9 Jul 1699 conveyed unto one JOHN BITTLE, and on 10 Nov 1699 conveyed the same unto one THOS ENGLAND, who on 1 Mar 1702/3 conveyed the same unto one JACOB USHER, who on 1 Jan 1703 conveyed the same to the sd DANIEL FLOWER . . . [illegible] . . . . Wit: RICHD MOORE, JACOB HOLCOMBE. Ackn 7 Mar 1709 before NATHAN STANBURY justice of the peace. RICHARD HEATH dep recorder of deeds. (E6:pg 67)

15 Feb 1709. Deed. DANIEL FLOWER of Phila carpenter for 75 pounds discharge the yearly rent of WILLIAM CARTER of same city blockmaker issueing out of the messuage & lot of land . . . whereas an indenture on 8 Feb instant [see above] . . . [illegible] . . . . Wit: ROBERT JOHNSON, JOSHUA LAWRENCE. Ackn 7 Mar 1709 before NATHAN STANBURY justice of the peace. RICHARD HEATH dep recorder of deeds. (E6:pg 71)

22 Feb 1709. Deed. WILLIAM LAWRENCE of Phila taylor for 20 pounds sold to CHRISTOPHER THOMPSON of same city bricklayer pt/o a tr of land 20 ft breadth 100 ft length bounded by TIMOTHY STEVENS & residue of the lot . . . whereas on 8 Oct 1692 ROBERT LONGSHORE of Phila Co yeoman conveyed to sd WILLIAM LAWRENCE a lot of land in Phila 20 ft breadth 426 ft length bounded then by lot of RICHD DAVIS but now of JAMES THOMAS, Fourth St, lot then of ROWLAND ELLIS but now of THOMAS PEART & Second St . . . . Wit: JOHN MIDLEFIELD, CHAS HUNT, JOSHUA LAWRENCE. Ackn 8 Mar 1709 before NATHAN STANBURY justice of the peace. RICHARD HEATH dep recorder of deeds. (E6:pg 73)

15 Sep 1695. Patent. WILLIAM PENN proprietary of PA for 25 pounds grant unto JOHN PIERSON (PEIRSON) son of LEONARD PIERSON of Haveningham Suffolk Co yeoman 750 a. clear of Indian incumber between the Rivers Susquehannah & DE . . . until the end of the term of 1000 years . . . it shall be seated . . . . Wit: HARBERT SPRINGETT, FRANCIS HARDING. Recorded 8 Mar 1709. (E6:pg 75)

16 Sep 1695. Patent. WILLIAM PENN proprietary of PA for 25 pounds granted unto JOHN PIERSON (PEIRSON) son of LEONARD PIERSON of Haveningham Suffolk Co yeoman 750 a. clear of Indian incumber between the Rivers Susquahannah & DE . . . until the end of the term of 1000 years . . . it shall be seated . . . . Wit: HARBERT SPRINGETT, FRANCIS HARDING. Recorded 8 Mar 1709. (E6:pg 76)

16 Dec 1709. Deed. MATHIAS VAN BEBBER of Cecil Co MD merchant for 25 pounds sold to ANDREW SHRAGE of Phila Co basket maker a parcel of land in Brebbin Twp adj HERMAN STEVENS & JACOB COBB[?] . . . 100 a. pt/o a 6166 a. tr granted unto the sd MATHIAS VAN BEBBER by patent dated 22 Feb 1702/3 (Patent Book A vol 2 pg 463-465) . . . . Wit: CLAM RITTENHOURER, FRANCIS DANIEL PASTORIUS. Ackn 9 Mar 1709 before NATHAN STANBURY justice of the peace. RICHARD HEATH dep recorder of deeds. (E6:pg 78)

4 Oct 1708. Deed. BRIDGET FORD of London widow & relict & executrix of the will of PHILIP FORD late of London merchant decd, JOHN HALL citisen & draper of London, THOS MORRIS (MORSE) of London merchant & PHILIP FORD of London merchant son of the sd PHILIP FORD decd for 10 shillings sold to WILLIAM PENN of London esqr 5000 a. in Phila devised to the sd PHILIP FORD the son by his father by his will and also all that tr called PA . . . [illegible] . . . also all that town of Newcastle DE & all that tr on River DE, & also all that tr s of New Castle DE . . . [illegible] . . . . Wit: JOHN ROUND, HERBERT SPRINGETT, JOHN PAGE, JOSEPH DAVIS. (E6:pg 80)

5 Oct 1708. Deed. BRIDGETT FORD of London widow the relict & executrix of the will of PHILIP FORD late of London merchant decd, JOHN HALL citizen & draper of London, THOMAS MORSE of London merchant, PHILIP FORD the younger of London merchant son & heir of sd PHILIP FORD decd, JAMES AYREY of London merchant & BRIDGETT his wife one of the daus of sd PHILIP FORD decd, ANN FORD of London spinster & SUSANNAH FORD of London spinster two other daus of sd PHILIP FORD decd for 7600 pounds sold to WILLIAM PENN of London esqr 5000 a. with a city lot in Phila & Liberty lands . . . whereas the sd WILLIAM PENN by indenture of lease & release dated 12&13 Jul 1681 conveyed to the sd PHILIP FORD decd 5000 a. and the sd WILLIAM PENN afterward by several deeds conveyed unto the sd PHILIP FORD decd all the land called PA . . . and whereas the sd PHILIP FORD decd in his will dated 20 Jan 1699 recited a city lot in Phila & the Liberty lands & did devise the same unto his only son the sd PHILIP FORD, excepting the 5000 a. which he devised to sd BRIDGETT FORD, JOHN HALL & THOMAS MORSE who should within 6 months after his

decease (in case WM PENN should not redeem the same) sell the same the money to be devided among his children . . . [illegible] . . . . Wit: JOHN ROUND, HARBERT SPRINGETT, JOHN PAGE, JOSEPH DAVIS. Ackn 4 Mar 1708 before Sir CHAS DURRAMT knight lord mayor & alderman of London. (E6:pg 82)

6 Oct 1708. Deed. WILLIAM PENN the elder of London esqr & WILLIAM PENN the younger of London gent for 10 shillings sold to HENRY GOULDNEY of London linen draper, JOSHUA GEE of London silkman, SILVANUS GROVE of London merchant, JOHN WOOD of London merchant, THOMAS CALLOWHILL of Bristole merchant, THOMAS OADE of Bristol gent, JEFFERY PENNELL of Bristol merchant, JOHN FIELD of London haberdasher & THOS CUPPAGE of Lambertowne[?] Whitehurst Parish Wexford Co Ireland gent then executors & adminrs of the land called PA & all that town called New Castle DE . . . [illegible] . . . 4000 a. . . . . Wit: JAMES THOMAS, HERBERT SPRINGETT, JOHN PAGE, JOSEPH DAVIS. (E6:pg 92)

7 Oct 1708. Deed. WILLIAM PENN the elder of London England & WILLIAM PENN of London gent heir apparant of the sd WILLIAM PENN the elder for 6600 pounds sold to HENRY GOULDNEY of London linen draper, JOSHUA GLEE of London silkman, SILVANUS GROVE of London merchant, JOHN WOODS of London merchant, THOMAS CALLOWHILL of Bristoll merchant, THOMAS OADE of Bristoll gent, JEFFRY PENNELL of Bristoll merchant, JOHN FIELDS of London haberdasher & THOMAS CUPPAGE of Lambertown[?] Whitehurst Wexford Co Ireland gent . . . [illegible] . . . . Wit: JAMES THOMAS, HERBERT SPRINGETT, JOHN PAGE, JOSEPH DAVIS. (E6:pg 95)

26 Dec 1709. Deed. GEORGE SIMCOE (SIMCO) (SENCOE) of Phila hatter for 100 pounds sold to ALEXANDER ROSS of Chester joyner a messuage & two pieces of ground . . . whereas GRIFFITH JONES of Phila merchant conveyed unto JOHN RICHARD of Phila cordwinder 1/2 pt/o his DE Front lot 20 ft breadth 42 ft length bounded by ROBERT WALTER & Jones Alley . . . and whereas the sd JOHN RICHARD sold but not conveyed effectually the messuage & piece of ground unto JAMES JACOB of Phila cordwainer who sold the same unto GEORGE SIMMS, whereupon the sd JOHN RICHARD & JAMES JACOB on 19 Dec now current did convey the same to the sd GEORGE SIMCOE (Book E4 vol 7 pg 371) and the sd GRIFFITH JONES conveyed the rent of 6 pounds with the residue of his DE Front lot unto his son JOSEPH JONES, and whereas on 8 Sep 1704 the sd JOSEPH JONES conveyed unto JOHN PARKER of Phila leather draper a parcel of ground in Phila bounded by Jones Alley & EDMOND DAVIS . . . whereas on 29 Sep

last past the sd JOHN PARKER conveyed unto the sd GEORGE SIMCOE the last mention piece of ground (Book E6 vol 7 pg 1) .... Wit: CORNELIUS VANDER GAIGHE, JOSHUA LAWRENCE. Ackn 14 Mar 1709 before NATHAN STANBURY justice of the peace. RICHARD HEATH dep recorder of deeds. (E6:pg 106)

30 Dec 1709. Deed. ALEXANDER ROSS of Chester, Chester Co joyner for 100 pounds sold to GRIFFITH JONES of Phila merchant a messuage & tr of land [same as above] .... Wit: CORNELIUS VANDER GAIGHE, JOSHUA LAWRENCE. Ackn 15 Mar 1709 before NATHAN STANBURY justice of the peace. RICHARD HEATH dep recorder of deeds. (E6:pg 114)

30 May 1709. Deed. PETER MATSON of Little Marst[?] Cr Glocester Co w NJ yeoman son & heir of PETER MATSON late of Phila Co yeoman decd for 120 pounds sold to JOHN HENRY SPROGELL of Phila merchant a parcel of land ... 100 a. .... Wit: THOMAS HUNT, EVAN EVANS minister of Phila, ANDREW SANDEL minister of Niccor[?]. Ackn 15 Mar 1709 before NATHAN STANBURY justice of the peace. RICHARD HEATH dep recorder. (E6:pg 115)

25 Mar 1710. Deed. SAMUEL RICHARDSON of Phila Co merchant in consideration of the rent sold to HUGH LONDON of Phila merchant a parcel of land ... whereas on 9 Sep 1703 JAMES RICHARDSON farm let unto HERBERT CORRIE of Phila innholder a pt/o his front lot in Phila 17 ft breadth 110 ft length bounded by GRIFFITH JONES, JOHN GRIFFITH & High St for the term of 60 years under the yearly rent of 30 shillings 8 pence, and whereas the sd HERBERT CORRIE on 23 Nov 1709 conveyed to HUGH LONDON of same place merchant the sd parcel of ground during the residue of the sd term ... [illegible] .... Wit: JNO MORSE, CHAS [?]. Ackn 16 Mar 1709 before NATHAN STANBURY justice of the peace. RICHARD HEATH dep recorder of deeds. (E6:pg 118)

7 Sep 1709. Deed. RICHARD DILLWORTH of Bristoll Twp Phila Co yeoman for 200 pounds sold to JOHN WORRELL of Oxford Twp Phila Co yeoman a tr of land in Bristoll Twp adj EDMUND GRAY & land formerly of WILLIAM DILLWORTH ... 140 a., also another piece of land adj land formerly of JOSEPH WILLCOX ... 6 a. pt/o 146 a. conveyed by ANN SIBTHORP to the sd RICHARD DILLWORTH 7 Sep 1709 ... [illegible] . ... Wit: JOHN WARDE, FRANCIS COOKE, JOSHUA [?]. Ackn 16 Mar 1709 before NATHAN STANBURY justice of the peace. RICHARD HEATH dep recorder of deeds. (E6:pg 122)

-- Sep 1709. Deed. ANN SIBTHORP of Phila Co widow for 146 pounds sold to RICHARD DILLWORTH of Bristol Twp Phila Co yeoman two parcels of land in Bristoll Twp adj JOHN WORRELL . . . both trs 146 a. being front of 400 a. made over unto her by endorsement on back of a deed by CHRISTOPHER SIBTHORP & ADANY his wife to WM DILLWORTH and the sd WM DILLWORTH unto the sd ANN SIBTHORP 7 Sep 1709 . . . . Wit: HOWELL JAMES[?], JOHN WORRELL, RICHD PRIGG. Ackn 16 Mar 1709 before NATHAN STANBURY justice of the peace. RICHARD HEATH dep recorder of deeds. (E6:pg 124)

26 Nov 1709. Deed. JOHN BOWYER of Phila shipwright for 175 pounds sold to SAMUEL CARPENTER of sd city merchant a tr of land in Shadgamaxon[?] Twp adj sd CARPENTER & land late of ROBERT TURNER but now of FRANCIS RAWLE . . . 100 a. which was hereby granted unto PETER COCK the elder & afterward by virtue of several conveyances in the tenure of GUNCE RAMBO who on 17 Jul 1699 conveyed the same unto the sd JOHN BOWYER (Book A2 vol 3 pg 194), and the sd JOHN BOWYER conveyed 25 a. unto the sd SAMUEL CARPENTER . . . . Wit: RICHARD MOORE, JOSHUA LAWRENCE. Ackn 7 Mar 1709 before NATHAN STANBURY justice of the peace. RICHARD HEATH dep recorder of deeds. (E6:pg 127)

19 Dec 1709. Deed. WILLIAM FISHER of Phila carpenter for 22 pounds 10 shillings sold to MORRIS MORRIS of Abington Phila Co yeoman a piece of ground in Phila e side of Second St 25 ft breadth 100 ft length adj CICELY TITTERY & sd WILLIAM FISHER, which is pt/o a front lot by patent dated 10 Dec 1701 was granted unto the sd WILLIAM FISHER (Patent Book A vol 2 pg 277) . . . . Wit: SAMUEL MEALER. Ackn 17 Mar 1709 before NATHAN STANBURY justice of the peace. RICHARD HEATH recorder of deeds. (E6:pg 129)

17 Dec 1706. Deed. MATHIAS VAN BEBBER of Cecil Co MD merchant sold to HENRY SELLEN of Siserhum[?] in Germantownship Phila Co husbandman . . . whereas HANNS PETER UMSTETT of Germantown Phila Co husbandman on 6 Oct 1694 sold unto the sd HENRY SELLEN a 25 a. tr of land at Krisheim between sd HENRY SELLEN & DIRK SELLEN pt/o 200 a. conveyed to the sd HANNS PETER UNSTATT by DIRK SIPMAN of Crefeld Nieurs[?] Co Germany 16 Aug 1685 . . . being confirmed unto the sd MATHIAS VAN BEBBER by patent dated 22 Feb 1702 (Patent Book A vol 2 pg 463-465) . . . . Wit: HENRY PANNEBECKER, ISAAC SHUMAKER, FRANCIS DANIEL PASTORIUS. Ackn 26 Mar 1710 before NATHAN STANBURY justice of the peace. RICHARD HEATH dep recorder of deeds. (E6:pg 132)

25 Oct 1709. Deed. WILLIAM BRANSON of Phila joyner for 135 pounds sold to WILLIAM BETRIDGE of same city glaser a messuage & two pieces of ground . . . whereas there is a piece of ground e side of Second St in Phila 5 ft breadth 20 ft length bounded by THOMAS GRIFFITH & sd WILLIAM BRANSON & another piece bounded by BENJAMIN WRIGHT & afsd lot 20 breadth 40 ft length . . . which two pieces of ground are pt/o ground which EDWARD CHURCH & SUSANNA CARTER executors of the will of HENRY CARTER decd on 4 Aug last past sold to sd WILLIAM BRANSON . . . ground rent of 30 shillings payable unto ANTHONY MORRIS . . . . Wit: CORNELIUS VANDER GAEGH, JOHN HENRY SPRIGETT. Ackn 31 Mar 1710 before GRIFFITH JONES justice of the peace. RICHARD HEATH dep recorder of deeds. (E6:pg 134)

14 Jan 1709/10. Deed. SAMUEL JONES of Dublin Twp Phila Co cordwainer for 20 shillings sold to JOSEPH WOOD of Bucks Co yeoman, GRIFFITH MILES of Bristol Twp Phila Co yeoman, EDWARD CHURCH of Phila cordwainer & GEORGE EATON of Phila Co yeoman, a piece of land in Dublin Twp adj ALLEN FOSTER near the burying ground & sd SAMUEL JONES . . . 1 a. pt/o 25 a. which GEORGE EATON on 27 Oct 1699 conveyed unto the sd SAMUEL JONES . . . . Wit: THOMAS POTTS, JOHN HART, JOSEPH TODD, WILLIAM BETRIDGE. Ackn 1 Apr 1710 before NATHAN STANBURY justice of the peace. RICHARD HEATH dep recorder of deeds. (E6:pg 137)

17 Feb 1709. Deed. JOSEPH COOKE (COOK) of Phila cooper & MARY his wife dau of HANNAH the now w/o DANIEL STREET of Phila Co carpenter who is one of the daus of JOHN WEST late citizen & girdler of London (the sd MARY being the sister of JOHN EAST late son of sd HANNAH by her former husband BENJ EAST decd) for 100 pounds sold to sd TOBY LEECH the younger of Phila Co yeoman a tr of land . . . the sd JOHN WEST was seized in 1250 a. by a warrant dated 26 Aug 1682 in Cheltenham Twp adj land late of NEHEMIAH NUTCHER[?] but now of RICHARD HALL, land late of BENJ EAST but now of DANIEL STREET . . . 198 a. and the sd JOHN WEST made his will dated 25 May 1698 & did devise all his lands unto his grandchildren JOHN EAST, MARY EAST & BENJAMIN STREET . . . and the sd JOHN EAST [sic] died intestate seized of 1/3 of the land & the same descended unto the sd MARY COOKE his only heir . . . . Wit: DANIEL STREET, JOHN BILLERY. Ackn 1 Apr 1710 before NATHAN STANBURY justice of the peace. RICHARD HEATH dep recorder of deeds. (E6:pg 139)

24 Feb 1707. Deed. ELIZABETH SHORTER of Abington Twp Phila Co widow for 5 shillings sold to JOHN RUSH a tr of land in sd twp adj ISAAC KNIGHT, land formerly of JOHN RUSH & SAMUEL CART . . . 103 a.

granted unto the sd ELIZABETH SHORTER by patent on 1 Mar 1684 . . . .
Wit: ISAAC WRIGHT, JOHN LINTON, SAMUEL POWELL. Ackn 3 Apr
1710 before NATHAN STANBURY justice of the peace. RICHARD HEATH
dep recorder of deeds. (E6:pg 142)

27 Feb 1709/10. Deed. DIRK JANSON (JOHSEN) of Germantown Phila Co
weaver for 27 pounds sold all his right unto JOHN DOEDEN in 100 a. . . .
whereas HUMPHRY EDWARDS from same place husbandman on 26 Nov
1708 (Book E4 vol 7 pg 267) sold to the sd DIRK JANSON & JOHN
DOEDEN of same place cooper 100 a. whereof 76 1/2 a. lies in Germantown
adj HERMAN VAN BON & lot formerly of ISAAC SCHEFER & the 23 a.
residue lies in the side land of the town of Plimouth adj afsd HERMAN VAN
BON & ISAAC SCHEFER . . . under the yearly rent of 24 shillings payable
every year to the Frankford Company the other 12 shillings 6 pence old
currently to SENERT ARITON . . . . Wit: PETER KEYSER[?], FRANCIS
DANIEL PASTORUS. Ackn 3 Apr 1710 before NATHAN STANBURY
justice of the peace. RICHARD HEATH dep recorder of deeds. (E6:pg 143)

2 Jul 109. Deed. JOHN RUSH of Abington Twp Phila Co yeoman for 53
pounds sold to JOHN ROBERTS of same province blacksmith a messuage &
tr of land in Abington Twp adj ISAAC KNIGHT & SAMUEL CARTER . . .
103 a. pt/o 250 a. granted unto ELIZABETH SHORTER by patent 1 Mar 1684
and she conveyed the same unto the sd JOHN RUSH by deed of gift 24 Feb
1707/8 . . . [illegible] . . . . Wit: JOHN DUN, THOMAS RINDADUN[?],
GEORGE BOWLY, THOS RUSH, ISAAC KNIGHT. Ackn 4 Apr 1710
before WILLIAM CARTER justice of the peace. RICHARD HEATH dep
recorder of deeds. (E6:pg 145)

6 Mar 1709. Deed. SAMUEL PAINTER of Chester Co paviour for 82 pounds
10 shilings sold to EDWARD WARTNALY of Phila joyner . . . whereas
DAMARIS CHICK of Phila widow on 8 Aug 1705 conveyed unto the sd
SAMUEL PAINTER a piece of ground in Phila 20 ft breadth 154 ft length
bounded by lot late of THOS TUNECLIFF but now of ELLEN JONES,
JAMES THOMAS & Second St . . . . Wit: PETER WELCH[?], SAMUEL
PAINTER, WILLIAM MORRINGTON. Ackn 4 Apr 1710 before NATHAN
STANBURY justice of the peace. RICHARD HEATH dep recorder of deeds.
(E6:pg 147)

11 Mar 1709/10. Deed. JOHN WALKER of Gloucester Co w NJ yeoman but
now of Phila for 65 pounds sold to JAMES PARROCK (PANOCK) of Phila
shipwright . . . whereas NATHANIEL [?] on 29 Sep 1701 conveyed unto
the sd JOHN WALKER a back pt/o his DE front lot in Phila 51 ft breadth 126
ft length bounded by WILLIAM GOULDNY[?] & JOHN TURNER . . . .

Wit: ROBERT BARROW, WM DRASON, FRANCIS COOKE. Ackn 5 Apr 1710 before GRIFFITH JONES justice of the peace. RICHARD HEATH dep recorder of deeds. (E6:pg 150)

21 Mar 1710. Deed. WILLIAM SLUBY of Phila merchant & SARAH his wife one of the daus of NICHOLAS MOORE late of Phila Co doctor of phisic decd for 40 pounds sold to THOMAS MORRIS of same co yeoman a tr of land adj JOSEPH PAUL, JOHN CADWALADER & DAVID MARPLE . . . 105 a. pt/o a greater tr called "Manor of Mooreland" granted to the sd NICHOLAS MOORE decd by patent dated 21 Aug 1684 . . . the sd WILLIAM SLUBY by his letter of atty dated 23 Jun 1709 did appoint JOHN BUDD of Phila brewer his atty to sell the afsd land . . . . Wit: ELIAS HUGG, STANELY TARRY. Ackn 5 Apr 1710 before NATHAN STANBURY justice of the peace. RICHARD HEATH dep recorder of deeds. (E6:pg 152)

1 Apr 1710. Quit Claim. NICHOLAS MOORE of Phila gent only surviving son & heir of NICHOLAS MOORE of Phila Co doctor of physic decd for 7 pounds 10 shillings quit claims unto THOMAS MORRIS of Phila Co yeoman a tr of land . . . whereas WILLIAM SHUBY of Phila merchant & SARAH his wife one of the daus of the sd NICHOLAS MOORE decd by their indenture did sell unto the sd THOMAS MOORE a tr of land [same as above] . . . . Wit: ROSE PLUMLEY, ELIZABETH [?], JOHN BUDD. Ackn 6 Apr 1710 before NATHAN STANBURY justice of the peace. RICHARD HEATH dep recorder of deeds. (E6:pg 153)

7 Apr 1710. Deed. ABRAHAM GRIFFITH of Phila cordwainer son of HOWELL GRIFFITH late of same place cordwainer decd for 10 pounds sold to ABRAHAM (ABRAM) BICKLY of Phila merchant a lot of land adj SAMUEL RICHARSON & GRIFFITH JONES . . . whereas by virtue of an indenture dated 3 Feb 1689 between GRIFFITH JONES of Phila merchant & HOWELL GRIFFITH the sd HOWELL GRIFFITH became seized in a lot of ground upon the bank of DE River in Phila 25 ft breadth 250 ft length . . . . Wit: JOSHUA LAWRENCE. Ackn 7 Apr 1710 before NATHAN STANBURY justice of the peace. RICHARD HEATH dep recorder of deeds. (E6:pg 158)

22 Dec 1709. Deed. SAMUEL BORDEN (BOURDEN) of Phila cooper for 70 pounds sold to JOSEPH REDMAN of same place bricklayer a piece of ground in Phila 22 ft 6 inches breadth 74 ft length bounded by High St, THOS MARTIN, LATITIA PENN & SAMUEL HARRIOTT together with the shop or workhouse . . . the sd SAMUEL BORDEN on 6 Mar 1705/6 did convey unto RICHD STILE (STILL) of sd city merchant, and the sd RICHD STILE on 7 Mar year afsd conveyed the same unto the sd SAMUEL BORDEN (Book

B vol 2 pg 444) . . . . Wit: HUGH DUR[?], DIANA DAVIS, NOAH
LAWRENCE Junr. Ackn 7 Apr 1710 before NATHAN STANBURY justice
of the peace. RICHARD HEATH dep recorder of deeds. (E6:pg 161)

13 Dec 1709. Deed. JOHN POWELL of Phila Co cooper for 300 pounds sold
to GEORGE ROCH of Phila merchant two trs of land 250 a. & 3 a. . . .
whereas WM POWELL the father of the sd JOHN POWELL on 8 Nov 1799
[sic] conveyed unto the sd JOHN POWELL a tr of land s side of Schuylkill
River adj land late of BARNABUS WILLCOX & WILLIAM SMITH . . . 250
a. (Book E3 vol 5 pg 317), and whereas PETER YOKOM late of Phila Co
yeoman decd in his lifetime on 5 Nov 1697 conveyed unto the sd JOHN
POWELL a piece of meadow land in Kingsess Twp adj PETER RAMBO &
THOMAS JENNER . . . 9 a. and whereas the sd JOHN POWELL conveyed
the 6 a. of the meadow to one WILLIAM WARNER, and the sd GEORGE
ROCH purch of ESTER the now w/o EDWARD SHIPPEN who was the relict
& executrix of PHILIP JAMES decd . . . . Wit: GRIFFITH JONES, JOSEPH
WILLCOX, DAVIS LLOYD, JOSHUA LAWRENCE. Ackn 8 Apr 1710
before NATHAN STANBURY justice of the peace. RICHARD HEATH dep
recorder of deeds. (E6:pg 164)

15 Dec 1709. Deed. MATHIAS VAN BEBBER of Cecil Co MD merchant for
31 pounds 10 shillings sold to JACOB KOLB of Germantown Phila Co
weaver a parcel of land in Bebbers Twp adj sd MATHIAS & JOHANES
KOLB . . . 150 a. pt/o 6166 a. granted by patent unto the sd MATHIAS VAN
BEBBER 22 Feb 1702/3 (Patent Book A vol 2 pg 463-465) . . . . Wit: PETER
SHOEMAKER, JACOB GAEDTSEHALEK, HENDRICH SELLEN. Ackn
10 Apr 1710 before NATHAN STANBURY justice of the peace. RICHARD
HEATH dep recorder of deeds. (E6:pg 167)

15 Dec 1709. Deed. MATHIAS VAN BEBBER of Cecil Co MD merchant for
31 pounds 10 shillings sold to JOHANES KOLB of Bebbers Twp Phila Co
weaver a tr of land in Bebbers Twp adj sd MATHIAS & JACOB KOLB
(COLB) . . . 150 a. pt/o 6166 a. granted by patent dated 22 Feb 1702/3 (Patent
Book A vol 2 pg 463-465) unto sd MATHIAS VAN BEBBER . . . . Wit:
PETER SHUMAKER, JACOB GARTHSIFALCH, HENDRICH SELLEN.
Ackn 10 Apr 1710 before NATHAN STANBURY justice of the peace.
RICHARD HEATH dep recorder of deeds. (E6:pg 169)

15 Dec 1709. Deed. MORRIS SLEWELYN of Haverford Chester Co yeoman
for 7 pounds 10 shillings sold to JOHN THOMAS of Glockley Phila Co
yeoman a tr of land in the Liberties of Phila adj JOHN THOMAS Senr . . . 10
a. pt/o 500 a. which WILLIAM PENN proprietary & governor of PA by his
indenture of lease & release dated 19&20 Jan 1686 (Book B vol 125)

conveyed unto the sd MORRIS SLEWELYN & by virtue of a warrant dated 16 Feb 1701 for lay out of the same .... Wit: DAVID LLOYD, DAVID SLEWLEN, JOSHUA LAWRENCE, RICHD NEWCOMBE. Ackn 11 Apr 1710 before NATHAN STANBURY justice of the peace. RICHARD HEATH dep recorder of deeds. (E6:pg 171)

31 Mar 1710. Deed. JOHN CARVER of Phila Co yeoman for 100 pounds sold to his son & heir apparent RICHARD CARVER of same co yeoman 386 a. . . . whereas the sd JOHN CARVER & one FRANCIS SEARLE of Bucks Co yeoman purch two trs of land, the one 200 a. was conveyed by JOSEPH FISHER executor of the will of THOMAS TERRWOOD decd unto the sd FRANCIS SEARLE & JOHN CARVER 1 Nov 1697 (Book E3 vol 5 pg 101), and the other tr 500 a. was conveyed by SILAS CRISPUN executor of the will of THOMAS HOLME decd unto the sd FRANCIS SEARL & JOHN CARVER 10 Dec 1697 (Book E3 vol 5 pg 317) ... on 5 Jun 1700 the sd FRANCIS SEARLE & JOHN CARVER made a division of the land.... Wit: [?] THOMAS, JOSHUA LAWRENCE. Ackn 11 Apr 1710 before WILLIAM CARTER justice of the peace. RICHARD HEATH dep recorder of deeds. (E6:pg 173)

5 Oct 1709. Deed. WILLIAM PRIGG of Phila taylor for 41 pounds 5 shillings sold to SAMUEL HOODLEY of Phila Co husbandman a parcel of land ... whereas YEAMAN GILLINGHAM of Phila Co yeoman on 11 Feb 1701 conveyed unto the sd WILLIAM PRIGG a parcel of land e side of Frankford Mile Bridge adj Kings Rd, ROBT ADAMS & sd YEAMAN ... 1/2 & 1/4 a. .... Wit: THOMAS VAUGHAN, JOSHUA LAWRENCE. Ackn 12 Apr 1710 before NATHAN STANBURY justice of the peace. RICHARD HEATH dep recorder of deeds. (E6:pg 176)

21 Aug 1705. Deed. HOWELL JAMES of Bristoll Twp Phila Co but now of New Castle Co DE yeoman for 400 pounds sold to RICHD DILLWORTH of Phila Co yeoman 300 a. pt/o a 500 a. tr of land ... whereas there is a 500 a. tr of land in Bristoll Twp adj Tacony Cr, BARNIBUS MILLER & JOHN LEIGHURST[?] purch by one JOHN BARNES of WILLIAM PENN proprietary & governor of PA by patent dated 12 Jun 1684, and the sd JOHN BARNES on 3 Aug 1687 conveyed the same unto EDWARD BALSFORD, and whereas PATRICK ROBINSON, HENRY WADDY & WILLIAM SALWAY attys of the sd EDWARD BALSFORD on 10 Nov 1691 conveyed the same unto the sd HOWELL JAMES, and the sd HOWELL JAMES conveyed unto his son JAMES JAMES 200 a. pt/o the 500 a. .... Wit: JOSIAH HARPER, ELLIS DAVIS, FRANCIS COOK. Ackn 12 Apr 1710 before NATHAN STANBURY justice of the peace. RICHARD HEATH dep recorder of deeds. (E6:pg 178)

16 Mar 1710. Deed. DENIS KONDERS (KUNDERS) of Germantown Phila Co for 37 pounds 10 shillings sold to JOHN LUCKEN of Bristol Twp sd co weaver a tr of land adj JOB GOODSON & JAMES PETERS . . . 275 a. pt/o 500 a. conveyed unto the sd DENIS KONDERS by LENART ARETS[?] of Crefelt Mours Co Germany weaver 18 Jun 1683 (Book E7 vol 8 pg 9) & confirmed by patent dated 3 Dec 1705 (Patent Book A vol 3 pg 183) . . . . Wit: FRANCIS DANIEL PASTORIA. Ackn 13 Apr 1710 before NATHAN STANBURY justice of the peace. RICHARD HEATH dep recorder of deeds. (E6:pg 181)

16 May 1696. Deed. MARY BROADWELL (BRADWELL) of Phila widow for 96 pounds sold to EVAN MORRIS of Phila glover a parcel of land adj JOSEPH PHILIPS & RICHD DINGWORTH . . . 300 a. now in possession of the sd MARY BROADWELL by virtue of a patent granted to WILLIAM CHAMBERLAN by THOMAS LLOYD, JAMES CLAYPOOLE & ROBERT TURNER commissioners 6 Jul 1686 (Book A vol 155) which patent was signed over to the sd MARY BROADWELL by the attys of the sd WILLIAM CHAMBERLAN 7 Jul 1686 . . . [illegible] . . . . Wit: FRANCIS HORNE, THOMAS MAKEN. The afsd EVAN MORRIS hath made THOMAS PRITCHARD his atty to receive this deed for him in open court. Ackn 4 Jun 1696 before JOHN CLAYPOOLE clerk. (E6:pg 183)

30 Dec 1709. Deed. WILLIAM TRENT of Phila merchant for 345 pounds sold to ANDREW HANEY of Phila Co blacksmith several trs of land . . . whereas by virtue of sundry conveyances duly executed by MARTHA COCK of Passyunk Phila Co widow, RICHD ROADS (RODES) of Passyunk yeoman & KATHERINE (CATHERINE) his wife one of the daus of LAWRENCE COCK decd, ANDREW COCKE, ROBERT COCKE & PETER COCK sons of sd LAWRENCE COCK decd, ANTHONY MORRIS of Phila merchant & ALEXANDER CRUICKSHANK and RICHARD CRUICKSHANK both of Phila Co yeoman sons of ALEXANDER CRUICKSHANK late of Passyunck decd, the sd WILLIAM TRENT is seized in a messuage & tr of woodland in Passyunk Twp adj Specks Cr, River Schuylkill, Jones Cr, JOHN THOMAS Senr & land late of JOSEPH KIRLL . . . 50 a. formerly sold to JOHN GARDNER & 50 a. of meadow formerly sold to MAT HOLSTON and 2 a. formerly sold to JOHN COX all of which are comprehended within the boundarys afsd, and whereas the sd WILLIAM TRENT is seized in another piece of cripple in Passyunk adj Sepekin Cr, WM CARTER & JOSEPH KIRLL . . . 15 a. . . . . Wit: EDMOND KEARNS, JOHN MOORE. Ackn 13 Apr 1710 before JASPER YEATES justice of the peace. RICHARD HEATH dep recorder of deeds. WILLIAM TRENT received of ANDREW HANEY 345 pounds. Wit: JOSEPH ROLFE, EDMOND KEARNS. (E6:pg 185)

15 Apr 1703. Deed. JOHN BETHELL (BETHALL) of Darby Chester Co miller sold to RICHD PARKER of same place yeoman & JANE his dau, 1/4 pt/o a grist mill or corn mill called "Darby Mill" in Darby and 1/4 pt/o the fulling mill now in possession of JAMES COOPER, and 1/4 pt/o several parcels of land, and 1/4 pt/o a 100 a. tr which the sd JOHN BETHELL purch of EDWARD PIRSON in Darby . . . in consideration of a marriage intended to be had & solemonized between the sd JOHN BETHELL & the sd JANE in case she shall outlive the sd JOHN BETHELL and in full recompence of all dower which the sd JANE after the death of the sd JOHN BETHELL shall have to any lands . . . . Wit: JAMES CHANDERS, DAVID LLOYD, RICHARD HEATH. Recorded 29 Sep 1710. (E6:pg 190)

10 Sep 1708. Deed. THOMAS ELISON (ELLISON) of Hempsted Queens Co, Nashaw Island NY and ELIZABETH his wife for 50 pounds sold to WALTER NEWMAN of Middletown Monmouth Co e NJ a tr of land near Matananay adj River Schuylkill, MATHIAS NATCHIOUS & MAURICE PRICE . . . 500 a. . . . . Wit: THOMAS WARNER, MARY WARNER, WILLIAM WATSON. Ackn 14 Sep 1708 at Perth Amboy before PETER SONMANS one of her majesties councils for NY. (E6:pg 192)

3 May 1682. Deed of Lease. WILLIAM PENN of Worminghurst, Sussex Co England for 5 shillings granted unto RICHARD PEARCE of Symonerich[?] Ireland apothecary 1000 a. for the term of 1 year paying unto the sd WILLIAM PENN rent of 1 pepper corn upon the last day of the term . . . . Wit: HARBERT SPRINGETT, THOMAS COXE, BENJAMIN GRIFFITH. Recorded 11 Feb 1710. (E6:pg 195)

4 May 1682. Deed. WILLIAM PENN of Worminghurst, Sussex Co England for 20 pounds sold to SAMUEL TAVERNER of Suprerich[?] Ireland merchant, in the sd SAMUEL TAVERNER's possession by virtue of a sale for 1 year dated day before this date, 1000 a. . . . whereas KING CHARLES the second by letters of patent under the great seal of England dated 4 Mar -- granted unto the sd WILLIAM PENN a tr of land in America with the islands bounded by DE River & 12 miles distance n of New Castle town, late a province called PA to the establishing a coloney . . . . Wit: HARBERT SPRINGETT, THOMAS COXE, BENJA GRIFFITH. Recorded 12 Feb 1710. (E6:pg 196)

23 Aug 1704. Deed of Lease. JOHN PHELPS of Bristol merchant son & heir of THOMAS PHELPS late of Sunerich Ireland merchant decd, SAMUEL TAVERNER of Sunerich apothecary, THOMAS PEARCE of Sunerich apothecary son & heir of RICHD PEARCE late of same place merchant & RICHD CRAVEN of Sunerich merchant son & heir of JAMES CRAVEN late

of same place merchant also decd for 5 shillings a piece granted unto JAMES SHALTICK & EDWARD LAINE of PA yeoman 5000 a. . . . (to wit) JOHN PHELPS 1000 a., SAMUEL TAVERNER 1000 a., THOMAS PEARCE 2000 a., RICHARD CRAVEN 1000 a. . . . . Wit: ANTHONY WHATLY, JOSEPH PENNOCK, ROWLAND THRUPPER, ROWLEY COLHOYS (COLSROYS), WM HIGGENS. (E6:pg 199)

24 Aug 1704. Deed. JOHN PHELPS of Bristoll merchant son & heir of THOMAS PHELPS late of Sunerich Ireland merchant decd, SAMUEL TAVERNER of Sunerich apothecary, THOS PEARCE of Sunerich apothecary son & heir of RICHARD PEARCE late of same place apothecary decd & RICHD CRAVEN of Sunerich merchant son & heir of JAMES CRAVEN late of same place merchant decd for 150 pounds sold to JAMES SHALTICK & EDWARD LAINE (LANE) of PA yeoman 5000 a. . . . (to wit) JOHN PHELPS 30 pounds, SAMUEL TAVERNER 60 pounds, THOMAS PEARCE 30 pounds and the residue to RICHD CRAVEN . . . in the possession of sd JAMES SHALTICK & EDWARD LAINE by virtue of the [above] deed of lease . . . . Wit: ANTHONY WHATLY, JOSEPH PENNOCK, ROWLAND THRUPPER. Recorded 13 Feb 1710. (E6:pg 201)

11 Jul 1693. Deed. FRANCIS RAWLE of Phila merchant & NICHOLAS PEARCE of same place weaver for 11 pounds 10 shillings sold to JOHN LOWDON of Phila weaver 1/2 of a lot of land in Phila called the "Plymouth Lot" 20 1/2 ft breadth 102 ft length bounded by FRANCIS FOX now RALPH JACKSON's lot, High St & other 1/2 lot sold to WM SNEAD . . . . Wit: ROBERT WALLIS, FRANCIS COOKE. Ackn 16 Mar 1710 before NATHAN STANBURY justice of the peace. RICHARD HEATH dep recorder of deeds. (E6:pg 209)

4 May 1704. Deed. ELIZABETH WEBB of Phila widow lately called ELIZABETH BARBER sole executrix of the will of JOHN BARBER late of Shiply Sussex Co England yeoman her former husband decd for 46 pounds 13 shillings sold to THOMAS FAIRMAN of Shakamaxun Phila Co gent 666 a. 2/3 pt/o 2400 a. . . . [illegible] . . . whereas WILLIAM PENN proprietary & governor of PA by his lease & release dated 12&13 Jul 1681 granted unto the sd JOHN BARBER 2500 a., the sd JOHN BARBER being seized in the land made his will dated 20 Sep 1682 & devised "to my loving wife ELIZABETH the eldest dau of JOHN SONGHURST & her child that she now goes with . . . the disposal of my estate . . . both in England & PA . . ." whereas the child with which the sd ELIZABETH was then bigg is also dead . . . . Wit: JNO PERSONS, SAML POWELL. Ackn 27 Mar 1711 before NATHAN STANBURY justice of the peace. RICHARD HEATH dep recorder of deeds. 13 Jun 1704 ELIZABETH WEBB received of THOMAS FAIRMAN the consideration money. Wit: JOHN PERSONS, MARY WEBB. (E6:pg 210)

20 Mar 1710. Deed. JAMES POULTER of Phila wheelwright for 18 pounds 15 shillings sold to GEORGE HATFIELD of same place carpenter pt/o a lot of land adj lot late of GEORGE RANDALL now of sd JAMES POULTER & lot late of WILLIAM HARMER now of sd JAMES POULTER . . . whereas WILLIAM MARKHAM & JOHN GOODSON commissioners of property by a patent dated 25 May 1687 did grant unto THOS HARRIS a parcel of land in Phila 50 ft breadth 306 ft length adj Mulberry St (Patent Book A pg 207), and whereas on 11 Dec 1689 DANIEL MACKARTY of New Castle Co planter & MARGARET his wife the relict of the sd THOS HARRIS decd conveyed unto RICHD HALLIWELL of Appoquinamink Cr New Castle Co merchant 1/2 pt/o the afsd tr, 25 ft breadth 124 ft length . . . and whereas SAPUNS[?] HARRIS (son & heir of sd THOMAS HARRIS & MARGARET his wife) on 6 Aug 1706 released unto the sd RICHD HALLIWELL the last mentioned tr . . . whereas the sd RICHD HALLIWELL on 12 Jun 1707 conveyed the same unto the sd JAMES POULTER . . . . Wit: HEN BADCOCK Junr, JOSHUA LAWRENCE. Ackn 7 Apr 1711 before NATHAN STANBURY justice of the peace. RICHARD HEATH dep recorder of deeds. (E6:pg 213)

15 Jun 1700. Deed. WM SNOWDEN of Phila yeoman for 12 pounds sold to CHAS READ of sd town a lot of land adj JAMES JACOB which he purch of WM SALWAY . . . the sd lot was granted to SAML RICHARDSON of Phila Co gent and by the sd RICHARDSON granted unto JOHN WHITE & MARY his relict by his deed & assignment dated 24 Apr 1693 & 15 Nov 1695, and by WM PAXTON & MARY his wife who was the relict of JOHN WHITE in conjunction with the children of sd JOHN WHITE granted unto the afsd WM SNOWDEN by their deeds dated 22&26 Oct 1698 . . . . Wit: NICHOLAS PEARCE, MARY PEARCE (PEARSE). Ackn 7 Apr 1711 before NATHAN STANBURY justice of the peace. RICHARD HEATH dep recorder of deeds. (E6:pg 216)

29 Mar 1711. Deed. NICHOLAS MOORE of Mooreland Phila Co gent & PRISCILLA his wife (he being son & heir of NICHOLAS MOORE of sd co gent decd) for 168 pounds 2 shillings 6 pence sold to WILLIAM ALLEN of Phila merchant a tr of land bounded by PETER CHAMBERLIN & LAWRENCE TOMSON . . . 555 a. pt/o a 9815 a. tr of land adj JOHN HURT granted by patent 7 Aug 1684 unto the sd NICHOLAS MOORE the father (Patent Book A vol 4 pg 210) . . . . Wit: THOS GRIFFITH, JOSHUA LAWRENCE. Ackn 7 Apr 1711 before WM CARTER justice of the peace. THOMAS STORY recorder of deeds. (E6:pg 218)

13 Apr 1711. Deed. JOHN GARDNER of Blockly Twp Phila Co yeoman for 19 pounds 11 shillings 3 pence sold to BENJAMIN CHAMBERS of Kinsids Twp sd co yeoman two trs of land w side of Schuylkill in Blockly Twp adj

land formerly belonging to THOS LLOYD . . . 15 a. pt/o 50 a. formerly purch by the sd JOHN GARDNER from THOS JENNER 6 Mar 1698/9, the other tr adj w side of afsd tr & sd BENJAMIN CHAMBERS . . . 3/4 a. pt/o a tr first granted by patent to PAUL SANDERS & lately sold by RICHD HILL to the afsd JOHN GARDNER . . . . Wit: WILLIAM ROBINS, JOSHUA LAWRENCE. Ackn 13 Apr 1711 before NATHAN STANBURY justice of the peace. THOMAS STORY recorder of deeds. (E6:pg 222)

9 Apr 1711. Deed. RICHD HILL of Phila merchant & HANNAH his wife for 63 pounds 15 shillings sold to JOHN GARDNER of Blockley Twp Phila Co yeoman 8 a. adj land late of PHILIP ENGLAND and 8 a. adj land of BENJAMIN EAST . . . whereas by patent dated 3 Dec 1692 granted unto PAUL SANDERS of sd co taner a tr of land adj Beaver Run, THOMAS LLOYD, JOHN GARDNER & River Schuylkill . . . 20 1/2 a. of fast land & 36 a. of marsh (Patent Book A vol 1 pg 326), and whereas the sd PAUL SANDERS on 20 Feb 1699 conveyed the land unto EVAN PROTHERA, and the sd EVAN PROTHERA on 22 Oct 1703 conveyed the land with other lands unto the sd RICHD HILL . . . . Wit: BENJAMIN CHAMBERS, CESAR GHISELINS. Ackn 13 Apr 1711 before JONATHAN DICKINSON justice of the peace. THOMAS STORY recorder of deeds. (E6:pg 224)

10 Apr 1711. Deed. THOS FAIRMAN of Shackamaxon Phila Co gent & ELIZABETH his wife for 24 pounds sold to PETER WENTZ of Chesnut Hill Germantown yeoman a tr of land adj HENRY FREY & PETER VIRBIN . . . 100 a. pt/o 666 2/3 a. granted to the sd THOS FAIRMAN by ELIZABETH WELD on 4 May 1704 (Book E6 vol 7 pg 170) & by virtue of a warrant dated 8 Sep 1704 was on 8 Jun 1709 laid out & surveyed unto the sd THOS FAIRMAN . . . . Wit: CASPER HOODT, WILLIAM BETTRIDGE. Ackn 14 Apr 1711 before WM CARTER justice of the peace. THOS STORY recorder of deeds. (E6:pg 228)

24 Apr 1711. Quit Claim. WILLIAM SLUBY of Phila merchant & SARAH his wife (by JOHN BUDD of sd city brewer atty for sd WILLIAM SLUBY) for 8 pounds 10 shillings quit claim unto WILLIAM ALLEN of sd city merchant a tr of land adj PETER CHAMBERLIN, Manor of Moreland (of which this is part), THOS SHUTE & LAWRENCE TOMSON . . . 555 a. . . . whereas the sd WM SLUBY by his letter of atty dated 23 Jun 1709 (Book D2 vol 5 pg 148) impowered the sd JOHN BUDD to sell the afsd tr of land . . . . Wit: JOSEPH YARD, OWEN ROBERTS, HUGH GRAHAM. Ackn 8 May 1711 before WM CARTER justice of the peace. RICHARD HEATH dep recorder of deeds. (E6:pg 231)

16 Feb 1702/3. Deed. JOHN WILLIAMSON of Phila wheelwright for 80 pounds sold to MATHIAS BELLAR of sd city shopkeeper a piece of ground near the market place in Phila 30 ft breadth 70 ft length adj Second St, lot late of GRIFFITH JONES, JOHN DAVIS & WILLIAM KELLEY ... confirmed unto the sd JOHN WILLIAMSON by JOHN DAVIS of sd city carpenter 22 Jan 1701/2 .... Wit: JOHN DAVIS, SAML BORDEN, FRANCIS COOKE. Ackn 8 May 1711 before NATHAN STANBURY justice of the peace. RICHARD HEATH dep recorder of deeds. (E6:pg 234)

18 May 1711. Deed. MATHIAS BELLAR of Phila shopkeeper & MAGDALIN his wife for 250 pounds sold to WILLIAM RUDD of same city baker & REBECCA his wife a tr of land ... whereas WILLIAM HARWOOD of Phila carpenter on 4 Jan 1708 conveyed unto WALTER WORRELAN a lot of land in Phila (Book E vol 3 pg 112) 30 ft breadth 70 ft length adj lot then of GRIFFITH JONES but now of JOHN COLLEY, lot then of SAML RICHARDSON but now of widow DAVIES & lot then of WILLIAM HARWOOD but now of sd MATHIAS BELLER ... and THOS WORRELAN the father & JOHN WORRELAN the brother & heir of the sd WALTER WORRELAN on 17 May 1694 conveyed the sd piece of ground unto WILLIAM KELLEY of Phila weaver, and the sd WILLIAM KELLEY on 11 Jun 1695 conveyed the same unto THOS TREESE of Phila ironmonger, and the sd THOS TRESSE on 24 Sep 1700 conveyed the same unto JOHN DAVIES of Phila carpenter, and the sd JOHN DAVIES on 22 Jan 1701/2 conveyed the same unto JOHN WILLIAMSON of Phila wheelwright, and the sd JOHN WILLIAMSON conveyed the same unto the sd MATHIAS BELLER [see above] .... Wit: WILLIAM WORRINGTON, ELIZABETH HILL. Ackn 21 May 1711 before NATHAN STANBURY justice of the peace. RICHARD HEATH dep recorder of deeds. (E6:pg 236)

17 Mar 1710. Deed. PHILIP HOWELL late of Phila but now of New Castle DE taylor & ANN his wife for 5 shillings sold to BENJAMIN MORGAN of Phila cooper pt/o a lot of land bounded by DE Front St, SAML CRICK, King St & lot formerly of DANIEL SIM[?] but now of sd DARBY GREEN ... whereas WILLIAM MARKHAM & JOHN GOODSON commissioners of property by patent dated 29 Oct 1689 granted unto WM BRADFORD of Phila printer a lot of land on the bank of DE River in Phila 25 ft breadth 250 ft length bounded by PHILIP HOWELL & DANL SMITH (Patent Book A vol 4 pg 177), and on 13 Feb 1696/7 the sd WM BRADFORD conveyed the lot unto the sd PHILIP HOWELL (Book B vol 2 pg 337), and on 16 Aug 1705 the sd PHILIP HOWELL conveyed to DARBY GREEN of Phila blacksmith 1/2 of the stone & brick wall adj to the afsd lot and 1/2 of the ground whereon the stone & brick wall is built (Book E5 vol 7 pg 366) ....

Wit: GEORGE PAINTER, PHILIP HILLIARD, SAMUEL CRICK. Ackn 21 May 1711 before NATHAN STANBURY justice of the peace. RICHARD HEATH dep recorder of deeds. (E6:pg 240)

17 Mar 1710. Deed. PHILIP HOWELL late of Phila but now of New Castle DE taylor & ANN his wife for 5 shillings sold to SAML CRICK late of the Island of Barbados but now of Phila merchant pt/o a lot of land bounded by King St, sd PHILIP HOWELL, other pt/o lot belonging to BENJAMIN MORGAN & Front St . . . whereas WILLIAM MARKHAM & JOHN GOODSON commissioners of property by patent dated 29 Oct 1689 granted unto WM BRADFORD of Phila printer a lot of land on the bank of DE River in Phila 25 ft breadth 250 ft length bounded by the sd PHILIP HOWELL & DANL SMITH (Patent Book A vol 4 pg 177), and on 13 Feb 1696/7 the sd WM BRADFORD conveyed the lot unto the sd PHILIP HOWELL (Book B vol 2 pg 337) . . . . Wit: GEORGE PAINTER, PHILIP HILLIARD, BENJAMIN MORGAN. Ackn 23 May 1711 before NATHAN STANBURY justice of the peace. RICHARD HEATH dep recorder of deeds. (E6:pg 245)

6 May 1711. Deed. ABLE COTTEY of Phila watchmaker & MARY his wife for 225 pounds sold to LIONEL BRITTEN of sd city shopkeeper a messuage & tr of land 25 ft breadth 100 ft length . . . whereas on 18 Oct 1699 GRIFFITH JONES of Phila merchant conveyed to SARAH COLEMAN widow pt/o a lot of land w side of DE Front St adj SAML RICHARDSON, and the sd SARAH with her husband CASPER HOODT on 9 Sep 1701 conveyed the same unto REECE PETERS, and the sd REECE PETERS having built a brick messuage did leave 2 ft in breadth to make up the 3 ft left by one ROBERT WALLIS adj an alley or passage for the use of the sd REECE & ROBERT (indenture dated 27 Jun 1703), and afterwards the sd REECE PETERS together with one JACOB COFFREY on 16 May 1706 conveyed the brick messuage & land unto ABEL COTTEY (Book -- vol 3 pg 285) . . . . Wit: SAML COOMBE, WM PRIGG, JOSHUA LAWRENCE. Ackn 18 Jun 1711 before WM CARTER justice of the peace. THOMAS STORY recorder of deeds. (E6:pg 250)

15 Sep 1710. Deed. JOSEPH TAYLOR of Phila cordwainer for 195 pounds sold to JACOB KOLLUCK (COLLUCK) of Sussex Co DE cooper several rents to be issueing out of several parcels of land . . . whereas on 30 Apr 1703 the sd JOSEPH TAYLOR conveyed unto BARBARA PEGG (BIGG) of Phila widow a piece of ground in Phila 20 ft breadth 50 ft length bounded by Second St, HENRY PRISTORIS, RALPH JACKSON & JOHN VAUGHAN, paying unto the sd JOSEPH TAYLOR the rent of 3 pounds on 1 Aug yearly forever, and whereas on 20 Mar 1704 the sd JOSEPH TAYLOR conveyed unto ANDREW BIRD of Phila brasier a piece of ground in Phila 24 ft breadth 62

ft length bounded by RANDALL JENNEY, High St, RALPH JACKSON & HENRY PRISTORIS, paying unto the sd JOSEPH TAYLOR the rent of 4 pounds on 25 Mar & on 29 Sep by equal portions, and whereas on 16 Aug 1705 the sd JOSEPH TAYLOR conveyed unto THOMAS COATS of Phila shopkeeper a messuage & piece of ground 26 ft breadth 62 ft length bounded by Second St, High St, ANDREW BIRD & HENRY PRESTON paying unto the sd JOSEPH TAYLOR the rent of 2 pounds on 16 Nov & 16 May by equal portions, and whereas on 20 Mar 1709 the sd JOSEPH TAYLOR conveyed unto PENTICOST TEAGUE of sd city merchant a piece of ground late in the tenure of the sd HENRY PRESTON bounded by Second St, High St & JOHN HAWARD . . . . Wit: DAVID LLOYD, JOSHUA LAWRENCE. Ackn 18 Jun 1711 before WILLIAM CARTER justice of the peace. RICHARD HEATH dep recorder of deeds. (E6:pg 253)

27 Mar 1682. Deed. THOMAS WINN of Conwist Flint Co chirurgeon & JOHN ap JOHN of Parish Rueabon[?] Denbigh Co yeoman for 40 shillings sold to DANIEL JONES of Ruthin[?] Denbigh Co 400 a. granted by WM PENN of Worminghurst Sussex Co esqr who purch from KING CHARLES the second now King of England being pt/o 4000 a. WM PENN sold to THOS WINN & JOHN ap JOHN on 11 Sep 1681 . . . . Wit: RICHARD DAVIS, KATHERINE EDDI, EDWARD RES, JANE PERRY, GEORGE THOMPSON. Ackn 18 Jun 1711 before NATHAN STANBURY justice of the peace. RICHARD HEATH dep recorder of deeds. (E6:pg 257)

29 May 1711. Deed. DANIEL ENGLAND of Phila marriner to extinquish the yearly ground rent & also for 20 pounds sold to GRIFFITH JONES of Phila merchant two lots of land . . . whereas on 10 Aug 1703 the sd GRIFFITH JONES conveyed unto the sd DANIEL ENGLAND a lot of land upon the bank of DE River in Phila (opposite to a front lot formerly granted to the sd GRIFFITH JONES to remove the Blew Anchor upon) 16 ft breadth 250 ft length bounded by sd GRIFFITH JONES . . . the other lot (being opposite of JAMES BOYDEN) 20 ft breadth 250 ft length bounded with Front St & the other lot of sd GRIFFITH JONES . . . paying the rent of 4 pounds 10 shillings on 1 May yearly forever . . . . Wit: JOSHUA LAWRENCE. -- Jun 1711 before WM CARTER justice of the peace. RICHARD HEATH dep recorder of deeds. (E6:pg 259)

2 Apr 1711. Deed. JOHN LEWDON late of Phila but now of Christeen[?] New Castle Co DE weaver and MARGARET his wife for 100 pounds sold to JAMES BINGHAM of Phila a piece of ground 20 1/2 ft breadth 102 ft length . . . whereas WILLIAM MARKHAM, ROBERT TURNER & JOHN GOODSON late commissioners of property by a patent dated 25 Feb 1692/3 granted unto FRANCIS RAWLE a lot of land in Phila 41 ft breadth 102 ft

length bounded by JAMES FOX & High St (Patent Book A vol 4 pg 226), and whereas the sd FRANCIS RAWLE & one NICHOLAS PEARCE of Phila weaver on 11 Jul 1693 conveyed unto the sd JOHN LEWDON a lot of ground pt/o the afsd lot 20 1/2 ft breadth 102 ft length bounded by lot of JAMES FOX but now of RALPH JACKSON, High St & residue of afsd lot now belonging to WM SNEAD decd (Book E6 vol 7 pg 109) . . . . Wit: JOSHUA LAWRENCE, JOHN SNOWDEN Junr. Ackn 19 Jun 1711 before NATHAN STANBURY justice of the peace. RICHARD HEATH dep recorder of deeds. (E6:pg 262)

2 Jun 1711. Deed. GARRET GARRET of [?] Blockley Twp Phila Co yeoman & RUANA his wife & MORTON GARRET of same place yeoman & BRIDGET his wife for 30 pounds sold to ROWLAND ELLIS Junr of Mizion Phila Co gent & ANTHONY MORRIS Junr of Phila brewer a parcel of land in Blockly Twp adj River Schuylkill, JOHN SCOOTON (SKUTTEN), GEORGE SCOTSON & sd GARRAT & MORTON . . . 50 a. and also a parcel of land adj sd GARRAT, JOHN ROBERTS & River Schuylkill, which land is the same mentioned in an award under the hand & seal of TOBY LUCK of sd co gent 10 Jan now last past and the first described tr is pt/o 150 a. granted by ANDREW WHEELER & ANNA MARIA his wife & JOHN BROWN & YOTSO his wife unto the sd GARRAT GARRAT & MORTON GARRAT 26 May now last past . . . . Wit: ISREAL PEMBERTON, JOSHUA LAWRENCE. Ackn 20 Jun 1711 before NATHAN STANBURY justice of the peace. THOMAS STORY recorder of deeds. (E6:pg 265)

11 Nat 1711. Deed. WILLIAM SLUBY of Phila merchant & SARAH his wife (she being one of the daus of NICHOLAS MOORE late of Phila Co gent decd) for 18 pounds 15 shillings by JOHN BUDD of sd city brewer (WILLIAM SLUBY by his letter of atty dated 23 Jun 1709 did impower the sd JOHN BUDD to sell his manor lands (Book D2 vol 5 pg 128)) & NICHOLAS MOORE of Mooreland Phila Co gent son & heir of the sd NICHOLAS MOORE & PRISCILLA his wife sold to DAVID WILLIAMS of the Manor of Mooreland yeoman a parcel of land adj land late of GEORGE BENSON, THOS PERRY & JOSEPH HALL . . . 66 a. . . . whereas by patent dated 7 Sep 1684 granted unto the sd NICHOLAS MOORE the father a tr of land bounded by a br of Potquipen Cr & JOHN KENT[?] . . . 9815 a. (Patent Book A vol 4 pg 210) . . . . Wit: JOHN LOBER, LAWRENCE THOMASON, JOSHUA LAWRENCE, PATRICK FLEMING. Ackn 20 Jun 1711 before NATHAN STANBURY justice of the peace. RICHARD HEATH dep recorder of deeds. (E6:pg 269)

10 Apr 1711. Deed of Mortgage. JOHN GARDNER of Blockly Twp Phila Co yeoman for 37 pounds 10 shillings sold to CEASER GUESLING of Phila silversmith a tr of land adj Beaver Run, THOS LLOYD, sd JOHN GARDNER,

River Schuylkill & THOMAS STORY . . . 20 1/2 a. of fast land & 36 a. of marsh, and also a parcel of land adj land late in the tenure of PHILIP ENGLAND . . . 8 a., and also a parcel of land adj BENJAMIN EAST & the ferry land . . . 8 a. . . . provided that if the sd JOHN GARDNER shall pay unto the sd CESAR GUESLING 37 pounds 10 shillings with interest within 2 years, then this present indenture shall cease . . . . Wit: JOHN BUDD, BENJAMIN CHAMBERS. Ackn 21 Jun 1711 before JONATHAN DICKINSON justice of the peace. THOMAS STORY recorder of deeds. 29 Nov 1714 before CHAS BROCKDEN dep recorder of deeds CAESAR GUESLING ackn that he received of JOHN GARDNER the full sum of 37 pounds 10 shillings & interest in full satisfaction of this mortgage. (E6:pg 275)

16 Feb 1710. Deed. JAMES SHATTICK of Phila Co yeoman to better enable the conveyance of the land & for 5 shillings sold to WILLIAM WOODLEY & JONATHAN WOODLEY both of same co husbandman a tr of land adj RICHD PEIRCE & residue of sd JAMES SHATTICK's land . . . 300 a. . . . for the term of 1 year . . . . Wit: ROWLAND ELLIS, RICHD HEATH, JOSHUA LAWRENCE. Recorded 24 Jul 1711. (E6:pg 278)

17 Feb 1710. Deed. JAMES SHATTICK of Phila Co yeoman for 40 pounds sold to WILLIAM WOODLY & JONATHAN WOODLY both of same co husbandman a tr of land [same as above] . . . whereas by an indenture of lease & release dated 3&4 May 1682 WM PENN of Worminghurst Sussex Co esqr proprietary & governor of PA conveyed unto SAML TAVERNER of Sunerick Ireland merchant 1000 a. (Book E6 vol 7 pg 156) & by virtue of a warrant dated 2 Sep 1700 surveyed out on 6 Nov next following unto the sd SAMUEL TAVERNER a tr of land in Sunerick Twp 500 a. pt/o the 1000 a., and whereas the sd SAMUEL TAVERNER on 23&24 Aug 1704 conveyed the 1000 a. unto the sd JAMES SHATTICK & EDWARD LANE of the sd co yeoman (Book E vol 7 pg 160) . . . and the sd EDWARD LANE died & after his decease the land accrued to the sd JAMES SHATTICK by right of survivorship . . . . Wit: ROWLAND ELLIS, RICHD HEATH, JOSHUA LAWRENCE. Recorded 25 Jul 1711. (E6:pg 279)

20 Jul 1711. Deed. EDWARD EVANS of Abington Twp Phila Co yeoman for 180 pounds sold to MORRIS MORRIS of same place yeoman a 198 3/4 a. parcel of land adj sd MORRIS MORRIS . . . whereas on 12 Oct 1696 JOSEPH PHIPPS of Abington yeoman conveyed to the sd EDWARD EVANS a 250 a. parcel of land in Abington Twp (Book E3 vol 5 pg 219) . . . . Wit: JOSHUA LAWRENCE. Ackn 28 Jul 1711 before NATHAN STANBURY justice of the peace. RICHARD HEATH dep recorder of deeds. (E6:pg 282)

3 May 1709. Deed. ROSE MOORE relict & widow of JAMES MOORE decd of Phila Co for 21 shillings sold to BENJAMIN CHAMBERS of Phila Co yeoman a bank lot on DE River n side of Phila bounded by BENJAMIN CHAMBERS, NATHANIEL POOLE & Front St . . . in Mar 1689/90 surveyed & laid out to the afsd JAMES MOORE . . . . Wit: WM BARTRAM, ROBERT POUND, NATHANIEL SYKES, JOHN MOORE, STEPHEN JACKSON. Ackn 17 Sep 1711 before WILLIAM CARTER esqr mayor of Phila & justice. RICHARD HEATH dep recorder of deeds. (E6:pg 285)

14 Mar 1711. Deed. ISAAC VAN SINTERN (SINTREN) (SINTON) of Germantown Phila Co weaver & NELTEI his wife & REINIER TISEN (TISSON) (TISON) (TISSEN) of Abington Phila Co yeoman for 15 pounds sold to CONRAD RUTTERS of Germantown yeoman two trs of land . . . whereas on 27 Mar 1708 the sd REINIER TISEN conveyed unto the sd ISAAC VAN SINTERN a 18 3/4 a. tr of land in the side land of Germantown between the inhabited pt/o the sd town & land of JAMES POTS (Book E5 vol 7 pg 78), and on 27 Mar 1708 the sd ISAAC VAN SINTERN conveyed unto the sd REINIER TISEN the afsd tr to be void upon payment of a sum of money (Book E5 vol 7 pg 80), and the sum was not paid . . . . Wit: EDMOND CARTLIDGE, JOSHUA LAWRENCE. Ackn 17 Sep 1711 before EDWARD FARMAR justice of the peace. RICHARD HEATH dep recorder of deeds. (E6:pg 287)

15 Mar 1711. Deed of Mortgage. CONRAD RUTTERS of Germantown Phila Co yeoman & ANN his wife for 15 pounds sold to REINIER TISON (TISSON) of Abbington Phila Co yeoman two parcels of land in Germantown adj land late of sd REINIER TISON but now of ISAAC VAN SINTERN, SAML POWELL & land late of ABRAHAM TUNIS now of JACOB GAETSCHALT . . . 29 2/3 a. . . . provided that if the sd CONRAD RUTTERS pay unto the sd REINIER TISON 19 pounds 16 shillings, that is 1 pound 4 shillings on 15 Mar next ensueing, 1 pound 4 shillings on 15 Mar 1712, 1 pound 4 shillings on 15 Mar 1713 & 16 pounds 4 shillings residue on 15 Mar 1714, then this present indenture shall cease . . . . Wit: EDMOND CARTLIDGE, JOSHUA LAWRENCE. Ackn 17 Sep 1711 before EDWARD FARMAR justice of the peace. RICHARD HEATH dep recorder of deeds. 14 Mar 1714 before CHAS BROCKDEN dep recorder of deeds REINIER TISEN ackn that he had received of CONRAD RUTTERS 19 pounds 16 shillings in full satisfaction of the mortgage. (E6:pg 289)

22 Sep 1711. Deed. JOHN IRONMONGER (IRONMUNGER) & SARAH his wife of Abington Twp Phila Co yeoman for 230 pounds sold to JAMES HAINES of same place carpenter a piece of land in Abbington Twp adj JOHN HUNTSMAN, THOMAS HALLOWELL & JOSEPH WOOD . . . 200 a. pt/o

500 a. granted unto THOMAS HOLMES late surveyor general by patent dated 29 Mar 1687, the sd THOMAS HOLMES conveyed the sd 200 a. unto EDMOND MCVEAGH, and the other 1/2 to ISAAC PAGE 16 Mar 1688 (Book E2 vol 5 pg 56&57) . . . and the sd EDMOND MCVEAGH conveyed the 200 a. unto the sd JOHN IRONMONGER 25 Jan 1695/6 . . . . Wit: EDMUND MCVEAGH, HENRY STRIKE. Ackn 24 Sep 1711 before WM CARTER justice of the peace. RICHARD HEATH dep recorder of deeds. (E6:pg 291)

1 Jun 1691. Deed. PETER BAYNTON (BAYTON) of New Castle Co PA gent with consent of REBECCA (relict & executors of WM STANLY son of WM STANLY both of Phila Co decd) now his wife for 112 pounds 10 shillings sold to JOHN JONES of Phila merchant a lot of land in Phila adj JOSEPH FISHER now ROBERT TURNER's lot, DE Front St, EDWARD DOUBTIN[?] & Second St 46 1/2 ft breadth 396 ft length & also a lot 76 1/2 ft breadth 350 ft length bounded by sd ROBERT TURNER, River DE & THOMAS TRESSE . . . now in the possession of sd PETER BAYNTON by virtue of a patent to the sd WM STANLY decd 5 Jul 1684, & by the sd WILLIAM STANLY his son conveyed unto THOMAS FAIRMAN 3 Dec 1688, and WILLIAM STANLY the son did quit claim all his right in the bank front lot (Book E vol 5 pg 104&105) & the sd THOMAS FAIRMAN & ELIZA his wife conveyed the same unto the sd PETER BAYNTON 3 May 1690 . . . and the back lot now in possession of sd PETER BAYNTON by virtue of a patent granted by WILLIAM MARKHAM, ROBERT TURNER, JOHN GOODSON & SAMUEL CARPENTER commissioners dated 16 Dec 1689 unto the sd PETER BAYNTON . . . against JOHN TAYLOR of Mary [sic] & DOROTHEA his wife, against THOMAS HOOTEN of Phila & ELIZA his wife & all the heirs of the sd WILLIAM STANLY father of the sd WILLIAM STANLY son . . . . Wit: JNO TEST, JEREMIAH ELFRETH, PAT ROBINSON. Ackn 7 Jun 1692. WILLIAM MARKHAM clerk. Recorded 15 Oct 1711. (E6:pg 294)

25 Sep 1711. Deed. BENJAMIN CHAMBERS of Kinsess Twp Phila Co yeoman for 5 shillings sold to STEPHEN JACKSON of Phila merchant a bank lot n side of Phila 25 ft breadth 250 ft length bounded by lot formerly of sd BENJAMIN CHAMBERS, DE River, NATHL POOL & Front St, being lately purch from ROSE MOORE relict and widow of JAMES MOORE formerly of Phila decd . . . . Wit: CASPER KLEINHOFF. DAVOD BREINTNALL. Ackn 15 Oct 1711 before NATHAN STANBURY justice of the peace. THOMAS STORY recorder of deeds. (E6:pg 297)

17 Jul 1711. Letter of Atty. THOMAS WILSON (WILLSON) of Sanernemerran Kings Co farmer hath appointed MARK CARTINGTON late of Ballyleaken Kings Co farmer to be his atty to enter & take possession of

1000 a. in PA & also a lot in Phila in the Liberty which were purch about 17 years since by the sd THOMAS WILSON of CHARLES HARTFORD of Bristol merchant who purch the same of WILLIAM PENN . . . and doth give unto the sd MARK CARLINGTON 125 a. pt/o the 1000 a. . . . . Wit: THOMAS MEREFIELD & ENOCH WHITLEY my servants, SAML WILKINSON, AMOS STRETTELL. Ackn 17 Jul 1711 before THOMAS SISSON notary public at Dublin. Recorded 10 Oct 1711. (E6:pg 299)

10 Jul 1711. Deed of Mortgage. JOHN FUNK lately an inhabitant of Switzerland but now of PA yeoman for 37 pounds 2 shillings sold to WILLIAM PENN esqr proprietary & governor of PA a tr of land in Streasburg Chester Co adj MARTIN KINDEY (KINDELY) & JACOB MILLER . . . 530 a. . . . provided that if the sd JOHN FUNK shall pay unto the sd WILLIAM PENN 54 pounds 18 shillings 1 1/2 penny, that is 2 pounds 19 shillings 4 pence farthing on 22 Oct 1712, 2 pounds 19 shillings 4 pence farthing on 22 Oct 1713, 2 pounds 19 shillings 4 pence farthing on 22 Oct 1714, 2 pounds 19 shillings 4 pence farthing on 22 Oct 1715, 2 pounds 19 shillings 4 pence farthing on 22 Oct 1716 & 40 pounds 1 shilling 4 pence farthing residue on 22 Oct 1717 . . . then this present indenture shall cease . . . . Wit: CASPER HOODT, JOSHUA LAWRENCE. Ackn 29 Oct 1711 before EDWARD SHIPPEN justice of the peace. THOMAS STORY recorder of deeds. 26 Sep -- before CHARLES BROCKDON . . . [illegible] . . . JAMES STEEL [?] general of the proprietary & did ackn that he had received of JOHN FUNK full satisfaction of all the money in full discharge of the mortgage. (E6:pg 300)

10 Jul 1711. Deed of Mortgage. CHRISTIAN HEIR lately an inhabitant of Switzerland but now of PA yeoman for 37 pounds 2 shillings sold to WILLIAM PENN esqr proprietary & governor of PA a tr of land in Strasburg Twp Chester Co adj MARTIN MELIN & MARTIN KINDEY . . . 530 a. . . . provided that if the sd CHRISTIAN HEIR shall pay unto the sd WILLIAM PENN 54 pounds 18 shillings 1 1/2 penny, that is 2 pounds 19 shillings 4 pence farthing on 22 Oct 1712, 2 pounds 19 shillings 4 pence farthing on 22 Oct 1713, 2 pounds 19 shillings 4 pence on 22 Oct 1714, 2 pounds 19 shillings 4 pence farthing 22 Oct 1715, 2 pounds 19 shillings 4 pence farthing on 22 Oct 1716 & 40 pounds 1 shilling 4 pence farthing residue on 22 Oct 1717 . . . then this present indenture shall cease . . . . Wit: CASPER HOODT, JOSHUA LAWRENCE. Ackn 29 Oct 1711 before EDWARD SHIPPEN justice of the peace. THOMAS STORY recorder of deeds. (E6:pg 302)

10 Jul 1711. Deed of Mortgage. STOPHEL FRANCISCUS late an inhabitant of Switzerland but now of PA yeoman for 37 pounds 2 shillings sold to WILLIAM PENN esqr proprietary & governor of PA a tr of land in Strasburg Twp Chester Co adj JOHN FUNK, JACOB MILLER, WENDEL BOWMAN

& JOHN RUDOLPH BUNDELY . . . 530 a. . . . provided that if the sd STOPHEL FRANCISCUS shall pay unto the sd WILLIAM PENN 54 pounds 18 shillings 1 1/2 penny, that is 2 pounds 19 shillings 4 pence farthing on 22 Oct 1712, 2 pounds 19 shillings 4 pence farthing on 22 Oct 1713, 2 pounds 19 shillings 4 pence farthing on 22 Oct 1714, 2 pounds 19 shilings 4 pence farthing on 22 Oct 1715, 2 pounds 19 shilings 4 pence farthing on 22 Oct 1716 & 40 pounds 1 shilling 4 pence residue on 22 Oct 1717 . . . then this present indenture shall cease . . . . Wit: CASPER HOODT, JOSHUA LAWRENCE. Ackn 29 Oct 1711 before EDWARD SHIPPEN justice of the peace. THOMAS STORY recorder of deeds. (E6:pg 305)

13 Oct 1711. Deed. SAMUEL PRESTON of Phila merchant & CLEMENT PLUNSTED of same place merchant devisees in trust in the will of JOHN JONES Senr late of sd city merchant decd for 212 pounds 10 shillings sold to SAMUEL TAYLOR of sd city boulter a lot of land . . . whereas JAMES CLAYPOOL & ROBERT TURNER commissioners by a patent dated 14 Apr 1686 did grant unto the sd JOHN JONES & one JOHN JENNINGS decd a lot of land in Phila on Second St 51 ft breadth 396 ft length adj Mulberry St (Patent Book A pg 121), and whereas on 4 May 1686 the sd JOHN JONES conveyed unto the sd JOHN JENNINGS 1/2 of the afsd lot (Book E vol 5 pg 222) . . . and the sd JOHN JENNINGS being seized of 1/2 of the lot made his will . . . "I do devise to JOHN JONES my brother all my money, negroes, houses, lands . . . in Barbadoes, England or elsewhere in all the world . . ." and made sd JOHN JONES executor . . . will proved 28 Jan 1688/9 . . . and the sd JOHN JONES being seized of the land made his will dated 28 Apr 1708 . . . "I give unto SAMUEL PRESTON & CLEMENT PLUNSTED all my messuage lot I now dwell in between Second & Third St in Phila . . . & to the survivor of them upon special trust to sell the messuage & land, the money to pay my just debts" . . . . Wit: JOHN SWIFT, THOMAS BROADGATE. SAMUEL PRESTON & CLEMENT PLUNSTED received 212 pounds 10 shillings of SAMUEL TAYLOR. Wit: JOSEPH SHIPPEN, SAML CARPENTER Junr. Ackn 2 Nov 1711 before NATHAN STANBURY justice of the peace. THOMAS STORY recorder of deeds. (E6:pg 307)

23 Aug 1711. Deed. JOHN GILBERT of Phila merchant for love & affection & 5 pounds sold unto my son JOSEPH GILBERT of Bibery Twp Phila Co yeoman a messuage & 20 ft lot of ground . . . whereas EDWARD SMOUT of sd city on 24 Aug 1704 conveyed unto WILLIAM HALL of sd city chysurgeon a water lot on three parcels under the bank of DE in Phila next to sd EDWARD SMOUT's other ground, 50 ft breadth extending to the River DE granted by ROBERT TURNER unto one FRANCIS JARVIS for 54 years from 24 Aug 1694, and the sd FRANCIS JARVIS sold & assigned unto one SUSANAH ELTON by whose executors the same was conveyed unto the sd

EDWARD SMOUT, & whereas the sd WILLIAM HALL on 5 Mar 1707/8 sold unto the sd JOHN GILBERT a new brick messuage pt/o the sd water lot adj King St . . . for the term of the first granted lease paying the rent unto the sd ROBERT TURNER . . . . Wit: ELIAS JONES, RICHD HARDING, JOHN CADWALADER. Ackn 13 Nov 1711 before NATHAN STANBURY justice of the peace. THOMAS STORY recorder of deeds. (E6:pg 311)

25 Nov 1709. Deed of Lease. THOMAS CALLOWHILL (CADWALADER) of Bristol in Kingdom of Great Britain haberdasher & JAMES LOGAN of Phila gent farm let unto THOMAS TRESSE of Phila ironmonger a strip of land from 24 Jun last past during the term of 33 years paying the rent of 20 shillings 24 Jun & 25 Dec yearly (in equal portions) . . . whereas the sd THOMAS CALLOWHILL by virtue of a patent dated 3 Sep 1706 (Patent Book A vol 3 pg 340) standeth seized in a small strip of ground in Phila 8 ft breadth 396 ft length bounded by sd CALLOWHILL, DE Front St, FRANCIS CHADD & Second St which strip was laid out unto the sd THOMAS CALLOWHILL for his disappointment & loss sustained by being deprived of the bank lot lying before his great lot which was appurtenant to his original purch of 5500 a., and whereas the sd THOMAS CALLOWHILL by his letter of atty dated 29 Jan 1705 did appoint the sd JAMES LOGAN his atty impowering him to demand of the commissioners all or any pt/o the 5500 a. for the use of the sd THOMAS CALLOWHILL . . . . Wit: RICHARD HEATH, JOHN LOTCHER. Ackn 19 Nov 1711 before WILLIAM CARTER justice of the peace. THOMAS STORY recorder of deeds. (E6:pg 313)

4 May 1711. Deed. NICHOLAS MOORE of Phila Co yeoman (the only surviving son & heir of NICHOLAS MOORE late of same place doctor in physic decd) & PRISCILLA his wife for 25 pounds sold to JOHN WALTERS of sd co husbandman a tr of land pt/o a tr called "Mooreland Manor" bounded by Pennypack Cr, THOMAS WOODS & ANTHONY YERKAS . . . 68 a. . . . . Wit: ROWLAND HUGH, JOSHUA LAWRENCE, JOHN BUDD. Ackn 19 Nov 1711 before NATHAN STANBURY justice of the peace. THOMAS STORY recorder of deeds. (E6:pg 316)

10 Nov 1711. Deed. EDWARD JAMES of Phila bricklayer and ANN his wife for 65 pounds sold to WILLIAM SINGARD of Phila blacksmith a parcel of land n side of Chestnut St in Phila 40 ft breadth 178 ft length bounded by High St, lot formerly of HENRY PATRICK but now of ABEL NOBLE & house & lot formerly of WILLIAM NICHOLAS but now of HENRY STEPHENS . . . . Wit: WILLIAM GARRET, JOSHUA LAWRENCE. Ackn 20 Nov 1711 before WILLIAM CARTER justice of the peace. THOMAS STORY recorder of deeds. (E6:pg 318)

10 Nov 1711. Deed of Release. JOSEPH FISHER Junr of Dublin Twp Phila Co yeoman for 5 shillings and for the consideration received by JOSEPH FISHER Senr release unto FRANCIS SEARL of Bucks Co yeoman a tr of land ... whereas THOMAS TREEWOOD of Dublin yeoman decd became in his life time seized in a tr of land adj CORNELIUS STURGES, JOSEPH KNIGHT, [?] CRISPAIN & land formerly belonging to THOMAS HOLME ... 200 a., and the sd THOMAS TREEWOOD being so seized made his will dated 16 Dec 1696 and did "devise 1/2 of the remainder pt/o my estate unto JOSEPH FISHER Junr & the other 1/2 of my estate unto MARY & MARTHA FISHER" and did appoint JOSEPH FISHER the elder sole executor ... and the sd MARY & MARTHA FISHER afterwards died intestate without issue whose 1/2 descended to the sd JOSEPH FISHER the younger their only brother & heir, and whereas on 1 Nov 1697 the sd JOSEPH FISHER the elder executor of sd THOMAS TERWOOD decd conveyed unto the sd FRANCES SEARL & JOHN CARVER of Phila Co malster the afsd tr of land (Book E vol 5 pg 101), and whereas by one indenture of partition dated 5 Jun 1700 the sd FRANCES SEARL & JOHN CARVER did make division of the afsd 200 a. .... Wit: WILLIAM GARRATT, JOSHUA LAWRENCE. Ackn 22 Nov 1711 before WILLIAM CARTER justice of the peace. THOMAS STORY recorder of deeds. (E6:pg 321)

20 Nov 1711. Deed of Mortgage. HENRY TREGENY of Passyunk Phila Co mariner & ELIZABETH his wife for 36 pounds 10 shillings sold to HENRY STEVENS of Phila mariner & MARTHA his wife a tr of land adj River Schuylkill, MARTHA COCK, JOSEPH RIELE, HENRY BADROK & PETER COCK's widow ... 39 a. ... provided that if the sd HENRY TREGENY shall pay unto the sd HENRY STEVENS or MARTHA his wife 37 pounds 19 shillings 2 pence before 20 May next ensueing, then this indenture shall cease .... Wit: CHAS BROCKDEN, JOSHUA LAWRENCE. Ackn 29 Nov 1711 before NATHAN STANBURY justice of the peace. THOMAS STORY recorder of deeds. 26 -- -- HENRY STEVENS & MARTHA his wife ackn before CHAS BROCKDEN that they received from HENRY TREGENY 37 pounds 19 shillings 2 pence in full satisfaction in discharge of the mortgage. (E6:pg 324)

9 Feb 1710. Deed. GILES (GYLES) KNIGHT of Byberry Phila Co weaver and MARY his wife for 10 shillings sold to JOSEPH GILBERT of sd twp yeoman a parcel of land in Byberry Twp adj other land of sd GILES KNIGHT & Potquessink Cr ... 100 a. sold by JOHN GILBERT father of the sd JOSEPH unto JOHN his brother & by the sd JOHN GILBERT Junr back to the sd JOHN GILBERT the elder & by him on 1 Sep 1700 sold unto sd GILES KNIGHT .... Wit: RICHARD MOORE, JONATHAN LEVEZEN, RICHARD SCOTT. Ackn 1 Dec 1711 before NATHAN STANBURY justice of the peace. THOMAS STORY recorder of deeds. (E6:pg 326)

10 Feb 1710. Deed. GILES KNIGHT of Byberry Phila Co weaver & MARY his wife for 71 pounds 5 shillings sold to JOSEPH GILBERT of sd twp yeoman a 100 a. tr of land . . . whereas WILLIAM MARKHAM & JOHN GOODSON commissioners by patent dated 2 Jul 1688 did grant unto THOMAS HOLME (surveyor general of PA) in right of SAMUEL CLARIDGE original purchaser of 5000 a., a parcel of land adj Potquessink Cr & EDWARD GOODING . . . 600 a. . . . and whereas the sd THOMAS HOLME on 2 Jun 1685 sold unto NICHOLAS REDOUT of Phila the 600 a. (Book E vol 2 pg 70), and SILAS CRISPIN of sd co executor of the will of the sd THOMAS HOLME on 4 Jun 1695 confirmed unto the sd NICHOLAS REDOUT, and the sd NICHOLAS REDOUT on 19 Feb 1695 conveyed the same unto JOHN GILBERT of Potquesink Cr Bucks Co husbandman (Book E3 vol 5 pg 255), and the sd JOHN GILBERT on 4 Jun 1696 conveyed unto JOHN GILBERT Junr son of the sd JOHN GILBERT 100 a. pt/o the 600 a., and the sd JOHN GILBERT Junr on 20 Oct 1700 conveyed the 100 a. unto the sd JOHN GILBERT the elder, and the sd JOHN GILBERT the elder on 1 Sep 1700 conveyed the same unto the sd GILES KNIGHT . . . . Wit: RICHARD MOORE, JONATHAN LIVEREY, RICHARD SCOTT. Ackn 1 Dec 1711 before NATHAN STANBURY justice of the peace. THOMAS STORY recorder of deeds. (E6:pg 328)

16 Mar 1710. Deed of Lease. SOLOMON CRESSON of Phila turner & ANN his wife for 10 shillings leased unto THOMAS STORY of sd city gent a 35 a. parcel of land in Passynick Twp adj Hollanders Cr, PHILIP RICHARDS, Eagle Nest Cr, land late in tenure of JOHN JONES, land late in tenure of SAMUEL JOHNSON by him sold to sd THOMAS STORY & DE River . . . during the term of 1 year . . . . Wit: RICHARD WALLN, JOHN LUCK. Ackn 26 Jun 1712 before NATHAN STANBURY justice of the peace. THOMAS STORY recorder of deeds. (E6:pg 232)

17 Mar 1710. Deed. SOLOMON CRESSON of Phila turner & ANN his wife for 11 pounds 5 shillings sold to THOMAS STORY of sd city gent a 35 a. tr of land . . . whereas by patent dated 2 May 1694, WILLIAM MARKHAM, ROBERT TURNER & JOHN GOODSON commissioners of property granted unto LACEY COCK of Passynick gent a parcel of swamp in Passynick Twp adj Myamenson land, River DE & River Schoolkill . . . 875 a. (besides the several trs of mowing meadow, Leitbrick Island & small piece of Rankars Hook) (Patent Book A vol 1 pg 328) . . . and the sd LACY COCK (by the name of LAWRENCE COCK) on 3 May 1694 conveyed 100 a. pt/o the 875 a. unto SAMUEL ATKINS of Phila glover, and the sd SAMUEL ATKINS on 16&17 May next following conveyed the 100 a. unto WM SOUTHBE of Phila boatbuilder, and the sd WM SOUTHBE on 18 Nov 1706 (Book E3 vol 6 pg 44) conveyed 35 a. pt/o the 100 a. unto the sd SOLOMON CRESSON

bounded by DE River, land late of PHILIP RICHARDS, Hollanders Cr, DANIEL HODGSON, land late of JOHN JONES & land late of SAMUEL JOHNSON [see above] .... Wit: RICHARD WALLN, JOHN LUCK. Ackn 26 Jun 1712 before NATHAN STANBURY justice of the peace. THOMAS STORY recorder of deeds. (E6:pg 236)

7 Dec 1711. Deed. GEORGE GREY of Phila merchant for 80 pounds sold to ANTHONY MORRIS of sd city merchant a tr of land near the Liberty of Phila adj Germantwp, DIRECK SIPMAN & JOHN MOORE ... 80 a. and also a 4 a. parcel of land adj and also 36 a. pt/o Germantown lot .... Wit: CHAS BROCKDEN, JOSHUA LAWRENCE. Ackn 13 Dec 1711 before SAMUEL PRESTON justice of the peace. THOMAS STORY recorder of deeds. (E6:pg 341)

3 Feb 1709. Deed. SAMUEL RICHARDSON of Phila Co merchant for 150 pounds sold to WILLIAM HUDSON of Phila tanor a 1160 a. tr of land ... by virtue of a patent dated 19 Oct 1703 (Patent Book A vol 2 pg 595) & several good conveyances the sd SAMUEL RICHARDSON became seized in a 1160 a. tr of land in Willis Town Chester Co adj the Society lands, WM GARRIT, land formerly surveyed to GRIFFITH JONES & RICHD SNEAD .... Wit: JOHN ROADS, RICHD HEATH, DAVID LLOYD, JOSHUA LAWRENCE. Ackn 13 Dec 1711 before ANTHONY MORRIS justice of the peace. THOMAS STORY recorder of deeds. (E6:pg 344)

16 Nov 1711. Deed. EDWARD BEESON of New Castle Co yeoman & ELIZABETH his wife for 7 pounds sold to THOMAS BATSON of Phila carpenter several lots of land in Phila ... whereas by an indenture of lease & release dated 17&18 Oct 1681 WILLIAM PENN of Worminghurst Sussex Co esqr conveyed unto MARY PENNINGTON (now w/o DANIEL WHARLY of Giles Chasfont Bucks Co citizen & glover of London) 2250 a., and whereas by other indenture of lease & release dated 10&11 Mar 1703 the sd DANIEL WHARLY & MARY his wife conveyed unto the sd EDWARD BEESON 1250 a. . . . . Wit: PETER WISHART, RICHD MOORE, JOSHUA LAWRENCE. Ackn 13 Dec 1711 before EDWARD SHIPPEN justice of the peace. THOMAS STORY recorder of deeds. (E6:pg 347)

13 Sep 1711. Deed. JAMES SHATTICK (SHATTOCK) of Phila Co yeoman for 30 pounds sold to PETER BELLAR of same co husbandman & ALICE his wife 200 a. ... whereas by indentures of lease & release dated 3&4 May 1682 WILLIAM PENN of Worminghurst Sussex Co esqr proprietary & governor of PA conveyed unto RICHARD PEARCE of Limerick, Ireland apothecary 1000 a., and the sd RICHARD PEARCE afterwards died seized of the 1000 a. & the land descended to THOMAS PEARCE his son & heir, and the sd

THOMAS PEARCE by his indentures of lease & release dated 23&24 Aug 1704 conveyed the 1000 a. unto the sd JAMES SHATTICK & EDWARD LANE of Phila yeoman (Book E6 vol 7 pg 160) . . . the sd EDWARD died & the land did wholy accrue to the sd JAMES SHATTICK by right of survivorship, and by virtue of a warrant dated 26 Apr 1708 there was surveyed & laid out unto the sd JAMES SHATTICK a 200 a. tr of land adj DERICK RANSBURG, THOMAS FAIRMAN & PETER WENT . . . . Wit: EDMOND CARTLIDGE, JOSHUA LAWRENCE. Ackn 14 Dec 1711 before EDWARD FARMER justice of the peace. RICHARD HEATH dep recorder of deeds. (E6:pg 349)

1 Jul 1710. Deed. JOSEPH ROADS (RHOADS) (ROADES) of Chester Co cordwiner for 4 pounds sold to PHILIP HOWELL of Phila taylor a lot of land 51 ft breadth 306 ft length bounded by Second St & THOMAS STORY . . . whereas by commissioners EDWARD SHIPPEN, THOMAS STORY & JAMES LOGAN there was granted unto the sd JOSEPH ROADS a warrant dated 29 Dec 1702 directed to DAVID POWELL surveyor requiring him to survey & lay out a 500 a. lot of land in sd city which one THOMAS WHITLY purch of the proprietary & sold to JOHN ROADS late father of the sd JOSEPH ROADS, surveyed 9 Jun 1709 & laid out the sd lot next adj to sd THOMAS STORY w side of Second St from DE Bank . . . . Wit: FRANCIS COOKE, ADAM ROADS. Ackn 14 Dec 1711 before ANTHONY MORRIS justice of the peace. THOMAS STORY recorder of deeds. (E6:pg 352)

21 Dec 1711. Deed. WILLIAM HEARN of Phila whitesmith & SARAH his wife for 3 pounds sold to THOMAS STORY of sd city gent a piece of ground near Phila 50 ft breadth 100 ft length bounded by PETER LONG & Vine St . . . and also a parcel of ground in Phila bounded by lot of sd THOMAS STORY now in the occupation of Col[?] ROBERT QUARY, Second St & Third St 50 ft breadth 196 ft length . . . . Wit: CHAS BROCKDEN, JOSHUA LAWRENCE. Ackn 25 Dec 1711 before EDWARD SHIPPEN justice of the peace. THOMAS STORY recorder of deeds. (E6:pg 354)

10 Jul 1711. Deed of Mortgage. JACOB MILLER lately of Switzerland but now of PA yeoman for 70 pounds sold to WILLIAM PENN esqr proprietary & governor of PA a 1000 a. tr of land in Strasburg Twp Chester Co adj JOHN FUNK, WENDEL BOWMAN & STOPHEL FRANCISCUS . . . provided that if sd JACOB MILLER pay unto the sd WILLIAM PENN 103 pounds 12 shillings, that is 5 pounds 12 shillings on 22 Oct 1712, 5 pounds 12 shillings on 22 Oct 1713, 5 pounds 12 shillings on 22 Oct 1714, 5 pounds 12 shillings on 22 Oct 1715, 5 pounds 12 shillings on 22 Oct 1716 & 75 pounds 12 shillings residue on 22 Oct 1717 . . . then this present indenture shall cease . . . . Wit: DANIEL ENGLAND, JOSHUA LAWRENCE. Ackn 25 Dec 1711

before EDWARD SHIPPEN justice of the peace. THOMAS STORY recorder of deeds. 31 Dec 1720 before CHAS BROCKDEN recorder of deeds, JAMES STEEL proprietary receiver general ackn that he had received of JACOB MILLER on behalf of the proprietary all the mortgage monies & interest in discharge of the mortgage. (E6:pg 357)

20 Dec 1711. Deed. SAMUEL SHOURDS (alias SICERTS) late of Germantown Phila Co cooper (but now of Phila) & SARAH his wife for 30 pounds sold to EDWARD HADFIELD (HATFIELD) one of the sons of ADAM HADFIELD of Germantown yeoman a lot of land 3 perches breadth 45 perches length bounded by NELTJEN[?] OP PEN GRAEFF & JOSEPH SHIPPEN . . . . Wit: RICHARD WALLN, CHAS BROCKDEN, JOSHUA LAWRENCE. Ackn 26 Dec 1711 before WILLIAM CARTER justice of the peace. THOMAS STORY recorder of deeds. (E6:pg 359)

2 May 1711. Deed. WILLIAM CARTER of Phila blockmaker & CATHERINE his wife & JOSEPH WELLS of Passyunk Phila Co yeoman son & heir of EDWARD WELLS decd for 180 pounds paid to WILLIAM CARTER & 5 shillings paid to JOSEPH WELLS sold to JAMES LOWNES of Chester yeoman three trs of land . . . one 101 a. tr bounded by lot late of MATHIAS HOLSTEN now in the tenure of THEODORUS LORD, THOMAS MASTERS, Moyaminsing line, land late of ANTHONY MORRIS & PETER COCK, pt/o a farm MOUNTS COCK conveyed unto the sd WILLIAM CARTER on 27 Nov 1693 in Passyunck late in possession of the sd EDWARD WELLS . . . another 140 a. tr of swamp in Passyunk bounded by River DE & Hollanders Cr which on 10 Jun 1706 PETER COCK son & heir of LASSIE COCK decd with his mother MARTHA COCK & others conveyed unto the sd WILLIAM CARTER, and another 5 a. tr in Passyunck adj HENRY BADCOK which on 1 May 1691 JOHN COCK conveyed unto the sd WILLIAM CARTER . . . and the sd WILLIAM CARTER being seized of the lands sold but not conveyed unto the sd EDWARD WELLS in his life time . . . . Wit: WILLIAM HUDSON, JOSHUA LAWRENCE. Ackn 29 Dec 1711 before NATHAN STANBURY justice of the peace. THOMAS STORY recorder of deeds. (E6:pg 362)

10 Mar 1709. Deed. JOSEPH TAYLOR of Phila cordwinder sold to PENTECOST TEAGUE of same city merchant a piece of ground late in the possession of HENRY PRESTON adj Second St, DE River, High St, THOMAS COATS, RALPH JACKSON & JOHN HAWARD 20 ft breadth 50 ft depth . . . granted in part of a High St lot by patent dated 4 Aug 1684 (Patent Book A pg 21) unto ARTHUR COCK and by him conveyed to the sd JOSEPH TAYLOR 1 Jun 1697 . . . saving unto the sd THOMAS COATS all the right he has to a wall which the sd THOMAS COATS (COATES) built . . . .

Wit: SAMUEL RICHARDSON, DAVID LLOYD, JOSHUA LAWRENCE. Ackn 8 Jan 1711 before ANTHONY MORRIS justice of the peace. THOMAS STORY recorder of deeds. (E6:pg 367)

24 Jan 1711. Deed. THOMAS TRESSE of Phila ironmonger for 16 pounds 10 shillings sold to NATHANIEL POOLE of same place shipwright a lot of land in Phila 40 ft breadth 150 ft length bounded by JOHN JONES, River DE, THOMAS MAILE & Front St . . . & also a lot in Phila 25 ft breadth 250 ft length bounded by WILLIAM HARWOOD & JAMES MAILE . . . . Wit: JACOB SEVERNY, JOSHUA LAWRENCE. Ackn 25 Jan 1711 before WILLIAM CARTER justice of the peace. THOMAS STORY recorder of deeds. (E6:pg 370)

1 Jan 1711. Deed. THOMAS STORY of Phila gent for 10 shillings sold to ISREAL PEMBERTON of sd city merchant 27 a. of Liberty land & 768 a. & 1000 a. . . . whereas WILLIAM PENN proprietary & governor of PA by lease & release dated 26&27 Sep 1681 did grant unto RICHARD SNEAD (SNEADE) of Bristol, Kingdom of Great Britain merchant 1500 a., and the sd WILLIAM PENN by indentures dated 9&10 Nov 1703 granted by patent unto the sd RICHARD SNEAD 858 a. pt/o the 1500 a. into two trs, the one on Skuylkill the other in Coshan in the Welch Tr (Patent Book A vol 4 pg 109), and the sd RICHARD SNEAD on 13 Aug 1709 sold unto the sd THOMAS STORY the 1500 a. (Book E[?] vol 8 pg 57) . . . by virtue of a warrant dated 30 Nov 1708 there was laid out & resurveyed 26 Mar 1711 in right of the sd RICHARD SNEAD 27 a. pt/o the 1500 a. unto sd THOMAS STORY in the Northern Liberties of Phila adj EDWARD LUFF, JACOB SHUMAKER & HANS NEUS . . . by virtue of one other warrant dated 29 Nov 1708 there was laid out & surveyed 1 Dec 1710 in right of the sd RICHARD SNEAD 768 a. pt/o the 1500 a. unto the sd THOMAS STORY near Perquea Cr in Chester Co adj JOHN RUDOLPH BUNDELY . . . and whereas WILLIAM PENN by patent dated 8 Apr 1700 granted unto the sd THOMAS STORY 1000 a. adj the Mannor of Highlands & River DE (Patent Book A vol -- pg 268) . . . . Wit: CLEMENT PLUMSTED, CHAS READ. Ackn 25 Apr 1712 before WILLIAM CARTER justice of the peace. CHARLES BROCKDEN dep recorder of deeds. (E6:pg 373)

17 Dec 1711. Deed. ISREAL PEMBERTON of Phila merchant in pursuance of a special trust & discharge of the same & 10 shllings sold to THOMAS STORY of sd city gent three trs of land [same as above] . . . whereas the sd THOMAS STORY on 1 Jan last past sold to ISREAL PEMBERTON three trs of land [see above] that the sd ISREAL PEMBERTON might be inabled to accept a grant & confirmation of the lands by patent which sd patent was granted to be to the only use & behoof of the sd THOMAS STORY & upon

special trust that the sd ISREAL PEMBERTON would reconvey the lands unto the sd THOMAS STORY . . . . Wit: CLEMENT PLUMSTED, CHARLES READ. Ackn 26 Apr 1712 before WILLIAM CARTER justice of the peace. CHARLES BROCKDEN dep recorder of deeds. (E6:pg 377)

26 Mar 1713. Deed. MARTHA COCK of Passyunk Phila Co widow relict & sole executrix of the will of LAWRENCE COCK (also LACY COCK) late of same place gent decd for 5 pounds sold to THOMAS STORY of Phila gent pt/o a parcel of land in Passyunk Twp bounded by land of sd THOMAS STORY (late of PHILIP RICHARDS), River DE, land of JAMES LOWNE (late of WILLIAM CARTER) & Hollander Cr . . . whereas LAWRENCE COCK in his life time by virtue of a patent granted by WILLIAM MARKHAM, ROBERT TURNER & JOHN GOODSON late commissioners dated 2 May 1694 (Patent Book A 1 pg 328) became seized in 875 a. and being so seized made his will dated 1 Oct 1699 empowering MARTHA his executrix to sell his lands for payment of his debts . . . . Wit: PETER CHAMBERLIN, JOHN MORRIS. Ackn 13 Apr 1712 before ANTHONY MORRIS justice of the peace. CHARLES BROCKDEN dep recorder of deeds. (E6:pg 381)

13 Oct 1711. Deed. BENJAMIN BANKSON of Myamenson Phila Co yeoman & CATHERINE (KATHERINE) his wife, ANDREW BANKSON of Potquessink Bucks Co yeoman & GERTRUDE his wife, JOHN BANKSON of Passyunck Phila Co yeoman & HELEN his wife, JACOB BANKSON of Passyunck yeoman, DANIEL BANKSON of Phila & JOSEPH BANKSON of Phila carpenter (all sons of ANDREW BANKSON late of Passyunk yeoman decd) for 15 pounds sold unto THOMAS OKLEY of Phila feltmaker 500 a. . . . whereas WILLIAM PENN proprietary & governor of PA by his present commissioners EDWARD SHIPPEN, GRIFFITH ORVEY & JAMES LOGAN granted by patent dated 11 Jun 1705 unto the sd ANDREW BANKSON the father a 500 a. tr of land adj PETER COCK, JOHN COCK & Schuylkill River (Patent Book A vol 3 pg 208), and the sd ANDREW BANKSON the father being seized of the 500 a. made his will & devised the premises to his sons . . . . Wit: HENRY LINDLEY, JAMES LINNOX[?], THOMAS LANGLER, RICHARD RODES. Ackn 19 May 1712 before NATHAN STANBURY justice of the peace. CHARLES BROCKDEN dep recorder of deeds. (E6:pg 384)

18 May 1689. Deed. DENNIS ROCKFORD of Phila for 8 pounds sold to THOMAS FAIRMAN 200 a. pt/o 5000 a. granted from NILE [blank] on [blank] . . . DENNIS ROCKFORD appoints JOHN MURRAY of Phila his atty to present this deed in open court . . . . Wit: HUMPREY MURRAY, JOHN MURRAY. Recorded 25 -- 1713. (E6:pg 387)

19 Nov 1712. Deed. WALTER NEWMAN of Manataway Phila Co yeoman for 57 pounds 10 shillings sold to JOHN CARNELL of Manataway yeoman a parcel of land adj River Schuylkill, MATHIAS NATELION & MAURICE PEARCE[?] . . . 500 a. . . . . Wit: ANTHONY SADOWSKI, RICHARD CEANE. Ackn 22 Mar 1713/14 before NATHAN STANBURY justice of the peace. CHARLES BROCKDEN dep recorder of deeds. (E6:pg 388)

24 Apr 1713. Deed of Lease. WILLIAM AUBREY of London merchant for 5 shillings sold to REES (REESE) THOMAS of Marion Phila Co gent & ANTHONY MORRIS Junr of Phila brewer a messuage & lands (except 500 a.) for the term of 1 year . . . whereas RICHARD WHITEPAIN (WHITPAIN) late citizen & butcher of London did in his will dated 27 Apr 1689 authorize his wife MARY WHITEPAIN his executrix to sell his lands in PA 7000 a., that is a large messuage 60 ft front 56 ft depth with two back houses in Phila near River DE, one plantation called "Whitepain Cr" 4000 a., 1000 a. belonging to the liberty of Phila, 2500 a. in Chester Co, & 500 a. not set out and taken up, for the payment of his debts . . . and the sd MARY WHITEPAIN on 13 Jul 1689 conveyed the land (except the 500 a.) unto JOHN BLACKHALL (BACKHALL) of London draper & other persons (who are since dead) in trust for the creditors of the sd RICHARD WHITEPAIN . . . and by indenture of lease & release dated 27&28 Nov last past the sd JOHN BLACKHALL conveyed the same to the sd WILLIAM AUBREY . . . . Wit: JOHN HADDON, THOMAS EMBLY, DANL TOMPSON, ABRAHAM ANTHONY, DEBORAH THOMPSON, J SPRINGETT. Ackn 29 Feb 1713 before ANTHONY MORRIS justice of the peace. CHARLES BROCKDEN dep recorder of deeds. (E6:pg 391)

25 Apr 1713. Deed. WILLIAM AUBREY of London merchant for 500 pounds sold to REECE THOMAS of Meryon Phila Co gent & ANTHONY MORRIS Junr of Phila brewer messuage & lands [same as above] . . . . Wit: JOHN HADDEN, THOMAS EMLY (ENLY), ABRAHAM ANTHONY, DANIEL TOMPSON, DEBORAH TOMPSON, J SPRINGETT. Ackn 27 Feb 1713/14 before ANTHONY MORRIS justice of the peace. CHARLES BROCKDEN dep recorder of deeds. (E6:pg 393)

# INDEX

Alexander, 88
Baldwin, 86
Charles, 2, 100
Elizabeth, 104
Joshua, 100
Loetitia, 7
Nathaniel, 103
Nile, 128
Samuel, 47
Susannah, 81
Thomas, 94
William, 47

## A

ACENT
  Benjamin Furly, 73
ADAMS
  Richard, 59
  Robert, 47, 48, 74, 106
  Seemercy, 87
  Somerey, 72
ALFORD
  Philip, 67
ALLEN
  Jeremiah, 75
  Nathan, 5
  Nathaniel, 34, 80
  Nehemiah, 3, 70
  Samuel, 58
  William, 110, 111
AMBLER
  Joseph, 78
AMBLERS
  Joseph, 13
ANDREAS
  Edmund, 11
ANDREWS
  Esther, 46
  Simon, 46
ANDROS
  Edmund, 11, 34
ANTHONY
  Abraham, 129
AP DEN GRAES
  Abraham, 63
AP EDWARDS
  John Evan, 58
AP EVAN
  Robert, 20
AP HUGH
  Richard, 25
AP HUGHS
  Richard, 30
AP JOHN
  John, 21, 53, 54, 55, 114
AP THOMAS
  Richard, 17
ARENTS
  Jacob Classen, 81
ARETS
  Lenart, 107
ARITON
  Senert, 103
ARMITT
  Richard, 1
ARNETT
  Richard, 82
ARROWSMITH
  Sarah, 80
ARTHUR
  John, 28
ASHCOM
  Charles, 76
ASHETON
  Rob, 67
  Robert, 16, 72, 81, 85
ASHTON
  Joseph, 1, 66, 67, 74
  Robert, 26, 29, 65, 82
  Thomas, 71
ASKEW
  Elizabeth, 80
  John, 80

ASSHETON
  Robert, 61, 82
ASSON
  Thomas, 38, 50
ATKINS
  Samuel, 93, 123
ATKINSON
  James, 36
AUBREY
  Latitia, 35, 96
  Loetitia, 21
  William, 19, 21, 35, 96, 129
AUBRY
  William, 88
AUSTIN
  Jane, 7
  John, 7, 25, 31, 60
AUTROLAY
  Joseph, 45
AYREY
  Bridgett, 98
  James, 98

# B

B-
  John, 88
BADCOCK
  Henry, 15, 110
BADCOCK (BADCOKE)
  Henry, 13
BADCOK
  Henry, 126
BADCOKE
  Alexander, 2
  Henry, 22, 37, 38, 60, 69, 72
  Mary, 60, 69
BADROK
  Henry, 122
BAKER
  Samuel, 86
BALSFORD
  Edward, 106
BANKSON
  Andrew, 10, 17, 128
  Benjamin, 128
  Catherine (Katherine), 128
  Daniel, 128

  Gertrude, 128
  Helen, 128
  Jacob, 128
  John, 128
  Joseph, 128
BARBER
  Elizabeth, 109
  John, 109
BARKER
  Thomas, 76
BARNES
  John, 28, 65, 66, 106
BARRETT
  James, 11, 12
BARROW
  Robert, 104
BARTHOLOMEW
  George, 24
  Jane, 24
BARTLESON
  Sebis, 84
BARTRAM
  William, 117
BATE
  Humphrey, 40, 58, 85, 86
  Job, 40
  Joseph, 40, 58, 85, 86
BATES
  Job, 25, 47
BATSON
  Thomas, 124
BAYNTON (BAYTON)
  Peter, 118
  Rebecca, 118
BEARD
  George, 59
BEAZOR
  John, 76
BEER
  Edward, 6
BEERS
  Edward, 4, 5, 7
BEESON
  Edward, 124
  Elizabeth, 124
BEHAGELL
  Daniel, 72
BEHAGILL

133

Daniel, 76
BELLAR
  Alice, 124
  Madgalin, 112
  Mathias, 112
  Peter, 124
BELLONGE
  Eve, 73
BENNETT
  Elizabeth, 7
  Henry, 74
BENSON
  George, 115
BERTLES
  John, 10
BETHELL (BETHALL)
  Jane, 108
  John, 108
BETRIDGE
  William, 102
BETTRIDGE
  William, 111
BEVAN
  Mary, 2
  William, 2
BICKLEY
  Abraham, 67, 68
BICKLY
  Abraham (Abram), 104
BILES
  John, 87
  William, 29
BILLERY
  John, 102
BINGHAM
  James, 24, 52, 114
BIRD
  Andrew, 53, 113, 114
  John B, 73
  Thomas, 25
BITRIDGE
  W., 94
BITTLE
  John, 78, 97
BLACKHALL (BACKHALL)
  John, 129
BLACKLEDGE
  William, 49

BLACKLIDGE
  Benjamin, 84
BLAND
  Isaac, 60
BLANEY
  Andrew, 41
  John, 3, 42
  Katharine, 32
  Katherine, 28
BLANY
  Catherine, 93
  Katherine, 94
BLUNSTON
  John, 84
BOLTON
  Edward, 54, 59, 94
  Everard, 9, 10, 16, 57, 70, 71
BON
  Peter, 72
BOND
  Gonnstone, 92
BONDELIN
  Randolph, 15
  Rudolph, 15
BONELL
  Robert, 9
BONN
  Andrew, 26
BONSALL
  Abadiah, 71
BOON
  Andrew Swanson, 62
  Peter, 62
  Swan, 62
BOON (BOONE)
  Conver (Caure), 62
BOONE
  Andreas, 62
  Morton, 62
  Peter, 62
BOORE
  Lasse, 1
BORDEN
  Samuel, 8, 10, 19, 21, 26, 112
BORDEN (BOURDEN)
  Samuel, 104
BORKUS
  James, 43

BOTTIMS
  Stack, 1
BOUCHER
  John, 95
BOURCHIER
  John, 83
BOURCHUR
  John, 67
BOWDE
  Grimston, 4
BOWERS
  John, 54
BOWLY
  George, 103
BOWMAN
  Thomas, 43
  Wendel, 119, 125
BOWYER
  John, 65, 101
BOYDEN
  James, 24, 76, 114
BRADFORD
  William, 96, 112, 113
BRADING
  Nathaniel, 28
BRADWAY
  Mary, 60
BRANDT
  Albertus, 34
BRANIN
  Francis, 40
BRANSON
  Nathaniel, 79
  William, 79, 94, 102
BRANSON (BRANSTONE)
  Nathaniel, 79
BRANSTONE
  John, 79
  William, 79
BREINTNALL
  David, 3, 23
  Davod, 118
BRICH
  Widow, 74
BRISTOM
  Thomas, 89
BRISTOW
  Thomas, 49

BRITTEN
  Lionel, 74, 113
BRITTON
  Joanna, 39
  Lionel, 30
  Lionell, 25, 31, 32, 39, 67, 90
  Rebecca, 39
BROAD
  Jacob Gattschalk, 73
BROADGATE
  Thomas, 120
BROADWELL (BRADWELL)
  Mary, 107
BROCK
  John, 71
BROCKDEN
  Charles, 22, 45, 50, 73, 95, 116, 117, 122, 124, 125, 126, 127, 128, 129
BROCKDON
  Charles, 9, 119
BROCKMAN
  Charles, 33
BROWN
  John, 18, 115
  Joseph, 31, 38, 39
  Thomas, 20, 55, 56, 68, 73
  William, 10
  Yotso, 115
BRUCE
  John, 20
BRUNS
  Clauss, 15
BUCKHOLTS
  Henry, 53
BUDD
  John, 78, 92, 95, 104, 111, 115, 116, 121
  Thomas, 24
BUNDELY
  John Randolph, 127
  John Rudolph, 120
BURCH
  Edward, 70
BURCHALL
  John, 66
BURGE
  John, 83

Sarah, 83
BURGLEY
   Thomas, 18
BURKHOLDER
   Henry, 85
BURLING
   John, 46
   Sarah, 46
BURROW
   Robert, 68
BURSON
   George, 71
BURTHRN
   John, 29
BUSBY
   Edward, 91
   Nicholas, 91, 92
   Richard, 91
BUSHBY
   John, 55
BUTCHER
   Michael, 18
BUZBY
   Edward, 15
   John, 55
BYWATER
   Gervas, 31, 90
   Joan, 31
   William, 31, 90
BYWAYTER
   Jean, 90
   Joan, 90

# C

CADWALADER
   John, 83, 85, 86, 90, 94, 104, 121
CADWALLAD (CADWALAD)
   John, 15
CADWALLADER
   Edward, 41, 42, 44
   John, 41, 42
CALLOW
   John Morgan, 47
CALLOWHILL
   Thomas, 99
CALLOWHILL (CADWALADER)
   Thomas, 121

CANBY
   Thomas, 58
CAPELL
   Arnold, 50
CARLILE
   Abraham, 69
CARLILE (CARLIEL)
   Abaraham, 13
CARLINGTON
   Mark, 119
CARNELL
   John, 129
CARPENTER
   Abraham, 50, 51
   John, 27, 78, 88
   Joshua, 4, 8, 41, 92
   Samuel, 4, 13, 14, 15, 18, 19, 21, 24, 27, 32, 35, 37, 38, 39, 41, 42, 50, 51, 52, 55, 82, 83, 87, 88, 90, 92, 96, 101, 118, 120
CARPP
   John, 8
CARPP (CRAP)
   John, 14
CART
   Joshua, 12
   Samuel, 30, 37, 52, 68, 86, 102
CARTER
   Catherine, 126
   Henry, 2, 85, 87, 90, 94, 102
   Samuel, 7, 83, 84, 103
   Susanna, 94, 102
   William, 2, 3, 5, 6, 7, 9, 10, 12, 19, 22, 27, 28, 29, 31, 38, 39, 45, 52, 59, 61, 69, 71, 74, 83, 93, 97, 103, 106, 107, 110, 111, 113, 114, 117, 118, 121, 122, 126, 127, 128
CARTINGTON
   Mark, 118
CARTLIDGE
   Edmond, 117, 125
   Edmund, 12
   John, 13
CARTRIDGE
   John, 12
CARVER
   John, 106, 122

Richard, 106
CASDORP
  Herman, 73
CASH
  Caleb, 3, 4
CASSEL
  Arnold, 81
CASSELL
  Arnold, 23, 50, 86
CASTLEBERRY
  Henry, 85
CATON
  John, 95
CAULEY
  Thomas, 86
CEANE
  Richard, 129
CHADD
  Francis, 121
CHALKLEY
  Thomas, 3, 6, 19, 35, 38, 39
CHAMBERLAINE
  Lucy, 80
  Peter, 80
CHAMBERLAN
  William, 107
CHAMBERLIN
  Peter, 22, 110, 111, 128
CHAMBERS
  Benjamin, 14, 15, 31, 38, 65, 67, 68, 88, 110, 111, 116, 117, 118
  Elizabeth, 68
  John, 67, 68
CHANDERS
  James, 108
CHANDLER
  Samuel, 26
CHEETAM
  John, 60
CHESTNUT HILL, 15
CHICK
  Damaris, 103
CHISELUS
  Cesar, 34
CHURCH
  Edward, 19, 24, 27, 28, 94, 102
CICLE

John, 1
CLARIDGE
  Samuel, 123
CLARK
  Thomas, 16, 31
CLARKE
  Thomas, 4
  William, 55, 56
CLAYPOOL
  James, 24, 120
CLAYPOOLE
  George, 54, 59
  Helionah, 54
  James, 7, 38, 54, 74, 81, 107
  John, 36, 65, 81, 107
  Joseph, 13, 69, 79
  Nathaniel, 54
CLAYTON
  James, 30, 83
  William, 34
CLEAST
  James, 54
CLEMFRESS
  Paul, 84
CLEMSON
  Elizabeth, 68
COATES
  Thomas, 53
COATS
  Thomas, 114, 126
COBB
  Jacob, 98
COCK
  Arthur, 126
  Gabriel, 26
  John, 12, 88, 126, 128
  Jonathan, 25
  Lacey, 123
  Lacy, 128
  Lasse, 20
  Lassey, 10
  Lassie, 126
  Laurence, 55
  Lawrence, 7, 107, 123, 128
  Martha, 72, 107, 122, 126, 128
  Mounts, 126
  Peter, 10, 20, 26, 87, 88, 101, 107, 126, 128

Sasse, 88
Widow of Peter, 72, 122
COCKE
  Andrew, 107
  Robert, 107
COFFING
  Jacob, 4, 10
COFFING (COFING)
  Jacob, 90
COFFREY
  Jacob, 113
COFING (COFFING)
  Jacob, 97
COLEMAN
  Joseph, 68
  Sarah, 71, 113
  Stephen, 70, 71
  Thomas, 53, 55, 60
  William, 13, 69, 78
COLHOYS (COLSROYS)
  Rowley, 109
COLLEE
  John, 26, 32, 75
COLLET
  Richard, 78
COLLETT
  Jeremiah, 36, 45
  Richard, 88
  Weyntia, 36
  Weynty, 36
  Wynlie (Weynlie), 45
COLLEY
  Abell, 45, 46
  Ann, 84
  John, 28, 29, 30, 32, 84, 112
  Susanna, 30, 84
COLLINS
  Edward, 50
  John, 39
COLLUCK (KOLLACK)
  Jacob, 57
COMELY
  Henry, 29, 92, 95
COOK
  Francis, 10, 22, 26, 29, 35, 37, 70, 106
  Lape, 96
COOKE
  Arthur, 55
  Francis, 22, 42, 43, 53, 54, 65, 66, 67, 81, 82, 84, 91, 100, 104, 109, 112, 125
  John, 48
  Mary, 43, 84
  Peter, 97
COOKE (COOK)
  Joseph, 102
  Mary, 102
COOMBE
  Samuel, 113
COOPER
  James, 108
CORDRINGTON
  Margarett, 12
  Thomas, 12
CORDRY
  Hugh, 11
CORK
  Jonathan, 31
CORKER
  William, 87
CORRIE
  Harbert, 53
  Herbert, 93, 94, 100
  Robert, 94
CORRIER
  Harbert, 39
COTLEY
  Abel, 90
  Abell, 2
COTTEY
  Abel, 74, 113
  Able, 113
  Mary, 113
COULSON
  Joseph, 24
COUNTIS
  John, 42
COURRIE
  Harbert, 93
COX
  John, 107
  Thomas, 79
COXE
  Thomas, 108
CRAPP

John, 15, 19, 23, 27, 28, 29, 87
CRAPP (CRAP)
    John, 18
CRASHE
    Sell, 79
CRAVEN
    James, 108, 109
    Richard, 108, 109
CRESSON
    Ann, 123
    Solomon, 3, 7, 23, 123
CRICK
    Samuel, 112, 113
CRISCOM
    Andrew, 59
CRISP
    Silas, 36
CRISPAIN
    -, 122
CRISPEN
    Silas, 36
CRISPIN
    Esther, 58
    Silas, 17, 32, 52, 58, 86, 123
CRISPUN
    Silas, 106
CROSLEY
    Richard, 85
CROSS
    Joseph, 79
    Thomas, 18
CROSWHIT
    John, 57
CROSWHITE
    John, 61
CROW
    Mary, 78, 97
CRUICKSHANK
    Alexander, 107
    Richard, 107
CULLOCH
    Jacob, 34
CUPPAGE
    Thomas, 99
CUSTER
    Arnold, 73
    Arnoll, 51, 52
    Johannes, 65

CUSTERS
    Hermans, 63

# D

D-
    James, 5
DAVID
    Ellis, 58
    James, 7, 21
    Lewis, 44, 83
    Richard, 54
    William, 37
DAVIDS
    Thomas, 5, 55, 56
DAVIES
    John, 20, 112
    Philip, 40
    Widow, 112
DAVIS
    Diana, 105
    Edmond, 89, 99
    Ellis, 106
    John, 93, 112
    Joseph, 98, 99
    Richard, 70, 97, 114
    William, 30, 91, 92
DAWSON
    Emanuel, 69
    Hannah, 69
DAY
    John, 10, 26
DEAVES
    Isaac, 23, 60
DEEWEES
    Cornelius, 64
    William, 64
DELAPLAINE
    James, 65
DELAVALL
    Hannah, 11
    John, 4, 12
    Margarett, 12
    Rebecca, 12
DELWYN
    William, 56
DEN GRAES
    Abraham Ap, 63

DENNIS
  Abraham, 81
DENSEY
  John, 52
DENSEY (DENSIE, DENZIE)
  John, 32
DEPLOURYS
  John, 84
DESMONT
  Daniel, 64
DEWEESE
  Cornelius, 64
  William, 64
DICKINSON
  Jonathan, 111, 116
  William, 81, 82, 83
DILLWIN
  William, 57
DILLWORTH
  John, 82
  Richard, 100, 101, 106
  William, 100
DILWORTH
  James, 82
DILWORTH (DILLWORTH)
  Ann, 82
DINGWORTH
  Richard, 107
DOE
  John, 7
DOEDEN
  John, 77, 103
DORDEN
  Jane, 48
DOUBTIN
  Edward, 118
DRASON
  William, 104
DRAUGHTON
  Edmund, 34
DUCASTELE
  Edmund, 9
DUCKET
  Thomas, 69
DUCKETT
  Ruth, 13
  Thomas, 48
DUFFIELD

  Benjamin, 94, 95
DUFFILD
  Benjamin, 77, 78
DUN
  John, 103
DUPLOVY
  John, 34
DUPLOVY (DUPLOUVY)
  John, 33
DUR
  Hugh, 105
DURRAMT
  Charles, 99

# E

EAGLESFIELD
  George, 28
EAST
  Benjamin, 102, 111, 116
  Hannah, 102
  John, 102
EATON
  Edward, 74
  George, 102
  Joseph, 47
ECKLEY
  John, 83
EDDI
  Katherine, 114
EDGCOME
  Nathaniel, 72
EDGECOME
  Nathaniel, 43, 81
EDWARD
  Alexander, 40, 47
EDWARDS
  Alexander, 25, 30, 31, 58
  Ellen, 54
  Hugh, 85
  Humphrey, 77, 103
  John Evan ap, 58
  Maurice (Manzire), 59
  Moses, 83
  Thomas, 25
EFORD
  Joseph, 70
ELDERSLEY

Henry, 71
ELDRIDGE
  Thomas, 94
ELFRETH
  Henry, 72
  Hester, 65
  Jeremiah, 118
ELISON (ELLISON)
  Elizabeth, 108
  Thomas, 108
ELLIS
  Ellen, 44
  Francis, 83
  Humphrey, 61
  Josias, 18
  Rowland, 44, 48, 54, 93, 97, 115, 116
  Thomas, 44, 45
ELLOTT
  John, 62
ELPETH
  Samuel, 91
ELTON
  Susanah, 120
  Susanna, 49, 61
EMBLY
  Thomas, 129
EMLY (ENLY)
  Thomas, 129
ENDEHAVE
  Edward, 18
  Garrett, 18
ENDEHOOF
  Gerrard, 64
ENGELL
  Paul, 73
ENGLAND
  Daniel, 114, 125
  Philip, 111, 116
  Thomas, 2, 25, 42, 78, 97
ENOCH
  Enoch, 11
  Gartho, 11
  Hermon, 11
EVAN
  Cadwallader, 20
  George, 58
  Owen, 31

Robert ap, 20
Thomas, 47
EVANS
  David, 9, 46, 57, 61, 77
  Edward, 2, 14, 23, 33, 39, 40, 43, 44, 47, 48, 53, 58, 61, 75, 93, 116
  Evan, 100
  George, 54
  Hugh, 59
  John, 40, 44, 93
  Owen, 13, 20
  Peter, 42, 52, 66
EVERNDEN
  Thomas, 9
EWER
  Robert, 46, 72, 74
EWINER
  Robert, 71

# F

FAIRMAN
  Eliza, 118
  Elizabeth, 85, 86, 111
  Robert, 25, 30, 40, 47
  Thomas, 1, 12, 20, 22, 28, 38, 40, 47, 50, 59, 65, 71, 85, 86, 88, 109, 111, 118, 125, 128
FALCKNER
  Daniel, 15
  Justus, 15, 76
FALCONER (FALCKNER)
  Daniel, 72
FALKNER
  Daniel, 75, 76, 81
  Justus, 81
FARMAR
  Edward, 60, 81, 84, 86, 117
  Franklin, 81
  Jasper, 84
  John, 36
  Mary, 84
  Thomas, 72
FARMER
  Edward, 33, 84, 85, 125
  Thomas, 16, 71
FATHUIRE

Daniel, 48
FAWLE
  Francis, 115
FEARN
  Joshua, 83
FEENEY
  Samuel, 40
FELLOWS
  John, 11
FELNER
  Jacob, 33
FELNOR
  Jacob, 24
FIELD
  John, 99
FINCHOR
  Francis, 42
  John, 42
FINNEY
  John, 16
  Joseph, 41
  Rebecca, 41
  Samuel, 26, 27, 40, 41, 47, 50
FISH (FISHER)
  Caspar, 10
  Casper, 1
  Williamka, 10
FISHBOURN
  William, 80
FISHER
  Bridget, 71
  John, 26, 74, 75
  Joseph, 13, 20, 94, 106, 118, 122
  Martha, 122
  Mary, 122
  William, 1, 49, 71, 101
FISKBOURN
  William, 9
FITCH
  Robert, 47
  Thomas, 45
FITZWATER
  George, 4, 55, 66, 92
  Mary, 55
FLEMING
  Patrick, 115
FLETCHER
  John, 74

Mary, 48, 74
Robert, 58, 86, 87
Sarah, 48
FLOWER
  Daniel, 26, 78, 97
  Enoch, 33
  Henry, 14, 15, 19, 33, 39, 45, 50, 51, 67
FLOWERS
  Daniel, 13
  Enoch, 74, 75
  Henry, 12, 13, 29, 74, 75
FORD
  Ann, 98
  Bridget, 98
  Philip, 98
  Susannah, 98
FORREST
  Joam, 60
FOSTER
  Allen, 102
FOX
  Elizabeth, 7, 8, 14, 15, 18, 19, 27, 81, 82
  Francis, 109
  James, 7, 8, 14, 18, 19, 27, 28, 81, 115
FRANCISCUS
  Stophel, 119, 120, 125
FREDRICKS
  Michael, 11
FREEMAN
  William, 66
FREY
  Henry, 111
FROGG
  John, 61
FUNK
  John, 119, 125
FURLEY (HURLEY)
  Benjamin, 81
FURLOW
  Benjamin, 68
FURLY
  Benjamin, 76
FURNEY
  Samuel, 38

## G

**GAEDTSEHALEK**
  Jacob, 105
**GAEGH**
  Cornelius Vander, 102
**GAETSCHALT**
  Jacob, 117
**GAIGHE**
  Cornelius Vander, 100
**GARDNER**
  John, 107, 110, 111, 115, 116
**GARRATT**
  William, 122
**GARRATT (GERRATT)**
  John, 17
**GARRET**
  Bridget, 115
  Garret, 115
  Morton, 115
  Ruana, 115
  William, 121
**GARRETT**
  William, 6, 80
**GARRIT**
  William, 124
**GARTHSIFALCH**
  Jacob, 105
**GATFIELD**
  James, 79
**GAUNT**
  Daniel, 3, 4
**GHIRELIN**
  Nathan, 95
**GHISELINS**
  Cesar, 111
**GIBBS**
  John, 49
  Sarah, 49
**GIFFIN**
  David, 94
**GILBERT**
  John, 48, 120, 121, 122, 123
  Joseph, 120, 122, 123
  Joshua, 49
**GILLINGHAM**
  Yeaman, 106
**GLAZIER**
  John, 80
**GLEE**
  Joshua, 99
**GLOBE, THE**, 4
**GODFREY**
  Benjamin, 35, 36
**GODSHALK**
  Jacob, 3, 23
**GOLDNEY**
  Henry, 19, 21, 35, 37
**GOODFELLOW**
  Thomas, 45
**GOODING**
  Edward, 123
**GOODSOM**
  John, 70
**GOODSON**
  John, 24, 27, 34, 36, 38, 45, 50, 55, 56, 77, 78, 80, 85, 96, 97, 107, 110, 112, 113, 114, 118, 123, 128
**GOODSONN**
  Job, 83, 84
  John, 2
**GOULDING**
  Henry, 88
  William, 71
**GOULDING (GOLDNEY)**
  Henry, 87
**GOULDNEY**
  Henry, 96, 99
**GOULDNY**
  William, 103
**GRAEF**
  Abraham Opden, 60
  Abraham Opden (Opten), 24
  Dirk, 24
  Dirk Opden, 60
  Herman, 24
  Herman Opden, 60
**GRAHAM**
  H., 51
  Hugh, 111
**GRANGE**
  Joshua, 88
**GRANT**
  Alexander, 84
**GRAY**

Edmund, 100
Edward, 65, 66
George, 3, 9, 10, 23, 43, 46, 52
GREEN
   Darby, 112
   Giles (Gyles), 29
   John, 82
GREENE
   John, 81, 82
GREGORY
   William, 22
GREY
   George, 124
GRIFFIN
   David, 31
   William, 28
GRIFFITH
   Abraham, 18, 104
   Benjamin, 108
   David Hugh, 30
   Edward, 45
   Elizabeth, 46
   Evan, 41, 42, 43
   Howell, 43, 104
   Hugh, 13, 41, 42
   John, 93, 100
   Thomas, 11, 13, 19, 22, 46, 69, 102, 110
GRISCOMB (GRISCOM)
   Andrew, 2, 88
GROVE
   Silvanus, 99
GROVIN
   Thomas, 53
GROWDON
   Joseph, 74, 77, 78
GUESLING
   Ceaser, 115
   Cesar, 116
GUEST
   Alce, 53
   Alice, 8, 23, 87
   Elizabeth, 24
   George, 23, 24, 86, 87
   John, 24, 28, 53, 55, 60
GUY
   John, 89

# H

HADDON
   John, 129
HADFIELD
   Adam, 126
HADFIELD (HATRIELD)
   Edward, 126
HAIG
   Laury, 32
   Lawry, 27, 28
   Lowry, 29
   William, 75
HAINES
   Andrew, 94
   James, 117
   John, 94
HALL
   Jacob, 11, 38, 40, 41, 50
   John, 98
   Joseph, 29, 53, 92, 115
   Richard, 16, 43, 49, 57, 102
   William, 28, 30, 48, 57, 61, 120, 121
HALLIWELL
   Richard, 59, 110
HALLOWELL
   Thomas, 117
HANEY
   Andrew, 107
HARDIE
   David, 83
HARDIMAN
   Abraham, 14, 15, 17, 39, 45, 55
   Deborah, 55
   Hannah, 55
   Mary, 55
   Rebecca, 55
HARDING
   Francis, 97, 98
   Richard, 121
   Thomas, 50, 51, 67
HARMER
   George, 6, 19, 26, 52
   William, 110
HARMON
   George, 3
   Widow, 10

HARNER
　George, 32
HARP
　Thomas, 19
HARPER
　John, 48
　Josiah, 106
HARRIOT
　Samuel, 4
HARRIOTT
　Samuel, 36, 92, 104
HARRIS
　David, 82
　Edward, 3
　Hannah, 11
　John, 3
　Sapuns, 110
　Thomas, 94, 110
HARRISON
　Christopher, 75
　John, 30
HART
　John, 1, 17, 25, 38, 43, 50, 71,
　　74, 78, 80, 94, 102
　Mary, 74
HARTFORD
　Charles, 119
HARTLEY
　Thomas, 12
HARVEY
　Joseph, 1, 12, 13
HARWOOD
　William, 30, 45, 112, 127
HASENOELL
　Abraham, 76
HATFIELD
　George, 110
HAVARCH
　Mary, 48
HAVARD
　John, 16, 57
　William, 17
HAWARD
　John, 114, 126
HAWKINS
　Elizabeth, 2
　Henry, 2
　James, 80

HAYES
　Jonathan, 68
HAYES (HAYS)
　Jonathan, 67
HAYS
　Lowry, 26
HAYWOOD
　John, 50
HEAPLEY
　Daniel, 58
HEARN
　Sarah, 125
　William, 125
HEATH
　Richard, 4, 5, 6, 8, 9, 12, 13, 14,
　　15, 17, 19, 20, 22, 23, 24, 25,
　　26, 27, 28, 29, 31, 32, 33, 35,
　　37, 38, 39, 44, 45, 46, 47, 49,
　　50, 51, 53, 54, 55, 58, 59, 60,
　　61, 62, 63, 64, 65, 67, 68, 69,
　　70, 71, 72, 73, 74, 75, 76, 77,
　　78, 79, 80, 81, 83, 84, 85, 86,
　　87, 88, 89, 90, 92, 93, 94, 95,
　　96, 97, 98, 100, 101, 102,
　　103, 104, 106, 107, 108, 109,
　　110, 111, 112, 113, 114, 115,
　　116, 117, 118, 121, 124, 125
　Ro, 9
　Robert, 46, 82
HEATH (HATH)
　Richard, 1, 2, 4
HEATHCOLE
　George, 87
HEATON
　Robert, 20, 71
HEAVERD
　William, 10
HEIR
　Christian, 119
HENDRICKS
　Gerrard, 64
　Gerrat, 63
　John, 91
　Sarah, 63, 64
　William, 20
HENDRICKSON
　Ian, 34
HENLINGS

William, 32
HERMAN
  Ephraim, 34
HERMANS
  Reinier, 60, 61
  Renier, 63
HERRIOTT
  Mary, 34
  Thomas, 34
HEWLING
  Dorothy, 52
  William, 52
HIBBS
  William, 18
HILL
  Edgar, 41
  Elizabeth, 112
  Hannah, 11, 12, 111
  Richard, 2, 4, 11, 12, 39, 45, 46, 52, 78, 79, 90, 111
HILLIARD
  Philip, 113
  Phillip, 11
Hinton
  Rees, 58
HITCHCOCK
  Nicholas, 32
HITCHINGS
  Richard, 43
HOBBS
  Israel, 41
HODGES
  Hannah, 65, 66
  Thomas, 65, 66
HODGKINS
  Millisent, 30
HODGSON
  Daniel, 26, 124
  Sarah, 26
HOLCOMBE
  Jacob, 97
HOLLAND
  John, 81
HOLLINGSWORTH
  Henry, 88
HOLM
  John, 53
  Thomas, 36

HOLME
  John, 77, 78, 88
  Thomas, 106, 122, 123
HOLMES
  Thomas, 36, 45, 118
HOLMS
  Thomas, 36
HOLSTED
  Mathias, 10
HOLSTEN
  Frederick, 10
  Mathias, 126
HONNEY
  William, 18
HOOD
  John, 12, 13, 58, 62
  Jonathan, 62
HOODF
  Casper, 45
HOODLEY
  Samuel, 106
HOODT
  Caspar, 3, 14, 17, 23, 39, 52, 55, 71, 82
  Casper, 15, 52, 111, 113, 119, 120
  Sarah, 113
HOOL
  John, 18
HOOTEN
  Eliza, 118
  Thomas, 118
HOOTOON
  Thomas, 83
HORMER
  William, 30
HORNE
  Francis, 107
HOUGH
  John, 21
HOUSTON
  William, 75
HOWARD
  John, 51
  William, 91
HOWE
  Thomas, 57
HOWELL

Ann, 112, 113
Daniel, 57
Mordicai, 45, 49, 50
Philip, 25, 31, 32, 69, 87, 96, 112, 113, 125
Phillip, 30
Samuel, 46
Thomas, 61
William, 44
HOWLSTED
   Lawrence, 10
   Mathias, 10
HUDSON
   Ann, 8
   Elizabeth, 8, 9
   John, 8, 9
   William, 8, 19, 32, 33, 52, 60, 75, 124, 126
HUGG
   Elias, 14, 51, 104
HUGH
   Richard ap, 25
   Rowland, 121
HUGHES
   John, 37, 41, 47
   Mary, 47
HUGHS
   John, 20, 42
   Richard ap, 30
HUMPHREY
   Daniel, 44
   John, 13, 18, 41, 42
   Robert, 41, 42
HUMPHREYS
   Daniel, 44
   Daniel Haverford, 44
   John, 70
HUNT
   Charles, 97
   Thomas, 100
HUNTLEY
   William, 47
HUNTSMAN
   John, 117
HURFORD
   John, 60
HURT
   John, 110

HUTCHESON
   Robert, 43

# I

IBLE
   Elizabeth, 87
INDENHOOF
   Garrett, 7
IRONMONGER (IRONMUNGER)
   John, 117, 118
   Sarah, 117
IRREGULAR SLIP, 77
ISHER
   Jacob, 69
IVENSEN
   Charles, 34

# J

JACKSON
   Ralph, 20, 109, 113, 114, 115, 126
   Stephen, 117, 118
   Steven, 14
JACOB
   James, 88, 99, 110
   Samuel, 74, 92
JACOBS
   James, 74, 90
JAFFREY (JAFFERY)
   George, 84
JAMES
   Ann, 8, 121
   Edward, 8, 9, 77, 85, 121
   Howell, 66, 101, 106
   James, 65, 66, 106
   John, 32, 52, 75
   Philip, 23, 26, 53, 67, 87, 105
   William, 10, 65
JANERL
   Johannes, 48
JANNAN
   Jeremiah, 7
JANSEN
   Dirk, 77
JANSON (JOHSEN)
   Dirk, 103

JARROW
  Robert V, 75
JARVICE
  Francis, 89
JARVIS
  Francis, 49, 61, 120
JAWERT
  Johann, 15
  Johannes, 72
JAWERT (JANHERT)
  Balthazar, 72
JELSON
  Jane, 56
  Joel, 56
JENKINS
  Elizabeth, 14
JENNER
  Thomas, 87, 96, 105, 111
  Widow, 14
JENNETT
  Hester, 66
  John, 66, 72
  Widow, 35
JENNEY
  Randall, 114
JENNINGS
  John, 120
  Samuel, 39
  William, 80
JERVIS
  Francis, 49
  Martin, 2
  Martyn, 90
JESTES
  Mary, 65
JOHN
  Don, 70
  Griffith, 5, 7
  John ap, 21
  John Ap, 53, 54, 55
  John ap, 114
JOHNSON
  Claus, 5, 64
  Clein, 69
  Griffith, 47
  Henry, 89
  Joshua, 25, 26
  Robert, 97

Samuel, 123, 124
Thomas, 89
JOHNSTON
  Claus, 4
  John, 4, 20, 22
JONES
  -, 12
  Abraham, 80
  Charity, 39, 45
  Charles, 72
  Daniel, 32, 52, 93, 94, 114
  Dorothy, 52
  Edward, 44, 56
  Elias, 121
  Ellen, 103
  Griffith, 9, 11, 17, 24, 25, 28, 31,
    32, 39, 43, 55, 58, 60, 75, 79,
    88, 89, 90, 93, 94, 99, 100,
    102, 104, 105, 112, 113, 114,
    124
  Hugh, 13, 58, 59
  John, 8, 10, 11, 39, 40, 42, 60,
    71, 118, 120, 123, 124, 127
  Jonathan, 47, 48, 56, 90
  Joseph, 31, 75, 80, 89, 90, 99
  Lewis, 86
  Margaret, 42
  Peter, 93
  Rachel, 77
  Richard, 77, 85
  Robert, 48, 90
  Samuel, 102
  Thomas, 8, 25, 47, 48, 56
JUSTASON
  Justa, 86

# K

KADWALADER
  John, 59
KAIGHIN
  John, 23
  Sarah, 23
KEARNEY
  Joanna, 39
  Michael, 39
  Philip, 39
  Rebecca, 39

Susannah, 39
KEARNS
  Edmond, 107
KEEN
  -, 1
  Erick, 10, 11
  George, 3, 10
  Jonas, 10
  Mathias, 10, 11
KEETHE
  George, 81
KEINS
  Mathias, 91
KELLEY
  William, 75, 112
KELLY
  Patrick, 53, 95
KEMBLER
  Johannes, 72
KENELIS
  Peter, 46
KENT
  John, 115
KENZLIN
  Peter, 52
KEYSER
  Peter, 103
KIELL
  Joseph, 72
KINDEY (KINDELY)
  Martin, 119
KING
  Walter, 42, 65
KING CHARLES, 108, 114
KINGSBURY
  James, 38
KINGSTON
  Henry, 86
KINSEY
  John, 38
KIRK
  Joseph, 11
KIRKBRIDE
  Joseph, 86
  Mary, 87
KIRLL
  Joseph, 107
KLEINHOFF

Casper, 118
KNIGHT
  Giles, 18, 123
  Giles (Gyles), 122
  Isaac, 102, 103
  Joseph, 122
  Mary, 122, 123
KNOWLES
  Elizabeth, 46
  Francis, 46, 90
KOLB
  Jacob, 105
  Johannes, 105
  Mathias, 105
KOLLUCK
  Jacob, 53, 54
Kolluck
  Jacob, 57
KOLLUCK
  Mary, 57
KOLLUCK (COLLUCK)
  Jacob, 113
KONDERS (KUNDERS)
  Denis, 107
KOON
  Matthias, 91
KORKBRIDE
  Joseph, 58
KRESHEM
  -, 51
KREY
  John, 5, 6, 23, 64
KUNBER
  Thomas, 95
KUNDERS
  Peter, 60
  Thomas, 65, 72, 81
KUSTER
  Hermans, 63
KUSTERS
  Herman, 64
  Thomas, 64

# L

LACE
  Thomas, 91
LADD

Samuel, 90
LAINE
  Edward, 109
LAINE (LANE)
  Edward, 109
LANE
  Edward, 54, 62, 116, 125
  William, 54
LANGLER
  Thomas, 128
LARGE
  Ebenezer, 31
LAURENCE
  John, 92
  Joshua, 69, 71, 74, 76, 77, 78, 80,
    81, 86, 87, 88, 89, 96
LAURENSS
  Ian, 76
LAWRENCE
  Henry, 22
  Joshua, 24, 90, 93, 95, 97, 100,
    101, 104, 105, 106, 110, 111,
    113, 114, 115, 116, 117, 119,
    120, 121, 122, 124, 125, 126,
    127
  Noah, 97, 105
  William, 42, 97
LEA
  John, 20
LEAGUE
  Pentecost, 11, 21
LEAPLIDGE
  John, 15, 16
LEARY
  Richard, 91, 92
  Thomas, 91
LEBRUN
  Johan, 72
LEE
  William, 18, 27
LEECH
  Toby, 31, 74, 102
LEECH (LEICH)
  Toby, 60
LEESH
  Toby, 29
LEIGHURST
  John, 106

LEOCST
  Antona, 65
LEVEZEN
  Jonathan, 122
LEVIS
  Samuel, 80
LEWDEN
  John, 20
LEWDON
  John, 114, 115
  Margaret, 114
LEWELLYN
  Griffith, 7
LEWELYN
  Griffith, 3
LEWIS
  Henry, 49, 83
  Samuel, 83
  Thomas, 59
LICON
  Hans, 18
LINDERMAN
  John, 58
LINDLEY
  Henry, 128
LINNOX
  James, 128
LINTON
  John, 103
LISLE (LIELE)
  Maurice, 1, 2, 3, 5, 8, 11
LISTE
  Maurice, 81
LIVEREY
  Jonathan, 123
LLOYD
  David, 4, 5, 6, 7, 8, 9, 13, 14, 16,
    17, 18, 19, 20, 22, 23, 25, 26,
    27, 28, 29, 31, 32, 33, 35, 37,
    38, 39, 40, 41, 42, 43, 44, 45,
    46, 48, 49, 53, 54, 55, 57, 58,
    59, 61, 62, 63, 64, 65, 67, 69,
    74, 75, 77, 78, 81, 82, 85, 86,
    87, 88, 91, 93, 105, 106, 108,
    114, 124, 127
  Robert, 44
  Thomas, 7, 9, 21, 45, 48, 70, 76,
    107, 111, 115

LLOYD (LOYD)
   David, 1, 2
LOBER
   John, 115
LOFTUS
   Leeson, 91
LOGAN
   James, 7, 12, 17, 19, 21, 25, 27, 30, 32, 35, 37, 41, 58, 59, 68, 81, 87, 88, 96, 121, 125, 128
LONDON
   Hugh, 93, 94, 100
LONG
   David, 93
   Peter, 125
   Walter, 89
LONGALIN
   Robert, 36
LONGER
   Walter, 59
LONGHORN
   Jeremiah, 89
LONGHURST
   John, 2
LONGSHORE
   Robert, 36, 65, 97
LORD
   Theodorns, 72
   Theodorus, 126
LOTCHER
   John, 121
LOVE
   John, 34
LOVELACE
   Francis, 26
LOVELAGE
   Francis, 86
LOWDEN
   Hugh, 53
LOWDON
   John, 109
LOWMAN
   Samuel, 59
LOWNES
   James, 126, 128
LOWTHER
   George, 6, 7
   Henrietta, 6
LOYD
   David, 15, 16, 17, 22, 25
   Thomas, 1
LOYDD
   David, 16
LUCK
   John, 123, 124
   Toby, 115
LUCKEN
   John, 73
LUCKEN (LUCKENS, LURCKENS)
   John, 81
LUFF
   Edward, 127

# M

MACCONST
   John, 66
MACKALL
   John, 57
MACKARTY
   Daniel, 110
   Margaret, 110
MADOX
   Thomas, 86
MAHER
   Thomas, 85
MAILE
   James, 127
   Thomas, 127
MAKEN
   Thomas, 107
MALLETT
   William, 89
MALLOWS
   Henry, 18, 40, 41
MALTBY
   Mary, 9
MANNOR OF MOUNT JOY, 35
MANOR OF MOORELAND, 104
MARKHAM
   William, 24, 27, 34, 38, 55, 56, 66, 70, 77, 78, 80, 81, 96, 110, 112, 113, 114, 118, 123, 128
MARLE

151

Thomas, 50, 51, 71
MARPLE
  David, 47, 53, 104
MARSHALL
  Abraham, 15
  William, 53
MARTIN
  Benjamin, 2
  John, 26
  Richard, 20, 86
  Thomas, 94, 104
MASTERS
  Thomas, 3, 4, 5, 7, 8, 9, 10, 11,
    13, 14, 17, 18, 19, 20, 21, 23,
    24, 25, 26, 27, 28, 29, 30, 31,
    33, 34, 36, 49, 50, 51, 56, 59,
    60, 68, 69, 70, 126
MATLOCK
  Thomas, 20
MATSON
  Catrin, 86
  Katharin, 86
  Peter, 86, 100
MAULE
  Charity, 90
  John, 90
MC VEAGH
  Edmond, 118
  Edmund, 118
MCVEAGH (MCVAUGH)
  Edmund, 42
MEALER
  Samuel, 101
MEALES
  Samuel, 75, 85
MEALS
  Samuel, 26, 68
MELIN
  Martin, 119
MEREFIELD
  Thomas, 119
MERIAN
  Caspar, 76
MERRICK
  John, 11
MERSG
  David, 69
MIDDLETON

  Hugh, 21
MIDLEFIELD
  John, 97
MIFFIN
  John, 37
MIFFLAN
  John, 39
MIFFLIN
  Edward, 82
  John, 17, 30, 35
MILES
  Griffith, 102
MILES (MEALS)
  Samuel, 14
MILLAR
  Thomas, 31, 33, 90
MILLER
  Barnibus, 106
  George, 15, 51, 52
  Jacob, 119, 125, 126
  Thomas, 39, 40
MILLES
  John, 75
MILLS
  John, 25, 68
  Wissahocken, 76
MITCHELL
  Thomas, 96
MOLEN
  Charles, 18
MOODY
  John, 78
MOON
  John, 52
MOOR
  Elizabeth, 2
  James, 14
  John, 2
MOORE
  Ann, 80
  Charles, 69, 73, 83, 93, 94
  Elizabeth, 80
  James, 117, 118
  John, 29, 67, 78, 83, 93, 94, 107,
    117, 124
  Mary, 78
  Naomi, 80
  Nicholas, 5, 53, 56, 58, 73, 77,

88, 92, 94, 95, 104, 110, 115, 121
Priscilla, 110, 115, 121
Rachel, 80
Richard, 97, 101, 122, 123, 124
Rose, 117, 118
Samuel, 77, 78
Sarah, 92, 95, 104, 115
Urn Monington, 67
MOORELAND MANOR, 121
MORE
   Nicholas, 24
MORGAN
   Benjamin, 15, 26, 76, 112, 113
   Cadwalader, 58, 59
   Hugh, 29, 92
   John, 15, 17, 47
   Young, 60
MORNINGTON
   William, 87
MORREY
   Ann, 30
   Humphrey, 29, 30, 43, 78, 80, 97
   Sarah, 79
MORRINGTON
   William, 92, 103
MORRIS
   Anthony, 1, 9, 11, 24, 36, 42, 59, 75, 84, 85, 87, 95, 102, 107, 115, 124, 125, 126, 127, 128, 129
   Cadwalader, 47
   David, 82, 83
   Evan, 30, 107
   Henry, 41
   Isaac, 80, 83
   John, 68, 128
   Joshua, 41
   Morris, 43, 101, 116
   Phoebe, 24
   Richard, 14, 18, 61
   Thomas, 5, 56, 85, 104
MORRIS (MORSE)
   Thomas, 98
MORRIS (NORRIS)
   Isaac, 80
MORSE
   John, 100

MOURRY
   Thomas, 3
MULLEKER
   Erick, 11
MULLIKEN
   Andrew, 50
MULLIKIN
   Andrew, 40, 41
   Errick, 40
MURRAY
   Humprey, 128
   John, 128
   Thomas, 16

# N

NASH
   Ann, 84
   John, 29, 84
NATCHIOUS
   Mathias, 108
NATELION
   Mathias, 129
NEEL
   Widow, 11
NEFF
   John, 84
NELLSEN
   Olle, 34
NELLSON
   Olie, 1
NELSON
   Erick, 1
   Olle, 38
NEUS
   Hans, 127
   John, 24
NEWBERRY
   John, 6, 7, 63, 64
   Walter, 45
NEWCOMB
   Richard, 56, 57, 69, 70, 71, 76
NEWCOMBE
   Richard, 46, 47, 97, 106
NEWCOMBER
   Richard, 31
NEWMAN
   Walter, 108, 129

NICHOLAS
  Samuel, 49
  William, 121
NICHOLLS
  William, 75, 77
NICOLLS
  William, 25
NOBEL
  Abel, 77
NOBLE
  Abel, 85, 121
  Abell, 59
NOOKS
  John, 3
NORRIS
  Isaac, 1, 7, 12, 13, 14, 15, 18, 19, 27, 67, 78, 82, 96
NUTCHER
  Nehemiah, 102

O

OADE
  Thomas, 99
OGILBY
  Patrick, 42
OKLEY
  Thomas, 128
OLESON (OLSON)
  Hans, 34
OP PEN GRAEFF
  Neltjen, 126
ORLON
  John, 89
ORME
  Richard, 21
ORPWOOD
  Edmond, 82
ORVEY
  Griffith, 128
OSBORNE
  Charles, 57
OTTER
  John, 11, 12
OWEN
  Evan, 41, 42, 48, 54
  Griffith, 2, 4, 7, 17, 21, 25, 32, 40, 44, 55, 58, 68, 81, 93
  Richard, 21
  Robert, 48, 56
  Thomas, 76
OWENS
  Caynor, 47
  Evan, 47
  Griffith, 27
  Robert, 47
OYL MILL, 23

P

PAGE
  Isaac, 118
  John, 78, 98, 99
PAINTER
  George, 39, 90, 113
  Samuel, 103
PALMER
  George, 18
  John, 61
  Thomas, 94, 95
  William, 18, 61, 76
PANNEBECKER
  Henry, 101
PANNEBECKERS
  Hendrick, 64
  Henry, 7
PANNENBECKER
  Henry, 64, 72
PARKER
  Alexander, 85
  Jane, 89, 108
  John, 89, 99, 100
  Richard, 108
PARROCK (PANOCK)
  James, 103
PARRY
  John, 54
  Owen, 54
PARSONS
  Ann, 8, 9
  Grace, 73
  John, 8, 9
  Robert, 68, 73
PASCHALL
  Thomas, 29, 87
PASCOLL

Thomas, 14
PASTORIA
　Francis Daniel, 107
PASTORIUS
　Francis Daniel, 24, 51, 52, 63, 64, 65, 73, 98, 101, 103
PASTORRAY
　Francis Daniel, 48
PATRICK
　Henry, 77, 121
PAUL
　Joseph, 74, 82, 104
PAULL
　Henry, 25, 31, 45, 47
　Hervey, 44
　Joseph, 48
PAXTON
　Alexander, 35, 36, 43
　Mary, 110
　William, 110
PEARCE
　Maurice, 129
　Nicholas, 89, 109, 110, 115
　Richard, 108, 109, 124
　Thomas, 108, 109, 124, 125
PEARCE (PEARSE)
　Mary, 110
PEARL
　Thomas, 36
PEART
　Thomas, 97
PEDERSON
　Joseph, 92
PEGG (BIGG)
　Barbara, 113
PEIRCE
　Richard, 116
PEIRS
　Richard, 15
PEMBERTON
　Isreal, 97, 115, 127, 128
　James, 23
　Joseph, 2
PENN
　Gulielina Maria, 35
　Latitia, 30, 35, 37, 96, 104
　Letitia, 87, 88
　Loetitia, 21
　Loetitia (Latitia), 19
　William, 1, 2, 3, 4, 5, 6, 7, 9, 12, 18, 19, 21, 24, 25, 26, 27, 30, 31, 32, 34, 35, 36, 38, 39, 40, 41, 42, 54, 55, 56, 61, 62, 63, 67, 68, 69, 70, 72, 76, 78, 79, 80, 81, 82, 85, 87, 93, 96, 97, 98, 99, 105, 106, 108, 109, 114, 116, 119, 120, 124, 125, 127, 128
PENNEBECKER
　Hendrick, 63
　Henry, 62
PENNEBECKERS
　Henry, 59
PENNEL
　John, 17
PENNELL
　Jeffery, 99
PENNINGTON
　Mary, 124
PENNOCK
　Joseph, 109
PENROSE
　Bartholomew, 29, 31
PERMOCK
　Christopher, 44
PERRY
　Jane, 114
　Thomas, 71, 88, 115
PERSONS
　John, 109
PETERS
　James, 107
　Mathew, 3
　Reece, 113
　Rice, 10, 16, 57
PETERSON
　Garrett, 28
　Johan Wilhelm, 72
　Johanna Eleanora, 76
　Lavrs, 86
PHELPS
　John, 108, 109
　Thomas, 108, 109
PHILIPS
　Joseph, 107
PHILIPSON

Charles, 16
PHILLIPS
  Jerome, 61
  Mary, 46
PHIPPS
  Ann, 74
  Isaiah, 74
  John, 74
  Joseph, 44, 74, 116
PICKERING
  Charles, 8, 27, 38, 93
PIDGEON
  Joseph, 51, 52, 61, 67
PIERSON
  Leonard, 97, 98
PIERSON (PEIRSON)
  John, 97, 98
PIGGOTT
  John, 33, 55
  Rebeccah, 55
PIGGOTT (PIGGOT)
  John, 32
PIRSON
  Edward, 108
PLUMLEY
  Charles, 69
  Rose, 104
PLUMLY
  Charles, 12, 41, 46, 79
  John, 41
PLUMSTAD
  Clement, 34
PLUMSTEAD
  Clement, 59
PLUMSTED
  Clement, 29, 127, 128
  Francis, 78
PLUNSTED
  Clement, 120
PLYMOUTH LOT, 109
PODDARDS
  Jeffery, 92
POLLARD
  Jeffry, 4
POLLARDS
  Jessey, 79
POOL
  Nathaniel, 118

POOLE
  Nathaniel, 117, 127
  William, 87, 96
PORTER
  Abraham, 91
PORTNES
  James, 31
PORTNESS
  James, 90
PORTUES
  James, 40
POTS
  James, 117
POTTS
  David, 46
  Elizabeth, 7
  Jonas, 28, 59, 73
  Thomas, 9, 10, 17, 102
POULTER
  James, 29, 110
POUND
  Robert, 117
POWEL
  David, 16, 18
  Samuel, 30
POWELL
  David, 1, 6, 7, 13, 25, 28, 31, 32,
    57, 61, 70, 95, 97, 125
  Jeremiah, 70
  John, 9, 105
  Rowland, 69
  Samuel, 9, 13, 25, 31, 43, 57,
    103, 109, 117
  Samuell, 1
  William, 41, 70, 77, 105
POYLE
  David, 54
PRATT
  Abraham, 93
  Elizabeth, 93
  Thomas, 93
PREENAWAY
  Robert, 82
PREES
  John, 5
  Rees, 5, 56
PRESTON
  Abell, 23

Henry, 53, 114, 126
　　Samuel, 9, 14, 21, 22, 78, 120, 124
　　William, 48, 91
PRICE
　　Elizabeth, 33
　　Maurice, 108
　　Philip, 61, 82
　　Thomas, 33
PRICHARD
　　Benjamin, 42
　　DAn, 46
　　John, 88, 89
PRIE
　　Philip, 18
PRIGG
　　Richard, 101
　　William, 106, 113
PRISTORIS
　　Henry, 113, 114
PRITCHARD
　　Thomas, 60, 107
PROELL
　　Samuel, 29
PROSSMALE (PRESMALE)
　　Robert, 71
PROTHERA
　　Evan, 111
PRYER
　　Silas, 12
PRYTHRY
　　Robert Evan, 41, 42
PUGH
　　Ellis, 54
　　Henry, 93
PUSEY
　　Caleb, 46, 88

# Q

QUARY
　　Robert, 125

# R

RACHFORD
　　Dennis, 85
RADLEY
　　Daniel, 17, 33, 50, 56
RAINKES
　　Govert, 4
RAMBO
　　Gunce, 101
　　Guner, 96
　　Gunner, 88
　　John, 88, 96
　　Peter, 105
RAMBOE
　　Gunner, 19, 20, 37
　　Peter, 1
RAMKES
　　Govert, 6
RAMSBRYE
　　Dirick, 7
RANBERY
　　-, 7
RANDALL
　　George, 110
　　Nicholas, 29
RANDOLPH
　　Mary Fits, 43
RANSBURG
　　Derick, 125
RANSTED
　　Caleb, 15, 45
　　Calet, 39
RANSTEDD (RANSTED)
　　Caleb, 17
RAWLE
　　Francis, 39, 81, 101, 109, 114
RAWLINGS
　　Daniel, 56
REACH
　　Elias, 47
　　Mary, 47
READ
　　Charles, 74, 110, 127, 128
REDMAN
　　John, 1, 12, 24, 25
　　Joseph, 24, 25, 36, 104
　　Thomas, 36
REDOUT
　　Nicholas, 123
REDRANE
　　Rees, 83
REDWITSIOR

Johan, 13
REDWITZER
  John, 81, 82, 83
REECE
  John, 54
  Lewis, 54
REED
  Ann, 80
  William, 80
REES
  Edward, 56, 57
REESE
  Edward, 48
REIGNIER
  Jacob, 11, 95
RENBERT
  Dirk, 6
  William, 6
RES
  Edward, 114
REY
  John, 72
RHODES
  Katherine, 72
  Richard, 72
RICE
  Rowland, 38, 60, 75, 77, 80
RICHARD
  John, 99
  Rowland, 58, 59
RICHARDS
  Abraham, 86
  Philip, 50, 51, 61, 67, 93, 94, 123, 124, 128
RICHARDSON
  Abraham, 58
  Francis, 34, 43, 67, 80
  James, 100
  Joseph, 94
  Philip, 85
  Samuel, 39, 43, 60, 74, 93, 100, 104, 110, 112, 113, 124, 127
RICHMOND
  John, 70, 71, 78
RICKETTS
  Elizabeth, 90
  Isaac, 90
RIDGE

Daniel, 39
RIELE
  Joseph, 122
RINDADUN
  Thomas, 103
RINNEY
  John, 9
RITTENHOURER
  Clam, 98
RITTERIS
  Mark, 80
ROACH
  George, 38
ROADES
  John, 33, 86
ROADS
  Adam, 125
  John, 33, 84, 124, 125
ROADS (RHOADS, ROADES)
  Joseph, 125
ROADS (RODES)
  Katherine (Catherine), 107
  Richard, 107
ROBERTS
  Benjamin, 78
  Cadwallader, 20
  Edward, 13, 54, 69
  Evan, 44
  Hugh, 41, 48, 54, 55, 56, 69, 70
  John, 7, 17, 27, 44, 48, 55, 58, 60, 103, 115
  Owen, 54, 56
Roberts
  Owen, 58
ROBERTS
  Owen, 69, 111
  Robert, 48, 54, 56, 57, 69
  Thomas, 60
ROBESON
  Andrew, 32, 77
ROBINS
  William, 111
ROBINSON
  Andrew, 76
  Mathew, 13
  Nathan, 25
  Pat, 118
  Patrick, 10, 33, 36, 61, 74, 75,

106
William, 67, 93, 94
ROBISON
  Andrew, 33, 36
  Patrick, 38
  Samuel, 36
ROCH
  George, 105
ROCHFORD
  Ambrose, 35
  Druins, 35
  Herriott, 34, 35
  Jeriott, 34
  Mary, 34
  Solomon, 35
ROCKFORD
  Deinus, 37
  Dennis, 128
  Herriott, 37
  Mary, 37
RODES
  Richard, 10, 128
RODGERS
  James, 71
  Pernell, 71
ROESSEN
  Olle, 34
ROLFE
  Joseph, 107
ROMAN
  Philip, 19
  Phillip, 3
ROSS
  Alexander, 99, 100
ROSTERS
  John, 62
ROUND
  John, 98, 99
ROUTLIGE
  William, 74
ROWLAND
  Samuel, 24
RUDD
  Rebecca, 112
  William, 4, 112
RUDIMAN
  Andrew, 91
RUSH

John, 102, 103
Thomas, 103
RUSSELL
  John, 54
RUTTER
  Anna, 48, 51
  Thomas, 46, 60, 65
RUTTERS
  Ann, 117
  Conrad, 117

# S

SADOWSKI
  Anthony, 129
SALLWAY (SALWAY)
  William, 74
SALSBERRY
  William, 15
SALTER
  Anna, 38, 50
  Anna (Annie), 1
SALWAY
  William, 89, 90, 106, 110
SAMSON
  James, 17
SANDEL
  Andrew, 100
SANDERS
  Charles, 15, 16
  John, 69, 70
  Paul, 111
  Sarah, 15, 16
  William, 16
SANGSTONE
  Thomas, 57
SAUNDERS
  John, 70
SAVAGE
  Anna, 51
  Samuel, 48, 51, 52
SAXTON
  Henry, 72
SAY
  William, 53, 60
SAYCOCK
  William, 75
SCHEFER

Isaac, 103
SCHOLL
  Johannes, 63
SCHUTE
  Johan Jacob, 76
SCHUTZEN
  Catharine Elizabeth, 72
SCOOTON (SKUTTEN)
  John, 115
SCOTSON
  George, 115
SCOTT
  Richard, 122, 123
  Samuel, 53
  Thomas, 29, 53, 68, 92
SEARIES
  Thomas, 74
SEARL
  Francis, 106, 122
SEARLE
  Francis, 106
SELIN
  Hendrick, 63
SELL
  Hendrick, 60
SELLEN
  Dirk, 101
  Hendrich, 105
  Henry, 5, 63, 101
SERVANT
  Judith, 94
SEVERING
  Kreisheim, 48
  Wigard, 48, 51
  Wiggard, 51
SEVERNY
  Jacob, 127
SHALLCROSS
  John, 74, 91, 92
SHALLICK
  James, 81, 82
SHALTICK
  James, 109
SHANKLE
  William, 33
SHARDLOR
  William, 34
SHARDLOW
  William, 16
SHATTICK
  James, 65, 116, 125
SHATTICK (SHATTOCK)
  James, 124
SHEFER
  Isaac, 77
SHELLY
  Thomas, 53, 79
SHIPP
  Edward, 27
SHIPPEN
  Ann, 59
  Edward, 2, 7, 8, 22, 25, 27, 32,
    37, 39, 40, 46, 48, 50, 51, 52,
    58, 59, 68, 69, 81, 93, 94,
    105, 119, 120, 125, 126, 128
  Joseph, 3, 24, 34, 38, 47, 120
  Joshua, 126
SHOEMAKER
  George, 74
  Isaac, 3, 23, 63, 64
  Jacob, 9
  Peter, 50, 64, 105
  Sarah, 63, 64
SHOOMAKER
  Peter, 65
SHORE
  George, 56
SHORTER
  Elizabeth, 102, 103
SHOURDS
  Samuel, 126
  Sarah, 126
SHRAGE
  Andrew, 98
SHUBEY
  William, 77
SHUBY
  Sarah, 104
  William, 104
SHUMAKER
  Isaac, 101
  Jacob, 60, 127
  Peter, 61, 105
SHUMAKER (SHOEMAKER)
  Peter, 63
SHUTE

Thomas, 10, 17, 32, 34, 37, 39,
    81, 82, 84, 111
SHUTE (SUIT)
    Thomas, 28
SIBLEY
    John, 17
SIBTHORP
    Adany, 101
    Ann, 100, 101
    Christopher, 15, 17, 39, 45, 68,
        73, 101
    Cristopher, 14
SICERTS
    Samuel, 126
    Sarah, 126
SIGN OF THE CROOKED
    BILLETT, 23
SIKES
    Nath, 31
    Nathaniel, 33, 43
SIM
    Daniel, 112
SIMCOCK
    George, 69
SIMCOE
    George, 89, 100
SIMCOE (SIMCO, SENCOE)
    George, 99
SIMES
    George, 88, 89
    John, 49
Simm
    George, 99
SIMONS (SYMONS)
    Walter, 23
SINGARD
    William, 121
SIPMAN
    Derick, 52, 63
    Direck, 124
    Dirick, 4, 6
    Dirk, 61, 63, 64, 101
SIPTHORP
    Christopher, 9
SISK
    Maurice, 43
SISOM
    Thomas, 57, 61, 85, 94

SISSOM (SISOM)
    Thomas, 57
SISSON
    Thomas, 119
SIVERT
    Cornelius, 23
SKOOLKILL ISLAND, 26
SLEWELYN
    Morris, 105, 106
SLEWLEN
    David, 106
SLUBY
    Nicholas, 95
    Sarah, 92, 95, 104, 111, 115
    William, 92, 104, 111, 115
SMART
    John, 35
SMEDLEY
    George, 20
    Thomas, 20
SMITH
    Author, 94
    Daniel, 8, 72, 112, 113
    Francis, 32
    Morice, 26
    Sarah, 90
    William, 29, 105
SMOUT
    Edward, 31, 48, 49, 61, 92, 120,
        121
SMYTH
    Richard, 47
SNEAD
    Richard, 124
    William, 115
SNEAD (SNEADE)
    Richard, 127
SNOWDEN
    John, 24, 115
    William, 10, 110
SONGBURST
    John, 43
SONGHURST
    Elizabeth, 109
    John, 10, 65, 66, 109
SONGSHORE
    Robert, 70
SONGSTROTH

Bartholomew, 71
SONMANS
  Peter, 108
SOUTHBE
  William, 123
SOUTHBY
  William, 49
SOUTHEBE
  William, 7
SOUTHWORTH
  John, 2, 86
SPEAKMAN
  Randall, 84
SPENCER
  Hester, 66, 67
  James, 4
  Samuel, 66, 67
SPERING
  John, 85
SPIKMAN (SPECKMAN, SPAKMAN)
  Randle, 72
SPRINGETT
  Harbert, 97, 98, 99, 108
  Hartel, 79
  J., 129
  John Henry, 102
SPROGELL
  John Henry, 72, 75, 100
SPROGETT
  John Henry, 76
STACY
  John, 53
  Robert, 38
STADT
  William, 68
STALLS
  Casper, 33
STANBURY
  Nathan, 1, 3, 4, 8, 11, 12, 13, 14, 15, 17, 18, 19, 22, 23, 24, 25, 26, 28, 29, 34, 35, 39, 43, 45, 46, 47, 51, 52, 56, 59, 66, 67, 68, 69, 71, 72, 73, 74, 75, 76, 77, 79, 80, 81, 83, 84, 85, 86, 87, 88, 89, 90, 91, 92, 93, 94, 95, 96, 97, 98, 100, 101, 102, 103, 104, 105, 106, 107, 109, 110, 111, 112, 113, 114, 115, 118, 120, 121, 122, 123, 124, 128, 129
STANFIELD
  James, 89
STANLY
  Rebecca, 118
  William, 118
STAPLEFORD
  Thomas, 43
STARK
  Matthias, 62
STE
  Henry, 85
STEEL
  James, 49, 119, 126
  Jane, 55
STEIGLEET
  Johannes Nicholaus, 86
  Nicholas, 85, 86
STEPHENS
  Henry, 121
STEVENS
  Henry, 34, 61, 62, 75, 77, 122
  Herman, 98
  Martha, 34, 61, 75, 122
  Timothy, 97
STIALL
  Joseph, 95
STILE (STILL)
  Richard, 104
STIRKE
  Henry, 47
STORNYGARD
  William, 15
STORY
  Ann, 2, 59
  Enoch, 9
  Thomas, 2, 3, 4, 5, 7, 8, 9, 10, 11, 12, 13, 14, 15, 17, 18, 19, 20, 21, 22, 23, 24, 25, 26, 27, 28, 29, 30, 31, 32, 33, 34, 35, 36, 37, 39, 40, 41, 42, 43, 44, 45, 46, 47, 48, 49, 51, 52, 53, 54, 55, 56, 57, 58, 59, 60, 61, 62, 63, 64, 65, 66, 67, 68, 69, 71, 73, 75, 78, 86, 93, 110, 111, 113, 115, 116, 118, 119, 120,

121, 122, 123, 124, 125, 126, 127, 128
STRAUSS
  George, 76
STREET
  Daniel, 50, 102
  Hannah, 102
  Mary, 102
STREPER
  William, 72
STRETCH
  Peter, 45
STRETTELL
  Amos, 119
STRIKE
  Henry, 11, 71, 118
STURBARY
  Ann, 4
STUREY
  Sarah, 96
STURGES
  Anthony, 26
  Cornelius, 26, 33, 122
  Elizabeth, 33
STURGS
  Cornelius, 26
SULLEN
  Hendrick, 64
SUTTON
  Richard, 26
SWERT
  Cornelius, 23
SWIFT
  John, 25, 32, 71, 80, 120
SYKES
  Nathaniel, 80, 117

# T

TARRY
  Stanely, 104
TATE
  Robert, 79
TAVERNER
  Samuel, 108, 109, 116
TAYLOR
  Anthony, 26
  Christopher, 9, 82
  Dorothea, 118
  Isaac, 14
  Jacob, 15
  John, 118
  Joseph, 53, 54, 55, 113, 114, 126
  Peter, 42, 91, 92
  Richard, 69, 71
  Samuel, 120
TEAGE
  Pentecost (Pantecrost), 95
TEAGUE
  Pentecost, 126
  Penticost, 114
TELNOR
  Jacob, 34, 60, 63
TENNET
  Widow, 30
TERRWOOD
  Thomas, 106
TEST
  John, 34, 118
TEW
  Edward, 7
  Elizabeth, 7
THLEMAN
  Philip, 17
THOMAS
  -, 106
  Chieftan, 41
  Daniel, 74
  David, 13
  Evan, 57, 61, 89
  Hugh, 69
  James, 48, 78, 97, 99, 103
  John, 22, 40, 105, 107
  Lewis, 83
  Owen, 19
  Reece, 54
  Rees, 61
  Rees (Reese), 129
  Richard, 17
  Richard ap, 17
  Susanna, 54
  William, 18, 61
THOMASON
  Lawrence, 115
THOMPSON
  Christopher, 97

Deborah, 129
George, 114
Widow of Thomas, 1
THOMSON
    Thomas, 50
THORNTON
    Nathaniel, 30
THRUPPER
    Rowland, 109
TIBBEN
    Gerhard, 48, 51
TILL
    William, 3, 6, 35, 39
TILLEMAN
    Daniel, 63
TILLERY
    Joshua, 84
TILTERY
    Josh, 68
TISEN (TISSON, TISON, TISSEN)
    Reiner, 117
TISRON (TISRAN)
    Mathias, 29
TITTERY
    Cicely, 101
    Joshua, 49, 86
TIZACK
    John, 80
TODD
    Joseph, 102
TOMLINSON
    Richard, 48
TOMPSON
    Daniel, 129
    Deborah, 129
TOMS
    Nathaniel, 5
TOMSON
    Lawrence, 110, 111
    Thomas, 41
TOURCHIER
    John V, 72
TOWNSEND
    Richard, 54, 58
TREENAWAY
    Robert, 82
TREEWOOD
    Thomas, 122

TREGENY
    Elizabeth, 122
    Henry, 72, 93, 122
TREGRANEY
    Henry, 4
TRENT
    William, 1, 4, 12, 13, 20, 21, 22,
        25, 26, 27, 28, 29, 35, 36, 37,
        40, 49, 67, 78, 82, 83, 107
TRESSE
    Thomas, 1, 49, 57, 71, 89, 112,
        118, 121, 127
TROTTER
    Rebecca, 97
TRUMP
    Hans Michael, 86
TUCKER
    James, 70
    Margaret, 70
TUNECLIFF
    Thomas, 103
TUNIS
    Abraham, 72, 117
TURNER
    John, 17, 29, 92, 103
    Nicholas, 70
    Robert, 24, 27, 28, 38, 49, 61, 70,
        74, 80, 89, 96, 101, 107, 114,
        118, 120, 121, 123, 128

# U

UBERFELD
    Wilhelm, 76
UMSTAT
    Johannes, 72, 77
    John, 62
UMSTETT
    Hanns Peter, 101
USHER
    Jacob, 2, 13, 20, 78, 97
    John, 78
USTENBURG
    Erick, 1
    Olie, 1

# V

VACKRIS
-, 76
VAN BEBBER
Mathias, 4, 5, 6, 7, 72, 98, 101, 105
Matthew, 81
Matthias, 62, 63, 64
VAN BON
Herman, 48, 103
Hermann, 77
VAN BURKLOW
Renier Hermans, 63
VAN MASTRICH
Gerhardt, 72
VAN SINTERN
Isaac, 73
VAN SINTERN (SINTREN, SINTON)
Isaac, 117
Neltei, 117
VAN WILLING
Maria, 72
Thomas, 72
VANDER GAEGH
Cornelius, 102
VANDER GAIGHE
Cornelius, 100
VANDEWALLER
Jacob, 75
VANDWALL
Maria, 72
VANLEAR
John, 36
VANLEET
John, 34
VAUGHAN
John, 113
Thomas, 106
VAUGHN
John, 22, 55, 56
VIRBIN
Peter, 111

# W

WADDY
Henry, 106
WADY
Henry, 68
WAINWRIGHT
Elizabeth, 93
Samuel, 93
WAIT
William, 73
WAITE
William, 73
WALDENFEILD
Samuel, 21
WALDENFIELD
Samuel, 35, 37, 87, 88, 96
WALDINGFEILD
Samuel, 19
WALKER
Cadwalader, 93
Emanual, 26
George, 71
John, 49, 103
Richard, 78, 95
Samuel, 38
WALLES
Philip, 82
WALLIS
Philip, 83
Robert, 89, 109, 113
WALLN
Nicholas, 65, 82
Richard, 123, 124, 126
WALLON
Catharine Elizabeth, 72
Jacob Vand, 72
WALN
Nicholas, 35, 37, 82
WALN (WALLN)
Nicholas, 66
WALTER
Robert, 99
WALTERS
John, 121
Thomas, 42
WALTON
Daniel, 88
Michael, 89
Nathaniel, 17, 56, 88
Thomas, 29, 71, 88
William, 18
WALTON (WALLTON)

Michael, 30
WANSFORD
  Nicholas, 26
WARD
  Henry, 70, 94
WARDE
  John, 100
WARDER
  John, 66
WARNER
  Mary, 108
  Thomas, 108
  William, 105
WARTNALY
  Edward, 103
WARTON
  Walter, 1
WATERMAN
  Humphrey, 42
  Isaac, 42
  Margaret, 42
WATSON
  John, 17, 57
  William, 108
WAYNRIGHT
  Elizabeth, 93
  Samuel, 93
WEAVER
  Samuel, 53, 57, 75
WEBB
  Elizabeth, 85, 109
  John, 23, 25, 36, 86, 87, 92
  Joseph, 46
  Mary, 109
  Nathaniel, 60
  Sarah, 46
  Thomas, 84
WEBSTER
  John, 18
WEGG
  John Am, 51
WELCH
  Peter, 103
WELCH TRACT, 21
WELD
  Elizabeth, 111
WELLIS
  John, 42

  Mathias, 42
WELLS
  Edward, 126
  John, 91
  Joseph, 126
  William, 59, 89
WENT
  Peter, 125
WENTZ
  Peter, 111
WEST
  Hannah, 102
  John, 84, 102
WHARLEY
  Daniel, 19, 21, 35, 37, 87, 88, 96
WHARLY
  Daniel, 124
  Mary, 124
WHARTON
  Daniel, 96
  Thomas, 9, 25
WHATLY
  Anthony, 109
WHEELER
  Andrew, 115
  Anna Maria, 115
WHITE
  Edward, 54
  James, 65
  John, 74, 110
  Mary, 110
WHITEPAIN (WHITPAIN)
  Mary, 129
  Richard, 129
WHITEPAINE
  Richard, 76
WHITFIELD
  Richard, 38
WHITLEY
  Enoch, 119
WHITLY
  Thomas, 125
WHITTON
  Thomas, 29, 92, 95
WILCOX
  Ann, 82
  George, 82
  Joseph, 43, 82

WILKINS
  William, 46, 65
WILKINSON
  Gabriel, 26, 27, 29, 31
  Samuel, 119
  William, 65
WILLCOX
  Barnabas, 57
  Barnabus, 105
  Joseph, 25, 27, 33, 95, 100, 105
WILLIAM
  John, 44
WILLIAMS
  David, 82, 83
  John, 30, 44, 45
  Nichols, 18
  Robert, 16, 47
WILLIAMSON
  David, 115
  John, 84, 112
WILLILAMS
  Edward, 49
WILLIS
  Henry, 15
WILLISON
  Isaac, 78
WILLS
  William, 43
WILMERTON
  Attiwell, 92
  Attiwil (Attiwill), 91
  Hannah, 91
  John, 91
WILMOTE
  Attwell, 74
WILSON
  Thomas, 6, 119
WILSON (WILLSON)
  Thomas, 118
WINN
  Thomas, 114
WISEMAN
  Thomas, 4, 5, 6, 64
WISHART
  Peter, 124
WOOD
  John, 99
  Joseph, 102, 117
  Rebecca, 47
  Thomas, 88
WOODLEY
  Jonathan, 116
  William, 116
WOODLY
  Jonathan, 116
  William, 116
WOODS
  Henry, 57
  Thomas, 121
WOODWARD
  John, 92
WORRALL
  John, 38
WORRELAN
  John, 112
  Thomas, 112
  Walter, 112
WORRELL
  John, 50, 100, 101
WORRINGTON
  William, 112
WRIGHT
  Benjamin, 43, 61, 88, 94, 102
  Isaac, 103
WULF
  Paul, 50
  Paull, 50
WYN
  Jonathan, 21
  Thomas, 21
WYNE
  Thomas, 21
WYNNE
  Thomas, 21, 53, 54

# Y

YARD
  Joseph, 25, 31, 95, 111
  William, 79
YEATES
  Jasper, 107
YELDALL
  Robert, 79
YERCAS
  Anthony, 88

YERKAS
    Anthony, 121
YOCOM
    Peters, 14
YOCUM
    Charles, 37
    Peter, 37
    Widow, 37, 47
YOKOM
    Peter, 105

# Z

ZACHERY
    Daniel, 45
ZIMMERMAN
    Christopher, 63
    Mathew, 54
    Philip Christian, 54

www.ingramcontent.com/pod-product-compliance
Lightning Source LLC
Chambersburg PA
CBHW062223080426
42734CB00010B/1999